Che Guevara
and the

FBI

Che Guevara and the

FBI

The U.S. political police dossier on the Latin American revolutionary

Edited by Michael Ratner and Michael Steven Smith

OCEAN PRESS
Melbourne • New York

OCEAN PRESS DISTRIBUTORS
United States: LPC/InBook,
     1436 West Randolph St, Chicago, IL 60607, USA
Canada: Marginal Distributors,
     277 George St. N., Unit 102, Peterborough, Ontario K9J 3G9, Canada
Britain and Europe: Central Books,
     99 Wallis Road, London E9 5LN, Britain
Australia and New Zealand: Astam Books,
     57-61 John Street, Leichhardt, NSW 2040, Australia
Cuba and Latin America: Ocean Press,
     Calle 21 #406, Vedado, Havana, Cuba
Southern Africa: Phambili Agencies,
     PO Box 28680, Kensington 2101, Johannesburg, South Africa

❧ *Dedications* ❧

Michael Ratner

To the dear comrades that I have loved and worked with, particularly the ones who have died — many of them close friends. I remember Nora Astorga, Maurice Bishop, Haywood Burns, Chris Hani, William Kunstler, Benjamin Linder, Abi Lugo, Sandy Pollack and Guillermo Ungo. And I think about the thousands of others I never knew, fallen in Nicaragua, Guatemala, El Salvador, Haiti, Grenada and elsewhere. I continue to work so they will continue to be *presente.*

Michael Steven Smith

To my cousin Anti Orban and his wife, Manci (d. 1996). Hungarian Communists and Jews, they were arrested by fascists in Budapest, not for being Jewish, but for their political ideas. Imprisoned in slave labor camps at the start of World War II, they had been able to hide their very young son Vili with a sympathetic Christian woman. Manci remained a prisoner throughout the war. Anti was able to escape, taking up arms, and fighting the fascists in an underground partisan band. After the war Manci returned to Budapest and found young Vili, still alive. "I am your mother," she said. "No you are not," he replied, "my mother was beautiful." She was bald and weighed 90 pounds. Vili grew up as a supporter of Che and remains a socialist to this day.

Table of contents

★ ★ ★

List of Documents

Chapter 4: 1962
The Cuban Missile Crisis   83

Chapter 5: 1963–1964
Solidarity with the Third World   105

Chapter 6: 1965
Che's Farewell   121

Chapter 7: 1965–1966
Rumors of Che's Activities and Death
139

Chapter 8: 1967–1968
Che in Bolivia: His Disappearance, Reappearance and Murder   183

Chapter 9: 1968
Richard Goodwin Briefs the *New York Times*   201

Publisher's Note

"Sorting through the archives of the fallen Arbenz regime in Guatemala City a few weeks after the [1954] coup, [CIA official] David Atlee Phillips came across a single sheet of paper about a twenty-five-year-old Argentine physician who had arrived in town the previous January to study medical care amid social revolution. 'Should we start a file on this one?' his assistant asked. The young doctor, it seemed, had tried to organize a last-ditch resistance by Arbenz loyalists; then he sought refuge in the Argentine Embassy, eventually moving on to Mexico. 'I guess we'd better have a file on him,' Phillips replied. Over the coming years the file for Ernesto Guevara, known as 'Che,' became one of the thickest in the CIA's global records."

From *Gentleman Spy: The Life of Allen Dulles* by Peter Grosse

Readers of *Che Guevara and the FBI* may well ask why the documents that have been released still have significant sections deleted? How many other files remain classified? The CIA and FBI files on Che Guevara contained in this book edited by Michael Ratner and Michael Steven Smith are only a small portion of the secret files still held by these spy agencies. Of particular note is the fact that the presently declassified documents covering the last months and weeks leading up to Che Guevara's death in Bolivia in 1967 are remarkably scarce.

The publisher wishes to indicate that the speeches printed in this book are as they appeared in the FBI or CIA files and therefore makes no claim to their accuracy. The documents frequently contain lies, distortions and errors. The source of these falsifications sometimes comes from CIA informants, apparently providing "information" that they believe will be well-received in Washington, such as stories about a "conflict" between Fidel Castro and Che Guevara. FBIS (Foreign Broadcast Information Service) transcripts or reports should not be regarded as accurate transcriptions of speeches by Che Guevara or Fidel Castro.

The documents reproduced here have been numbered from 1 to 109. When multiple pages of the same document have been reproduced, the separate pages have been listed (a), (b), (c), etc. Occasionally these pages have been reproduced over two pages and have been indicated as "1 (a): continued."

Other books published by Ocean Press on Cuba and Che Guevara are listed at the end of this book.

Appreciations

The authors would like to thank Philip Agee, Chris Agee, Simone Benanti, Emily Jane Goodman, Sandra Levinson, National Security Archives, Karen Ranucci, Ann Schneider and Deborah G. Smith for their assistance.

About the editors

MICHAEL RATNER is an international human rights attorney, former Legal Director for the Center for Constitutional Rights and former president of the National Lawyers Guild. He has taught at Yale and New York University law schools and has won numerous awards for his work in defense of people from Haiti, Puerto Rico, El Salvador, Guatemala, Nicaragua and Grenada. In 1996 he was appointed by President Aristide of Haiti as special counsel for human rights prosecution. He has published several books, including *International Human Rights litigation in U.S. courts* (Transnational Publications, 1996), co-authored with Beth Stephens, and has been a regular contributor to *Yale Law Journal, Social Policy, Harvard Human Rights Journal* among others.

MICHAEL STEVEN SMITH practices law in New York City. He has testified on human rights issues before committees of the United Nations and the United States Congress. He is the author of the memoir *Notebook of a Sixties Lawyer: An Unrepentant Memoir* (Smyrna Press, 1992). He is on the editorial board of *Guild Notes*, the magazine of the National Lawyers Guild.

Ernesto Che Guevara

Ernesto Guevara de la Serna was born in Rosario, Argentina on June 14, 1928. As a medical student in Buenos Aires and after earning his degree as doctor, he traveled throughout Latin America. Living in Guatemala during 1954 — then under the elected government of Jacobo Arbenz — he became involved in political activity there and was an eyewitness to the overthrow of that government in a CIA-organized military operation.

Forced to leave Guatemala under threat of death, Guevara went to Mexico City. There he linked up with exiled Cuban revolutionaries seeking to overthrow dictator Fulgencio Batista. In July 1955 he met Fidel Castro and immediately enlisted in the guerrilla expedition Castro was organizing. The Cubans nicknamed him "Che," a popular form of address in Argentina.

From November 25 to December 2, 1956, Guevara was part of the expedition that sailed to Cuba aboard the cabin cruiser *Granma* to begin the revolutionary armed struggle in the Sierra Maestra mountains. Originally the troop doctor, he became the first Rebel Army commander in July 1957.

In September 1958, Guevara and Camilo Cienfuegos each led guerrilla columns westward from the Sierra Maestra to the center of the island. Through fierce fighting they successfully extended the Rebel Army's operations to much of Cuba. At the end of December 1958, Guevara led the Rebel Army forces to victory in the battle of Santa Clara, one of the decisive engagements of the war.

Following the rebels' victory on January 1, 1959, Guevara became a key leader of the new revolutionary government. In September 1959 he began serving as head of the Department of Industry of the National Institute of Agrarian Reform; in November 1959 he became President of the National Bank; and in February 1961 he became Minister of Industry. He was also a central leader of the political organization that in 1965 became the Communist Party of Cuba.

Guevara was a leading Cuban representative around the world, heading numerous delegations and speaking at the United Nations and other international forums

In April 1965 Guevara left Cuba to participate directly in revolutionary struggles abroad. He spent several months in the Congo in Africa, returning to Cuba secretly in December 1965. In November 1966 he arrived in Bolivia where he led a guerrilla detachment fighting that country's military dictatorship. Wounded and captured by U.S.-trained and supervised Bolivian counter-insurgency troops on October 8, 1967, he was murdered the following day.

★ ★ ★

Chronology

Che Guevara and the Cuban Revolution

June 14, 1928 Ernesto Guevara is born in Rosario, Argentina, of parents Ernesto Guevara Lynch and Celia de la Serna.

1945–51 Guevara is enrolled at medical school in Buenos Aires.

January–July 1952 Guevara visits Peru, Colombia, and Venezuela. While in Peru he works in a leper colony treating patients.

March 10, 1952 Fulgencio Batista carries out coup d'état in Cuba.

March 1953 Guevara graduates as a doctor.

July 6, 1953 After graduating, Guevara travels throughout Latin America. He visits Bolivia, observing the impact of the 1952 revolution.

July 26, 1953 Fidel Castro leads an armed attack on the Moncada army garrison in Santiago de Cuba, launching the revolutionary struggle to overthrow the Batista regime. The attack fails and Batista's troops massacre more than 50 captured combatants. Castro and other survivors are soon captured and imprisoned.

December 1953 Guevara has first contact with a group of survivors of the Moncada attack in San José, Costa Rica.

December 24, 1953 Guevara arrives in Guatemala, then under the elected government of Jacobo Arbenz.

January 4, 1954 Guevara meets Ñico López, a veteran of the Moncada attack, in Guatemala City.

January–June 1954 Unable to find a medical position in Guatemala, Guevara obtains various odd jobs. He studies Marxism and becomes involved in political activities, meeting exiled Cuban revolutionaries.

June 17, 1954 Mercenary forces backed by the CIA invade Guatemala. Guevara volunteers to fight.

June 27, 1954 Arbenz resigns.

September 21, 1954 Guevara arrives in Mexico City after fleeing Guatemala.

May 15, 1955 Fidel Castro and other Moncada survivors are freed from prison in Cuba due to a massive public campaign in defense of their civil rights.

June 1955 Guevara encounters Ñico López, who is also in Mexico City. Several days later López arranges a meeting for him with Raúl Castro.

July 7, 1955 Fidel Castro arrives in Mexico with the goal of organizing an armed expedition to Cuba.

July 1955 Guevara meets Fidel Castro and immediately enrolls as the third confirmed member of the future guerrilla expedition. Guevara subsequently becomes involved in training combatants, with the Cubans giving him the nickname "Che," an Argentine term of greeting.

November 25, 1956 Eighty-two combatants, including Guevara as doctor, sail for Cuba aboard the small cabin cruiser *Granma*, leaving from Tuxpan in Mexico.

December 2, 1956 *Granma* reaches Cuba at Las Coloradas beach in Oriente Province. The rebel combatants are surprised by Batista's troops and dispersed. A majority of the guerrillas are either murdered or captured; Guevara is wounded.

December 21, 1956 Guevara's group reunites with Fidel Castro; at this point there are 15 fighters in the Rebel Army.

January 17, 1957 Rebel Army overruns an army outpost in the battle of La Plata.

May 27–28, 1957 Battle of El Uvero takes place in the Sierra Maestra, with a major victory for the Rebel Army as it captures a well-fortified army garrison.

July 1957 Rebel Army organizes a second column. Guevara is selected to lead it and is promoted to the rank of commander.

May 24, 1958 Batista launches an all-out military offensive against the Rebel Army in the Sierra Maestra. The offensive eventually fails.

August 31, 1958 Guevara leads an invasion column from the Sierra Maestra toward Las Villas Province in central Cuba, and days later signs the Pedrero Pact with the March 13 Revolutionary Directorate, which had a strong guerrilla base there. Several days earlier Camilo Cienfuegos had been ordered to lead another column toward Pinar del Río Province on the western end of Cuba.

October 16, 1958 The Rebel Army column led by Guevara arrives in the Escambray Mountains.

December 1958 Rebel columns of Guevara and the March 13 Revolutionary Directorate, and Cienfuegos with a small guerrilla troop of the Popular Socialist Party, capture a number of towns in Las Villas Province and effectively cut the island in half.

December 28, 1958 Guevara's column begins the battle of Santa Clara, the capital of Las Villas.

January 1, 1959 Batista flees Cuba. A military junta takes over. Fidel Castro opposes the new junta and calls for the revolutionary struggle to continue. Santa Clara falls to the Rebel Army. Guevara and Cienfuegos are ordered immediately to Havana.

January 2, 1959 Cuban workers respond to Fidel Castro's call for a general strike and the country is paralyzed. The Rebel Army columns of Guevara and Cienfuegos arrive in Havana.

January 8, 1959 Fidel Castro arrives in Havana, greeted by hundreds of thousands of people.

February 9, 1959 Guevara is declared a Cuban citizen in recognition of his contribution to Cuba's liberation.

February 16, 1959 Fidel Castro becomes prime minister.

May 17, 1959 Proclamation of the first agrarian reform law, fixing legal holdings at a maximum of 1,000 acres and distributing land to peasants.

October 7, 1959 Guevara is designated head of the Department of Industry of the National Institute of Agrarian Reform (INRA).

October 21, 1959 Following an attempt to initiate a counterrevolutionary uprising, Huber Matos, military commander of Camagüey Province, is arrested by army chief of staff Camilo Cienfuegos.

October 28, 1959 Camilo Cienfuegos's plane goes down over sea. Cienfuegos is lost at sea.

November 26, 1959 Guevara is appointed president of the National Bank of Cuba.

July–October 1960 Cuba nationalizes all major foreign and domestic industries and banks.

April 17–19, 1961 1,500 Cuban-born mercenaries, organized and backed by the United States, invade Cuba at the Bay of Pigs on the southern coast. The aim was to establish a "provisional government" to appeal for direct U.S. intervention. They are defeated within 72 hours, with the last ones surrendering at Playa Girón (Girón Beach), which has come to be the name used by the Cubans for the battle. Guevara is sent to command troops in Pinar del Río Province.

October 22, 1962 President Kennedy initiates the "Cuban Missile Crisis," denouncing Cuba's acquisition of missiles capable of carrying nuclear warheads for defense against U.S. attack. Washington imposes a naval blockade on Cuba. Cuba responds by mobilizing its population for defense. Guevara is assigned to lead forces in Pinar del Río Province in preparation for an imminent U.S. invasion.

October 28, 1962 Soviet Premier Khrushchev agrees to remove Soviet missiles in exchange for U.S. pledge not to invade Cuba.

March 1964 Guevara meets with Tamara Bunke (Tania) and discusses her mission to move to Bolivia in anticipation of a future guerrilla expedition.

December 9, 1964 Guevara leaves Cuba on a three-month state visit, speaking at the United Nations. He then visits a number of African countries.

March 14, 1965 Guevara returns to Cuba and shortly afterwards drops from public view.

April 1, 1965 Guevara delivers a farewell letter to Fidel Castro. He subsequently leaves Cuba on an internationalist mission in the Congo (now Zaire), entering through Tanzania. Guevara operates under the name Tatú, Swahili for "number two."

April 18, 1965 In answer to questions about Guevara's whereabouts, Castro tells foreign reporters that Guevara "will always be where he is most useful to the revolution."

June 16, 1965 Castro announces Guevara's whereabouts will be revealed "when Commander Guevara wants it known."

October 3, 1965 Castro publicly reads Guevara's letter of farewell at a meeting to announce the Central Committee of the newly-formed Communist Party of Cuba.

December 1965 Castro arranges for Guevara to return to Cuba in secret. Guevara prepares for an expedition to Bolivia.

January 3–14, 1966 Tricontinental Conference of Solidarity of the Peoples of Asia, Africa, and Latin America is held in Havana.

March 1966 Arrival in Bolivia of the first Cuban combatants to begin advance preparations for a guerrilla detachment.

July 1966 Guevara meets with Cuban volunteers selected for the mission to Bolivia at a training camp in Cuba's Pinar del Río Province.

November 4, 1966 Guevara arrives in Bolivia in disguise and using an assumed name.

November 7, 1966 Guevara arrives at site where Bolivian guerrilla movement will be based; first entry in Bolivian diary.

November–December 1966 More guerrilla combatants arrive and base camps are established.

December 31, 1966 Guevara meets with Bolivian Communist Party secretary Mario Monje. There is disagreement over perspectives for the planned guerrilla expedition.

February 1–March 20, 1967 Guerrilla detachment leaves the base camp to explore the region.

March 23, 1967 First guerrilla military action takes place with combatants successfully ambushing a Bolivian army column.

April 10, 1967 Guerrilla column conducts a successful ambush of Bolivian troops.

April 16, 1967 Publication of Guevara's Message to the Tricontinental with his call for the creation of "two, three, many Vietnams."

April 17, 1967 Guerrilla detachment led by Joaquín is separated from the rest of the unit. The separation is supposed to last only three days but the two groups are unable to reunite.

April 20, 1967 Régis Debray is arrested after having spent several weeks with a guerrilla unit. He is subsequently tried and sentenced to 30 years' imprisonment.

May 1967 U.S. Special Forces arrive in Bolivia to train counterinsurgency troops of the Bolivian army.

July 6, 1967 Guerrillas occupy the town of Sumaipata.

July 26, 1967 Guevara gives a speech to guerrillas on the significance of the July 26, 1953, attack on the Moncada garrison.

July 31–August 10, 1967 Organization of Latin American Solidarity (OLAS) conference is held in Havana. The conference supports guerrilla movements throughout Latin America. Che Guevara is elected honorary chair.

August 4, 1967 Deserter leads the Bolivian army to the guerrillas' main supply cache; documents seized lead to arrest of key urban contacts.

August 31, 1967 Joaquín's detachment is ambushed and annihilated while crossing a river after an informer leads government troops to the site.

September 26, 1967 Guerrillas walk into an ambush. Three are killed and government forces encircle the remaining guerrilla forces.

October 8, 1967 Remaining 17 guerrillas are trapped by Bolivian troops and conduct a desperate battle. Guevara is seriously wounded and captured.

October 9, 1967 Guevara and two other captured guerrillas are murdered following instructions from the Bolivian government and Washington.

October 15, 1967 In a television appearance Fidel Castro confirms news of Guevara's death and declares three days of official mourning in Cuba. October 8 is designated Day of the Heroic Guerrilla.

October 18, 1967 Castro delivers memorial speech for Guevara in Havana's Revolution Plaza before an audience of almost one million people.

February 22, 1968 Three Cuban survivors cross border into Chile, after having traveled across the Andes on foot to elude Bolivian army. They later return to Cuba.

Mid–March 1968 Microfilm of Guevara's Bolivian diary arrives in Cuba.

July 1, 1968 Guevara's Bolivian diary published in Cuba is distributed free of charge to the Cuban people. The introduction is by Fidel Castro.

Excerpts from the declassified documents

CIA physical description of Che Guevara in the Sierra Maestra, 1958:

'Che' is between 25 and 30 years old [deleted]. He is about five feet nine inches tall and weighs about 160 pounds. He is stocky in build, and is strong rather than lean and sinewy. He has brown hair and a brown mustache and beard. His beard, but not the hair on his head, has a very reddish tinge.... The outstandingly noticeable thing about 'Che'... is that he has a severe and chronic case of asthma.... He is completely dependent for survival upon this inhalator [deleted] and always carries a spare with him in case of emergency....

★★★

CIA political description of Che Guevara in the Sierra Maestra, 1958:

'Che' speaks fluent Spanish, of course. He speaks French fairly well, although with a heavy Spanish accent. He speaks no English at all, and knows only one word of English. The word is 'golf,' a game of which he is inordinately fond....

Now, it is of course impossible to state whether or not 'Che' is or is not a Communist. He himself denies it.... There is no question that he does not entertain friendly feelings toward the US.... His political views are those of a very emotional 'Latino' nationalist.... He has the emotional hostility of the nationalist inhabitant of a small and backward and weak country towards the big and rich and strong country.... In sum, [deleted] 'Che's' attitude towards the U.S. is dictated more by somewhat childish emotionalism and jealousy and resentment than by a cold, reasoned, intellectual decision... Che is fairly intellectual for a 'Latino.'

★★★

CIA informant's view of Cuba and Che Guevara in 1964:

'Communist Cuba' is something of a paradox. From the Communist standpoint, it displays all the shortcomings of a country set in the tropics. Cubans, far from submitting to discipline, prefer to idle in the sun or dance to their native rhythms. They are a mercurial people, capable of sudden, swift bursts of emotional enthusiasm, but without the staying power which creation of a Communist state demands.

The real boss of Cuba is very probably Ernesto (Che) Guevara, Argentine-born and a life-long Communist. But, [deleted] Che is willing to let Fidel believe he is still running the country. Che is said to have a talent for planting ideas in Fidel's mind with such skill that Fidel believes them to be his own.

★★★

From "Socialism and Man"

At the risk of seeming ridiculous, let me say that the true revolutionary, is guided by great feelings of love. It is impossible to think of a genuine revolutionary lacking this quality. Perhaps it is one of the great dramas of the leader that he must combine a passionate spirit with a cold intelligence and make painful decisions without contracting a muscle. Our vanguard revolutionaries must idealize this love of the people, the most sacred cause, and make it one and indivisible.

Che Guevara, 1965

Che: *The Heroic Guerrilla*

A personal note by Michael Ratner

I was a college and law student during the 1960s. It was the generation of the civil rights struggle, the movement against the war in Vietnam and the era of black liberation and the Panthers. The Cuban revolution had occurred a few years earlier and for many of us seeking to change our society, Cuba was a desirable model. And it was Che Guevara, more than any other figure, who embodied both that revolution and solidarity with peoples fighting to be free from U.S. hegemony. Many of us had on our walls the poster of Che with his famous quote: "Let me say, at the risk of appearing ridiculous, that the true revolutionary is guided by a great feeling of love." It was a sentiment that combined what many of us in the 1960s were feeling: the need for revolutionary change with the need for compassion. Che has remained my hero ever since.

In 1976 I went on a Venceremos Brigade to Cuba where I worked on a construction project. After eight weeks of very difficult work, the Cubans took us on a vacation. One day of that vacation was spent hiking in the Sierra Maestra; we took a 30- or 40-kilometer walk following Che's path into the mountains. The Cubans, of course, left nothing to chance. They wanted no injury to befall us. There were doctors in front and behind; other Cubans carried water and at various points men were macheteing open coconuts and handing them to us as we passed. But it was still a very hot, exhausting and difficult hike. As we reached the top of a mountain, I could hear children singing. I could not believe it. What were they singing and why were they there? As I walked past I saw 40 or 50 neatly uniformed children standing in front of a school high in the mountains. These were the children of the revolution. Each was holding a handwritten placard and singing the words written thereon: "Seremos como el Che." "We will be like Che." Tears streamed down my cheeks, my energy was renewed and I completed the hike. To be like Che: To be selfless, to make a family of one's comrades, to give up comfort and material gain for the revolution, to risk and probably give one's life to free humanity.

I bumped into Che in many other places in Cuba. One evening our brigade arrived in the beautiful, white-washed city of Santiago. I wandered the darkened streets and saw lights on in one shop. I walked in; it was a chess parlor. On the wall opposite the door was an oil portrait of Che playing chess; it was not portrait size, but was huge and covered the wall. A few days later we returned to Havana in time to participate in the May Day parade; we marched in the Plaza de la Revolución in front of the huge portrait of Che on a major building. But Che also appeared in miniature. There was a beauty shop in our Havana hotel; it was an exemplary beauty shop. That year it had won the award of the Heroic Guerrilla and a small picture of Che was emblazoned on the certificate displayed in the shop window.

In 1988, twenty-one years after Che Guevara's death, I spent two months in Bolivia with my family. Prior to my trip I read everything I could get my hands on about Che in Bolivia. I knew the names of the peasants Che had befriended and I learned as much as I could about the area in southern Bolivia where Che had fought. My intention was to travel the route Che had traveled.

Our apartment in La Paz was a block or so from the university, a university which, like many in Latin America, was a center of radical political activity. At the university, Che had not been forgotten. Painted on an entire wall of the main courtyard was a portrait of Che.

Where Che had fought was far from La Paz. The roads were not paved and it would take days to get there. I would need supplies and a guide. But first I would need a good map of that area of Bolivia, one that showed roads and small towns. I went to the one and only map store in La Paz and asked to buy a map of the area near the Río Ñacahuazú — the locale where Che made the first entry in his diary. The clerk was polite and explained that she had no such map; that area was still a security zone and maps of that zone could not be obtained. I was stunned. More than twenty years had passed since Che's death, but the Bolivian authorities were still terrified of him. Che lives on.

INTRODUCTION
Che Guevara and the FBI

A note on the U.S. political police

"The use by the American government of political spies was regarded with revulsion by America's founders. Informing and political espionage was anathema to the great generation of Americans who made the revolution."[1]

This had totally changed when we were growing up in the 1950s. An extremely popular television program was aired weekly to millions of people. "I Lead Three Lives" featured the activities of one Herbert Philbrick. He was not only a red-blooded American citizen, but a secret police agent who posed as a member of the Communist Party for the Federal Bureau of Investigation (FBI). He was a hero. The FBI itself was viewed as a sacred institution. All the more so because of its revered director, the self-promoting J. Edgar Hoover, who relentlessly cowed the communists and kept these files on Che Guevara. Hoover was in charge of the FBI for four decades. Their massive building in Washington, D.C., is named after him.

The techniques they used, which are documented in this book, were those first brought to bear against the pioneers of the American Labor Movement in the 1870s. But the FBI was launched as "a mode of governess," in the words of Frank Donner, an expert on the FBI, under Democratic President Franklin D. Roosevelt in the late 1930s.

In the 1870s private detective agencies targeted labor organizations. They marshalled the techniques of physical surveillance, infiltration, informers, provocateurs, the recruitment of defectors, the identification of leaders, and the development of files and dossiers. They used the information they gathered to influence public opinion through fear mongering. This was the origin of the FBI.

The 1917 Russian revolution was the catalyst for the federalization of intelligence: local, state and private. Fear mongering about foreign subversion became the FBI's stock in trade. In January 1920, thousands of suspected radicals were rounded up by agents of the federal government in collaboration with local red squads. The suspected radicals were held incommunicado, subjected to extreme brutality, imprisoned, and many of them deported. J. Edgar Hoover got his first taste of suppressing the left in helping to plan and supervise the raids.

Hoover had been picked to head the General Intelligence Division, or "Radical Division," as it came to be called, of the Justice Department. Hoover set up an index of radicals, their organizations and publications, and collected some 450,000 names. He kept biographies of individuals and stenographic reports of their speeches. Articles in newspapers and periodicals were digested, briefed and made available for immediate reference. The "Radical Division" amassed the largest data bank on radicals available. Attorney General

---

[1] Frank J. Donner, *The Age of Surveillance* (Knopf, 1980)

Palmer, for whom Hoover worked and from whom he learned, treasured these files saying it sent a message: "The government is watching."

Hoover and the FBI, as the General Intelligence Division was later named, concentrated on personalities and individuals. They personalized unrest, detaching it from social and economic causes. Their politics are conservative: they blame unrest on malcontents who are unwilling to accept the sacrifice and discipline needed for an ordered society. The FBI then went after the malcontents.

The "reds" (communists and radicals) were attacked as godless, bestial, depraved and dirty practitioners of free love. When Hoover in 1968 warned against the depraved nature and "moral looseness" of the new generation of student rebels, he was playing an old song. But it began to resonate less and less. The prestige of the FBI and its personification, Hoover, plummeted as the great political movements of the 1960s and 1970s — the civil rights movement, the peace movement and the women's movement — caused their fall in public esteem. The relationship of forces in the United States had changed.

The 1950s image of the "G-Men" arresting counterfeiters, catching car thieves, imprisoning men who transported women across state lines for "immoral purposes," and fighting bank robbers, tommy guns in hand, was an image that faded. In its place came a more generalized public appreciation of the FBI as a political police force. Files "liberated" from the regional FBI office outside of Philadelphia in Media, Pennsylvania, showed that most of the activity in that office was not concerned with crime, but with radical politics.

Articles, books and anecdotes began to circulate about the FBI and about Hoover. He emerged as both evil and nutty. One story had it that he would never allow his chauffeur to turn left. So whenever Hoover went anywhere, in order to turn left the driver of his Cadillac had to make three right hand turns. Another story which appeared in print and then on public television had Hoover, a man who never hesitated to blackmail people for their sexual preferences, arriving at a Valentine's Day party. The party was hosted by Roy Cohen at New York City's Plaza Hotel. Hoover showed up with his sidekick Clyde Tolson, the number two man at the FBI, wearing a red chiffon dress with matching red pumps and was introduced to everybody at the party as Mary. The image of this pug ugly little bulldog so outfitted marked the nadir of the man's reputation.

When the FBI first took notice of Che Guevara in Miami in 1952, and again four years later when he had joined up with Fidel Castro in Mexico City, the organization was at its full strength. They not only followed Che and his associations in Mexico three years before the Cuban revolution, but sent spies into Che's rebel camp in the Sierra Maestra mountains prior to the overthrow of the Batista dictatorship.

The FBI kept tabs on Che Guevara, although legally it was not supposed to be involved in international political intelligence work anymore than its younger and bigger brother, the CIA, was supposed to involve itself in American domestic affairs. In reality, if not legally, as these documents show, the FBI was interested in Che no matter where he lived or what he did. The deep radicalization of the 1960s and the pressure it put on the American ruling elites caused deep tactical divisions among them. In the 1960s and 1970s, stories about the real crimes of the CIA and the FBI were exposed: assassinations, reactionary coups all over the world, de-stabilization operations, pay-offs and bribes to corrupt politicians and bloody dictators on five continents. Similar methods in America logically had to follow. If the spy agencies could conspire to assassinate Fidel Castro and sabotage the Cuban revolution, they would likewise attempt to destroy the defenders of the Cuban revolution and socialism in the United States.

In 1973, the Socialist Workers Party (SWP), an active defender of the Cuban revolution, with its attorney Leonard Boudin, the great Bill of Rights attorney, whose firm Rabinowitz, Boudin & Standard represented the government of Cuba, filed suit against the FBI. The suit charged that the FBI had conspired to disrupt and destroy a legitimate political party. It stated that the conspiracy "involved the use of informers, burglars, black lists, wire taps, bugs, mail openings, and other illegal acts." Inside the Justice Department, at the FBI, and inside the White House, the complaint drafted by Boudin hit like a bombshell because it was true. Every "wild accusation" that was put into the complaint was proven more or less accurate.

The lawsuit after many, many years was eventually won. But in the interim, the Freedom of Information Act, by which the documents in this book were obtained, was strengthened, reflecting the defensive posture and temporary loss of strength that the U.S. political police apparatus had to endure.

Despite the victory in the SWP case, which assessed a quarter of a million dollars in damages against the FBI and enjoined them from their illegal activities against a socialist party, the FBI persisted and persists today in its political police function.

In the 1980s, the decade of the Nicaraguan and Grenadian revolutions and the struggle of the Salvadoran and Guatemalan people for freedom, the FBI illegally conducted a covert spying and disruption operation in the United States. The targets were a nationwide network of U.S. groups opposed to the Reagan administration's brutal policies in Central America. The FBI conducted a wide-ranging assault on domestic dissent. It included death threats, break-ins, burglaries, harassment, intimidation and arson. The Committee in Solidarity with the People of El Salvador (CISPES) was targeted for destruction even as the U.S. government warred against the revolutions in Nicaragua and Grenada and the revolutionaries in El Salvador.

Whether in its battle against Che Guevara or those who supported self-determination for the countries of South and Central America, the goal for the U.S. government and its spy agencies was and is to prevent the spread of the Cuban revolution; and ultimately to destroy it. Policymakers in the United States do not want the Cuban revolution to stand as an example for other countries. They do not want, either in Cuba or in the region, an economy over which they have no control. At stake is the future of Latin America. Will the Caribbean continue to be "an American lake"? Will South America continue to endure poverty in order to enrich its North American neighbor? Or will the Cuban example of national self-determination, control of its resources, and the providing of a better life for the majority of its citizens spread the revolution south?

Overview of the documents

The documents in this book surfaced as a result of a Freedom of Information Act (FOIA) request made in 1984 to the Federal Bureau of Investigation (FBI). We received the documents in 1985. In early 1997, the year of the 30th anniversary of Che Guevara's death in Bolivia, we took another look at the materials and recognized that a wider audience ought to see the documents, some of which date back to the early 1950s.

Unfortunately, in 1984 we only applied for the FBI file and did not request Che Guevara's file from the many other U.S. spy agencies including the Central Intelligence Agency (involved in Che's murder), Navy, Army, and Air Force Intelligence, and the

National Security Agency.[2]   Thus, the documents in this book reveal only the tip of the iceberg; they represent a minuscule portion of material that is contained in the files of the other spy agencies in the United States concerning Che Guevara, Fidel Castro, other Cuban leaders and the Cuban revolution.

The FBI file is made up primarily of documents from other U.S. spy agencies. These agencies frequently disseminate information to a broad spectrum of U.S. agencies and government departments such as the National Security Council and State Department. Contained in the FBI file are numerous CIA documents including informant reports, CIA evaluations of Che Guevara when he was fighting in the Sierra Maestra and CIA biographical sketches. Another agency of the U.S. government, the Foreign Broadcast Information Service (FBIS), monitors all radio and TV broadcasts throughout the world; as a result, numerous live speeches of Che's, which probably exist nowhere else, were in the files, and some are published here.

The first document in the file is from 1952 and the last from 1968, a year after Che Guevara was killed. The FBI initially took notice of Che when he came to Miami in 1952; they copied his passport and took his fingerprints. It is unclear whether he was permitted to stay in the United States. One document says he was arrested during a demonstration against intervention in Korea; another says he was not permitted entry into the United States. Four years later, a few months prior to his leaving on the *Granma*, Che Guevara was arrested with Fidel Castro in Mexico City. By this time, the FBI had a fair amount of information regarding Che and his associates. In the Sierra Maestra there were informants in or near to Che's column; the FBI was interested in everything about Che — what he wore, what he read and even his bathing habits.

When the revolutionaries took power, the surveillance was maintained. What others said about Che and what he said were meticulously documented. When Che went abroad the spy agencies were there and when he dropped from public view the agencies speculated on his "disappearance." His guerrilla activities in Bolivia, his death, the controversy surrounding the whereabouts of his body and the authenticity of his Bolivian diary were chronicled.

A number of themes and spy agency concerns run through the documents. The stereotypes of Latin Americans confirm Che Guevara's views about the contempt the U.S. government has for its southern neighbors. Che is described as "fairly intellectual for a Latino," his attitude toward the United States "is dictated... by somewhat childish emotionalism and jealousy and resentment." The Cubans have shortcomings from the "Communist standpoint" as they prefer "to idle in the sun or dance to their native rhythms."

Frequently, the documents record what the U.S. government wants to hear and have nothing to do with reality. The Cuban exiles and the spy agencies wished for a split between Fidel and Che, so there are numerous reports of fights between Che and Fidel over who is the real leader, relations with the Soviet Union and China and other matters. There is even a report that Che is shot after a fight with Fidel. There is the claim, which some people still believe, that Che's speech in Algiers, a speech somewhat critical of certain socialist countries, forced him from Cuba. Yet it is obvious from reading the documents that Che's intention was always to carry the Cuban revolution elsewhere. After a lengthy analysis one of the spy agencies does acknowledge that Che's absence "was not motivated by problems with Fidel."

A lot of ink is wasted by the agencies on whether or not Che is a communist. They cannot really figure him out. Why does he hate the U.S. government unless he is a

---

[2] We have remedied this oversight and hopefully we will have additional documents in the future.

communist? Does he favor Beijing or Moscow? U.S. policymakers could only see the world through Cold War lenses; they never could understand the authentic grievances of someone growing up in Latin America who saw firsthand both U.S. exploitation and its overthrow of President Arbenz in Guatemala.

The spy agencies also wanted Che Guevara dead, although the documents we have thus far do not set forth assassination plots. There is an inordinate focus on Che's asthma and his need for medication; he "is completely dependent for survival upon his inhalator." It would not be surprising if, like the poisoned cigars the CIA prepared for Fidel, a similar scheme for Che's inhalator was proposed.[3]

When Che disappears, and even after he reappears, there are numerous reports from Latin American diplomats, governments and press that Che is dead; he was supposedly killed in many countries and in a variety of ways. This was certainly the wish of the agencies. For Che alive was dangerous to the status quo; his goal was revolution.

Che's legacy

Che Guevara lived as he spoke. He carried his thoughts into action. He understood the evils of capitalism and imperialism. He knew nothing would change without struggle, and that armed struggle might be, and frequently was, necessary. As he said, "The Cuban revolution has shown that in conditions of imperialist domination as exist in Latin America, there is no solution but armed struggle — for the people to take power out of the hands of the Yankee imperialists and the small group of the national bourgeois who work with them."

Che was murdered while putting his thoughts into practice. He was not only a dreamer. We idealize him because he was selfless. His survival and the victory in the Sierra Maestra was a miracle; he could have stopped there and lived as a hero, in relative comfort, while helping build the Cuban revolution. But he believed deeply in the liberation of all people from exploitation; so deeply that he left his young children knowing well that he might never see them again. He, like Fidel Castro, understood, that "no revolutionary is eternal... revolutionaries are always running great risks."

Although murdered in the Andes, Che inspired movements of armed struggle that continued in Colombia, Chile, Uruguay, Peru and other countries. These struggles reached a height in the early 1980s. The Sandinistas were successful in Nicaragua as was the New Jewel Movement in Grenada. In El Salvador and Guatemala, the FMLN and URNG fought almost to victory. Even where state power was not achieved, these armed struggles fundamentally changed many of their societies moving them in a more democratic direction. Even today, Che-inspired movements in Mexico and elsewhere are clear reminders that when oppression is great, and when democratic channels do not exist, people will resort to armed struggle.

Some would say that Che Guevara's thoughts and his emphasis on armed struggle are inappropriate for today's world. The dire economic and political situation in Mexico and the effectiveness of the Zapatista movement refutes this simplistic assertion. As long as there is repression and exploitation there will be a need for Che's example. While it is true that today the option of guerrilla warfare in Latin America is not generally part of political discourse on the left, that is not a permanent state of affairs. Poverty continues to grind Latin America down; the IMF and the World Bank continue practices of structural readjustment which throw thousands out of work and into forced immigration. There will come a time when once again, the poor and disenfranchised will fight back. As Che, anticipating his own death,

---

[3] For such plots against Castro see *CIA Targets Fidel* (Ocean Press, 1996)

said, "other hands will pick up the weapons." On reading some of Che's words contained in these documents, one is struck by how valid his thoughts are for today's world.

Che calls for an end to the economic and political subjugation of Latin America. He understood how foreign capital, particularly from the United States, exploited Latin America and pointed to the Nicaro Nickel company in Cuba, which removed the nickel, leaving only "an ox as a souvenir" for the Cubans. This was one of his examples of buying raw materials cheaply from the Third World and selling the finished products dearly. It was true in Cuba before the revolution and is still true elsewhere today. More than a decade after Che's critique, the former Prime Minister of Jamaica, Michael Manley, forcefully made the same point about the bauxite that corporations took out of his country to make aluminum. Che understood that this imbalance was, in part, the fault of the IMF, "established and based on Wall Street." He knew even then that the loans from such institutions frequently wound up purchasing luxury goods for the wealthy.

Che saw the United States as a great evil and not only because of its attacks on Cuba. He called it a "barbaric civilization," a "so-called democracy" where U.S. elections merely determine who is to be the "jailer" of the "North American people" for the next four years. He understood that there was little significant difference between Democrats and Republicans, stating that it made no difference whether Johnson or Goldwater became President. It is a sentiment that could not be more accurate if said today. He particularly condemned the divisions in U.S. society between blacks and whites, the unionized and nonunionized, the employed and the unemployed; he believed these were intentionally caused by the ruling class in the United States.

Che condemned the Organization of American States which had done the United States' bidding and barred Cuba; he called it the "Ministry of Colonies." He discussed ways the "colonialists" could attack revolutions. The OAS method is to use mercenaries as they did against Cuba, but there were also other models for defeating social change.

He had a firm belief in solidarity with the oppressed in Latin America. He frequently hailed the former President of Guatemala, Jacobo Arbenz, and specifically mentioned Albizu Campos, the Puerto Rican patriot, "a man who is free, although he is in a dungeon of the so-called North American democracy." Che believed that the Cuban people had to fight injustice everywhere; that the Cuban people "cannot be indifferent to any injustice any place on earth." This especially included support for African countries, and the "Congolese patriots fighting valiantly and stubbornly against U.S. imperialism." Che's commitment to African liberation was certainly a precursor of Cuba's later support for Angola.

Che understood what was necessary for the people in any society, particularly those of Latin America. First, that "no government in Latin America can call itself revolutionary if it does not undertake agrarian reform." Second, that literacy was a necessity and 1961 would be the year in Cuba to "wipe out that shame of illiteracy." Finally, by the end of 1962 Cuba had the "obligation of wiping out unemployment forever." These are lessons that most countries in Latin America still have not learned.

The words of Che Guevara herein demonstrate his profound understanding of the necessity of struggle and what needs to be achieved. It is for good reason that Che remains a hero and an example for people everywhere resisting oppression and tyranny. The U.S. spy agencies and their Latin American collaborators may have killed the man, but the battle for human liberty, as personified by Che, is eternal.

Michael Ratner
Michael Steven Smith

Deciphering the CIA-generated documents

A note by Philip Agee[4]

During the period of the CIA reports in this book there were two means of transmission from the field to Headquarters: diplomatic pouch or cable. TDCS before the serial number means cable — this is short for Teletyped Clandestine Services report. When the serial numbers are preceded only by "CS," which simply means Clandestine Services, the reports were sent by diplomatic pouch, no doubt from the Havana CIA station. ("Place and Date Acq. [Acquired]" was censored in all the reports.) "Date Distr. [Distributed]" is the date the report went into circulation within the Agency and to outside "customers" like the State Department, the Department of Defense, the FBI and others.

Clandestine Services meant what is now the Directorate of Operations (DO), but during the time of the reports it was the Deputy Directorate for Plans (DDP). The "CS" was used to identify the report as coming from the CIA's DDP as opposed to any of the other components that originated the reports.

"Precedence" means the priority with which a TDCS was processed by the Office of Communications and other Headquarters components in the distribution process. The terms for "Precedence," from fastest to slowest, were Flash [war or imminent war], Immediate, Priority, Routine and Deferred. "Source" description (censored in all the reports) was a vague characterization that gave the reader some idea of what the source was but was meant to impede identification (e.g. "A member of the Communist Party of Mexico.") "Appraisal of Content" and "Reliability of Source" (both also censored) were sliding scales: Appraisal of Content was a number from one to five: 1 for "Documentary," 2 for "Probably True," 3 for "Possibly True," 4 for "Possibly False," and 5 for "Cannot Be Determined." Reliability of Source went from A to E: A for "Highly Reliable," B for "Usually Reliable," on to E for "Reliability Cannot Be Judged."

---

[4] Philip Agee is a former CIA officer who wrote *Inside the Company: CIA Diary*, the first exposé by a former operations officer. He has lectured widely at U.S. and European universities and has worked in solidarity with Cuba and other revolutionary movements for 25 years.

March 1960, Havana (Photo: Korda)

First and last photographs of Che Guevara and Fidel Castro together. Top, Mexico, June 1956 at end of prison sentence. Above, Havana, 1966, Fidel Castro checking fake passport of Guevara in disguise before his departure for Bolivia.

Fidel Castro, Raúl Castro and Che Guevara in 1963 (Photo: Osvaldo Salas)

Photo: Osvaldo Salas

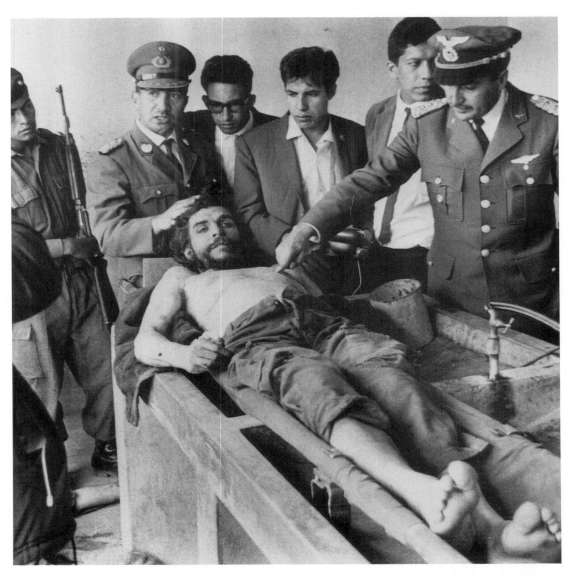

Che Guevara after being murdered by Bolivian Army on October 9, 1967, following capture the day before.

Resting after voluntary work, Havana, 1961. (Photo: Osvaldo Salas)

1

1952-1958

*Argentina, Mexico
and the
Sierra Maestra*

★ ★ ★

T he ten documents in this chapter demonstrate the early interest of the United States spy agencies in Che Guevara and, in particular, his days as a guerrilla fighter. It is clear from the documents that the United States had informants either in Che's column in Cuba's Sierra Maestra or close by. They contain information on him in Argentina, Guatemala, Mexico and Cuba. Primary themes concern his asthma (presumably a weakness the CIA and others want to exploit), questions about whether he is a communist, his views about the United States and his daily routine as a guerrilla, including his claimed bathing habits.

U.S. prejudices toward Latin Americans are perhaps best illustrated by the comment in Document 6 that "'Che' is fairly intellectual for a 'Latino'."

It was during this period, that Che met Fidel Castro in Mexico City in 1955. Che became part of the group led by Fidel Castro preparing to return to Cuba in order to overthrow the Batista dictatorship. In June 1956 he was arrested along with Fidel by the Mexican police. After almost two months in jail Che was released. He left with Fidel for Cuba on the yacht *Granma* on November 25, 1956, as the troop's doctor. They landed in Cuba on December 2, 1956. Fidel Castro victoriously entered Havana on January 8, 1959.

★ ★ ★

#261 746

<u>BIO DATA</u>

NAME: GUEVARA de la Serna, Ernesto
              aka Che

DPOB: 14 June 1928, Rosario, Argentina

TRAVEL: Visited United States August 1952.

FATHER: GUEVARA Lynch, Ernesto

1 (a). 1952: The first document in Che Guevara's file is a copy of his Argentine passport and tourist visa. Information was entered on a separate "Bio Data" sheet.

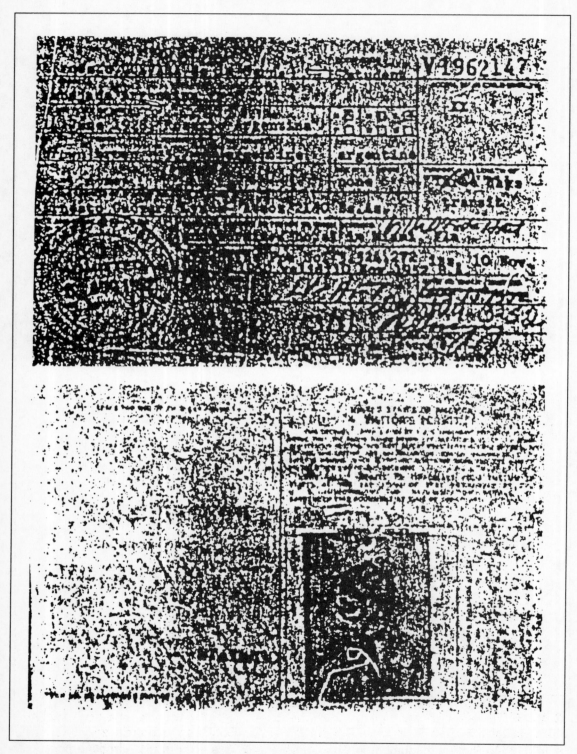

1 (b). 1952: Che Guevara's passport xeroxed by U.S. authorities in 1952.

GUEVARA, Ernesto

ARGENTINA
a/o July 1956

LOMBARDO TOLEDANO PROTEGE—Ernesto Guevara, an Argentine Communist recently arrested in Mexico in connection with the Fidel Castro plot against President Batista of Cuba, enjoys two official sinecures in Mexico, "one-as a doctor at General Hospital, although he has never studied medicine," for which he receives 1,500 pesos a month, and another as a teacher in the School of Medicine at the University, for which he is paid 800 pesos a month. At present he is still under arrest, with Dr. Fidel Castro. Nevertheless he continues to receive his salaries. Upon his arrival in Mexico City, after he was expelled from Guatemala following the fall of the Arbenz Government, Guevara became a protege of Vicente Lombardo Toledano, who accepted him as an active member of the Partido Popular, and it was Lombardo Toledano who obtained the two sinecures for him. (Mexico, D.F., CGV Agency, July 25, 1956, 1500 GMT—E)

Cárdena García Velaso Agency

FBIS Rept., July 26, 1956 OFF. USE ONLY

2. 1956: File card with information about Che Guevara shortly after his arrest on June 22, 1956, in Mexico as a member of the group led by Fidel Castro planning an invasion of Cuba. Contains erroneous information such as "never studied medicine." Typical of the file cards kept by U.S. spy agencies on any potential "trouble makers."

GUEVARA SERNA, Ernesto   Argentina

On July 2, Hilda Gadea de Guevara denied that she or Ernesto

Guevara Serna, Her Argentine physician husband, are communists. She was forced to leave Peru, she stated, not for Communist activities, but because she was statistical decretary of ;the APRA; neither she nor her husband have everh had Communist sympathies. She furhher denied the rumor that she and her husband had come to Mexico from Gustemala with Rogelio Cruz Wer and Jaime Rosenbery, chiefs of the Civil Guard and the Judicial Guard under the Arbenz regime, respectively. She stated that neither she nor her husband knew either of these men when they were in Guatemala.
Mexico City Excelsior, 3 July 56.

SO:CIA, FOreign Documentary Summary, # 1017, 30 July 56, For Official Use Only. at

Approved for Release
Date ~~14 APR 1984~~

3. 1956: Similar file card on Che Guevara's spouse, Hilda Gadea de Guevara.

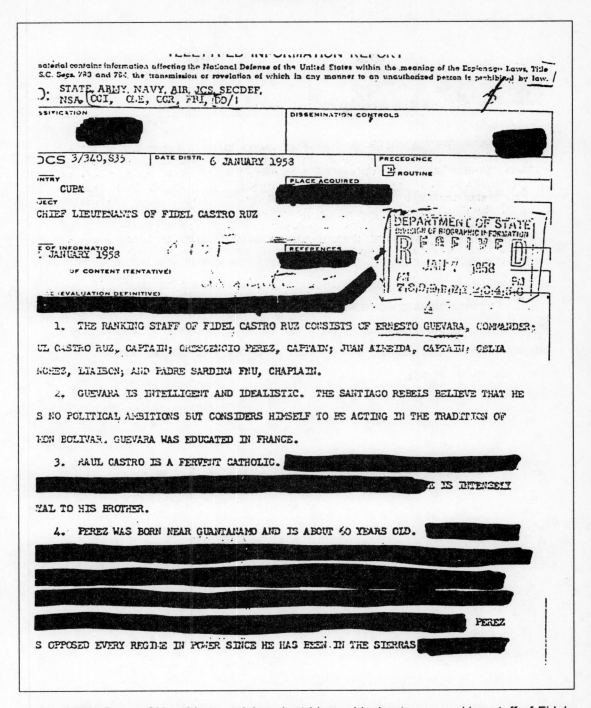

): STATE, ARMY, NAVY, AIR, JCS, SECDEF,
NSA, CCI, ORE, CCR, FBI, DD/I

SSIFICATION | DISSEMINATION CONTROLS

JCS 3/340,835 | DATE DISTR. 6 JANUARY 1958 | PRECEDENCE
B ROUTINE

NTRY CUBA | PLACE ACQUIRED

JECT CHIEF LIEUTENANTS OF FIDEL CASTRO RUZ

DEPARTMENT OF STATE
DIVISION OF BIOGRAPHIC INFORMATION
RECEIVED
JAN 7 1958

E OF INFORMATION
JANUARY 1958
OF CONTENT (TENTATIVE)

REFERENCES

E (EVALUATION DEFINITIVE)

1. THE RANKING STAFF OF FIDEL CASTRO RUZ CONSISTS OF ERNESTO GUEVARA, COMMANDER; UL CASTRO RUZ, CAPTAIN; CRESCENCIO PEREZ, CAPTAIN; JUAN ALMEIDA, CAPTAIN; CELIA NOMEZ, LIAISON; AND PADRE SARDINA FNU, CHAPLAIN.

2. GUEVARA IS INTELLIGENT AND IDEALISTIC. THE SANTIAGO REBELS BELIEVE THAT HE S NO POLITICAL AMBITIONS BUT CONSIDERS HIMSELF TO BE ACTING IN THE TRADITION OF MON BOLIVAR. GUEVARA WAS EDUCATED IN FRANCE.

3. RAUL CASTRO IS A FERVENT CATHOLIC. .... E IS INTENSELY WAL TO HIS BROTHER.

4. PEREZ WAS BORN NEAR GUANTANAMO AND IS ABOUT 60 YEARS OLD.

PEREZ

S OPPOSED EVERY REGIME IN POWER SINCE HE HAS BEEN IN THE SIERRAS

4 (a). 1958: Secret CIA cable containing short biographical notes on ranking staff of Fidel Castro's guerrilla force in the Sierra Maestra. Che Guevara is described as "intelligent and idealistic" and believes himself acting in the "tradition of Simon Bolívar." Note the distribution of cable to Department of State, Army, Navy, Air Force, Joint Chiefs of Staff, National Security Agency and others.

CS 3/340,835

 PEREZ IS IN CHARGE OF THE SECURITY
OF THE CASTRO HEADQUARTERS AND THE SURROUNDING AREA.

5. SANCHEZ, THE DAUGHTER OF A DOCTOR, STUDIED NURSING IN THE U. S. A. AND IS
VERY PRO-U. S.. HER OPINIONS ARE IMPORTANT TO CASTRO.

6. ALMEIDA, THE ONLY NEGRO OFFICER, WAS A TRACTOR MECHANIC IN HAVANA. HE
RECEIVED HIS POLITICAL EDUCATION FROM FIDEL CASTRO, WITH WHOM HE WAS IMPRISONED ON
THE ISLE OF PINES. HE CAME FROM MEXICO WITH CASTRO AND HAS HIS CONFIDENCE.

7. FIDEL CASTRO IS THE DOMINATING INFLUENCE, AND HIS STAFF IS VERY UNITED.
(COMMENT: THE SANTIAGO REBELS BELIEVE BLINDLY IN FIDEL CASTRO BUT ARE APATHETIC
TOWARDS HIS AIDES. THEY NEITHER KNOW NOR CARE ABOUT THE POLITICAL THOUGHTS AND
ASPIRATIONS OF THE LATTER.)

FLD DISTRIBUTION: NONE

(END OF MESSAGE)

4 (b). 1958

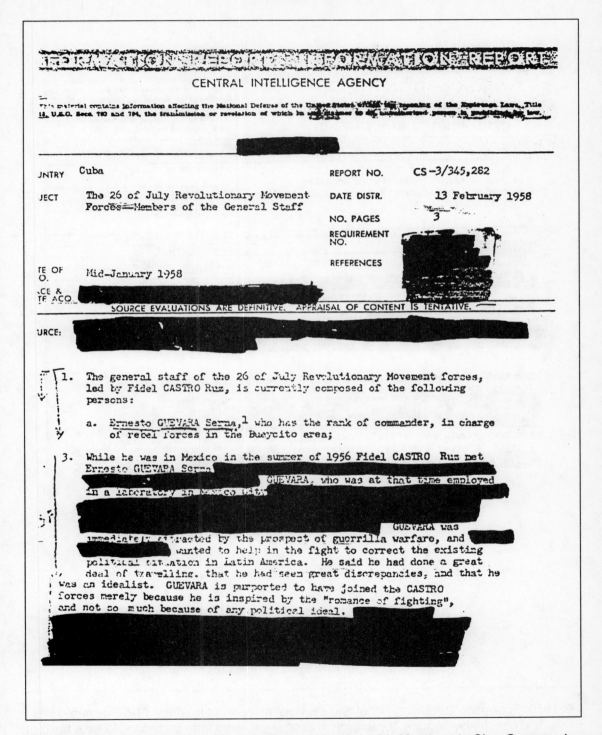

CENTRAL INTELLIGENCE AGENCY

This material contains information affecting the National Defense of the United States within the meaning of the Espionage Laws, Title 18, U.S.C. Secs. 793 and 794, the transmission or revelation of which in any manner to an unauthorized person is prohibited by law.

JNTRY	Cuba	REPORT NO.	CS-3/345,282
JECT	The 26 of July Revolutionary Movement Forces—Members of the General Staff	DATE DISTR.	13 February 1958
		NO. PAGES	3
		REQUIREMENT NO.	
TE OF O.	Mid-January 1958	REFERENCES	
CE & TF ACQ			

SOURCE EVALUATIONS ARE DEFINITIVE. APPRAISAL OF CONTENT IS TENTATIVE.

URCE:

1. The general staff of the 26 of July Revolutionary Movement forces, led by Fidel CASTRO Ruz, is currently composed of the following persons:

   a. Ernesto GUEVARA Serna,[1] who has the rank of commander, in charge of rebel forces in the Bueycito area;

3. While he was in Mexico in the summer of 1956 Fidel CASTRO Ruz met Ernesto GUEVARA Serna GUEVARA, who was at that time employed in a laboratory in Mexico City.

   GUEVARA was immediately attracted by the prospect of guerrilla warfare, and wanted to help in the fight to correct the existing political situation in Latin America. He said he had done a great deal of travelling, that he had seen great discrepancies, and that he was an idealist. GUEVARA is purported to have joined the CASTRO forces merely because he is inspired by the "romance of fighting", and not so much because of any political ideal.

5. 1958: CIA report on the general staff of the July 26 Movement. Che Guevara is described as wanting to "help in the fight to correct the existing political situation in Latin America."

SEE BOTTOM OF PAGE FOR SPECIAL CONTROLS, IF ANY

INFORMATION REPORT

PARED AND DISSEMINATED BY

CENTRAL INTELLIGENCE AGENCY

This material contains information affecting the National Defense of the United States within the meaning of the Espionage Laws, Title 18, U.S.C. Secs. 793 and 794, the transmission or revelation of which in any manner to an unauthorised person is prohibited by law.

RY

CT   Cuba

Biographic and Personality Information
Concerning "Che" (Ernesto Guevara), Henchman
of Fidel Castro

REPORT NO.   00—B-3,098,099

DATE DISTRIBUTED   13 Feb 58

NO. OF PAGES   4   NO. OF ENCLS.

SUPPLEMENT TO REPORT #

OF INFORMATION (Date or dates, on or between which events or conditions described in report)

AND DATE ACQUIRED (by source)

OO/C—   RESPONSIVE TO

THIS IS UNEVALUATED INFORMATION

CE

The individual who calls himself "Che" and who is one of Fidel Castro's chief lieutenants is an Argentine medical doctor named Ernesto Guevara.

The following represents the information concerning this man. "Che", incidentally, is a familiar form of address. Guevara is never known by any other name.

6. 1958: Four-page CIA biographical and personality report concerning Che Guevara, Fidel Castro's "henchman." Apparently this information is gathered from someone in Che's band. **(a):** This document emphasizes Che's asthma claiming that he "is completely dependent for survival upon his inhalator." Also, includes the statement that Che has no "negro strain in him" and derogatory comments concerning Che's teeth and bathing habits.

"Che" is between 25 and 30 years old, ████████████████ He is about five
feet nine inches tall and weighs about 160 pounds. He is stocky in build,
and is strong rather than lean and sinewy. He has brown hair and a brown
mustache and beard. His beard, but not the hair on his head, has a very
reddish tinge. By no stretch of the imagination, however, can "Che" be
described as red-bearded. He has a rather square face, a straight nose, an
olive complexion, and dark brown eyes. He is definitely of Spanish descent
and does not ████████████████ have any negro strain in him. In short,
he is a "Latino" and not a mulatto. He is, incidentally, extremely proud
of his "Latino" background. He bears a rather remarkable resemblance to
the Mexican artist Cantinflas and sometimes laughingly refers to himself as
"Cantinflas". However, he is never known by the name "Cantinflas". He has
rather clownish features. By ordinary middle class standards, "Che" has
bad teeth, but by the standards of his companions in the mountains his
teeth are perhaps better than the average. "Che" does not wear glasses
████████████████ and has no particularly outstanding mannerisms, with the possible
exception of his exuberance and his readiness to laugh. He smiles readily
and is extremely personable. "Che" possesses a long scar on the left side
of his neck, a scar caused, he says, by a wound received in combat against
the Cuban Government forces. ████████████████
████████████████
██████████ The outstandingly noticeable thing about "Che" from the
physical aspect is that he has a severe and chronic case of asthma. His
asthma is so severe that he always carries with him a portable asthma
inhalator which he uses almost constantly. He is completely dependent for
survival upon this inhalator ██████████ and always carries a spare with
him in case of emergency. One can always tell when "Che" is in a group,
even when he is not to be seen, because of the bellows-like noise which
this inhalator makes when in use. ████████████ he has had chronic
asthma ever since childhood and that he has always had to use the inhalator.
The remaining noticeable physical trait of "Che" is his filth. He hates
to wash and will never do so. He is filthy, even by the rather low standard
of cleanliness prevailing among the Castro forces in the Sierra Maestra.
Once in a while "Che" would take some of his men to a stream or pool, in

6 (a). 1958: continued.

- 2 -   00-B-3,098,099

order that they might wash. On those occasions "Che" would never wash either himself or his clothes, but would sit on the bank and watch the others. He is really outstandingly and spectacularly dirty.

"Che" speaks fluent Spanish, of course. He speaks French fairly well, although with a heavy Spanish accent. He speaks no English at all, and knows only one word of English. The word is "golf", a game of which he is inordinately fond. ▓▓▓▓ he had learned some Russian in a school in Buenos Aires ▓▓▓▓ that on that account he had been called a Communist. ▓▓▓▓ in his opinion the Western world is full of people who call Communists those who show any interest in the USSR. ▓▓▓▓ know whether or not he can actually speak any Russian ▓▓▓▓

Raul A. Lynch

"Che" told relatively little concerning his personal background. He claims that his uncle, whom he identified as Guevara-Lynch ▓▓▓ is or was the Argentine ambassador in Havana, Cuba, and is a naval officer. "Che" was born in Argentina ▓▓▓▓ in some city or town other than Buenos Aires. ▓▓▓ His father is a medical doctor in Argentina ▓▓▓▓ "Che" said that his father is still alive. "Che" has some brothers and sisters, ▓▓▓ He also has a wife and daughter, ▓▓▓ Certainly, they are not with him in the Sierra Maestra. ▓▓▓ "Che" does come from a middle-class background ▓▓▓ He is not by origin a "big-city" type. ▓▓▓

6 (b). 1958: The informant alleges that Che Guevara speaks only one word of English – "golf" – a game he supposedly loves and comments on his preference as a doctor to extract upper teeth. Describes Che as "the type which would joust at windmills."

"Che" asserts that he is a medical doctor and that he is a specialist in allergies. He gave as his reason for being an allergist the sympathy he feels for allergy sufferers. This natural sympathy has been increased ███████ ████ by his own troubles with asthma. In other words, his choice of a medical specialty was dictated by humanitarian, as much as by scientific, motives.

███ his medical specialization in allergies is a specialization of study rather than a specialization of actual medical practice. At any rate, he is the friend to and sympathizer with the allergy sufferer. ██

████████████████ he at least has had some medical training. medical examinations, ██ had been either an advanced medical student or intern or that of one who was ██

██████ "Che's" present medical activities are much more than those necessary to keep a force of men in being, ████████████████ among his medical duties is the extraction of teeth and ████████████ he much preferred to extract upper teeth. The reason for this taste in tooth extractions ████████████ is that he is never quite sure of the location of the nerves in the lower jaw. Consequently he prefers to defer extractions of lower teeth in the hope that the trouble will go away. If it does not, of course, he will undertake the operation.

"Che" smiles and laughs readily, ████████████████████████████ and has an engaging and exuberant personality. He appears ████████████████ quite a romantic figure in his own mind and to be just the type which would joust at windmills. For instance, although he is a medical doctor and although Castro took him on because a doctor was needed, "Che" delights in referring to himself as a warrior. ███████████████████████████ "I am not a doctor; I am a warrior".

6 (b). 1958: continued

"I am not a doctor; I am a warrior," Che is reported to have said.

- 3 -   CO-B-3,098,099

He is extremely proud of being the only one of Castro's officers in the
mountains to bear the title of "Comandante". ▓▓▓▓▓▓▓▓ he always had
been the rebel in his family. In 1954 he was in Guatemala when Castillo
Armas displaced Arbenz. He spoke strongly of this episode and denounced to
▓▓▓▓▓▓ what he claimed was US influence in the successful rebellion by
Castillo Armas. He rambled on at considerable length concerning alleged
actions against Arbenz by the US. These accounts of his were highly colored
and rather extreme and romantic in tone and character. ▓▓▓▓▓▓▓▓ he
explained that his reason for feeling as he does concerning the events in
Guatemala in 1954 was that he regards the whole thing as an affront to
Guatemalan national feeling and national dignity. Concerning the Hungarian
revolution of 1956, "Che" sticks straight to the Communist Party line and
asserts flatly that the US set off that revolt. He asserts that he left
Argentina because of the policies of Perón, but made no claim ▓▓▓▓▓▓
▓▓▓▓▓ that Perón had persecuted or exiled him. He merely chose to leave.
His subsequent history is not clear ▓▓▓▓▓▓ he spent some time in Bolivia.
Guatemala (see above), and then went to Mexico, where he first met Castro.
▓▓
▓▓▓▓▓▓▓▓▓▓▓▓▓▓▓▓▓▓▓▓▓▓ Apparently, he and Castro liked each
other from the start. Castro needed a doctor. "Che" liked the prospect of
action in Cuba and accompanied Castro when he went to Cuba in 1956. ▓▓▓▓

6 (c). 1958: Asserts that Che Guevara "always had been the rebel in his family."
"Apparently, he and Castro liked each other from the start. Castro needed a doctor. 'Che'
liked the idea of action in Cuba…".

Now, it is of course impossible to state whether or not "Che" is or is not a Communist. He himself denies it. There is no question but that his utterances regarding events in Guatemala and Hungary are definitely Communist in tone and approach. There is no question that he does not entertain friendly feelings towards the US. He repeated with great solemnity and emphasis that the US is planning to cut Cuba physically into two parts by means of a canal. His political views are those of a very emotional "Latino" nationalist. Despite "Che's" undoubted hostility to the US and despite his ███████ of the Communist line concerning Guatemala and Hungary, ███████ difficult to believe that he is a Communist in the sense of the dedicated Party member and revolutionary, and conspirator. One reason ████████ is that he does not talk consistently like an intellectually-disciplined Communist (despite the two examples above). He does not have the usual jargon, the usual phrases, the pat and stock answers which ████ characterize the real Communist. He does not display the patterned thinking which ████ characterizes the real Communist. Furthermore, "Che" is such an individualist and such a romantic that he doesn't sound like an "organization man" at all. Of course, this may be nothing but camouflage, ██████████████ ███████████████████ "Che's" attitude towards the US ██████ is an attitude which is fairly common among young "Latinos". He has the emotional hostility of the nationalist inhabitant of a small and backward and weak country towards the big and rich and strong country. It does not seem ████████████ the organized, directed hostility which characterizes Communist hostility. Curiously enough, in "Che's" case this unfriendly attitude towards the US is coupled with a desire to visit the US and admire its wonders (his phrase). In sum, ███████████ "Che's" attitude towards the US is dictated more by somewhat childish emotionalism and jealousy and resentment than by a cold, reasoned, intellectual decision. Of course, the effect may well be the same. It is the origin which is different. ████

"Che" is fairly intellectual for a "Latino". He is quite well-read in "Latino" literature and has an appreciation of the classics from other literatures. He is intelligent and quick. ███████████████████████ he has caused books to be brought into the Sierra Maestra and by the way he reads to the soldiers

6 (c). 1958: continued

Primarily concerned with whether or not Che Guevara is a communist and his attitude toward the United States. Comments that Che's attitude is "fairly common among young 'Latinos'." Concludes that "Che's attitude towards the U.S. is dictated more by somewhat childish emotionalism and jealousy and resentment than by a cold, reasoned, intellectual decision." States: "'Che' is fairly intellectual for a 'Latino'."

- 4 -   00-B-3,098,099

in his column █████ never saw him reading Karl Marx or other Communist authors. On the contrary, he confines to literature his efforts to educate his soldiers █████████████████████ reading to them from the works of Charles Dickens and of Alphonse Daudet, among others.

█████████████████████ "Che" has a conception of himself as a romantic, dashing, warrior figure. He claims that he has no political influence over Castro and that he does not want to have any. Politics, as such, does not interest him. █████████ that if Castro wins his fight, he ("Che") will leave Cuba and explore the upper reaches of the Amazon River. However, "Che" now considers himself a Cuban and as of the present moment intends to become a Cuban citizen after Castro wins his rebellion (which "Che" is sure he will). This is something he has always wanted to do, said he. He is an adventurer, not a politician or a professional revolutionar █████ "Che" has always been searching for something with which to give his life some meaning and significance and that for the time being he has found it in Castro, not Castro the politician, but in Castro the underdog, in Castro the fighter against tyranny.

████████████████████ He is an individualist. "Che" stated more than once █████████ that if Castro's rebellion does not succeed, he, "Che", will "die like a man" at the head of his troops. █████ he would probably make the effort to do just that, because he is a "combat man", because he would feel it incumbent upon himself to set the example to his troops of courage in the face of heavy odds. "Che" is not, █████ the leader to direct things from behind. He must be out in front, inspiring his troops by his own deeds of valor. If this sounds romantic, █████ "Che" is, a romantic.

████████████████████ "Che's" attitude concerning the burning of the sugar crop and concerning bombing and terrorism, but think that he would either consider these matters as beneath his dignity to consider or else would consider them childish, just as the mountain forces of Castro consider all other manifestations of the rebellion against Batista as childish.

- END -

6 (d). 1958: Che Guevara "has a concept of himself as a romantic, dashing, warrior figure." "Politics, as such, does not interest him" and "if Castro wins his fight, he ('Che') will leave Cuba and explore the upper reaches of the Amazon River." Reports that Che reads literature to his troops including Charles Dickens and Alphonse Daudet and descibes himself as an "individualist." Indicates that if Fidel does not succeed, he "will 'die like a man' at the head of his troops."

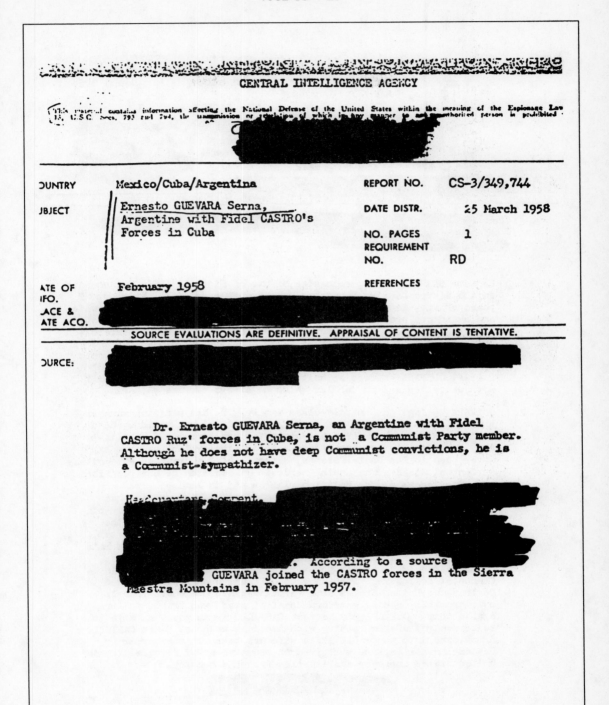

CENTRAL INTELLIGENCE AGENCY

This material contains information affecting the National Defense of the United States within the meaning of the Espionage Law 18, U.S.C. secs. 793 and 794, the transmission or revelation of which in any manner to an unauthorized person is prohibited.

COUNTRY	Mexico/Cuba/Argentina	REPORT NO.	CS-3/349,744
SUBJECT	Ernesto GUEVARA Serna, Argentine with Fidel CASTRO's Forces in Cuba	DATE DISTR.	25 March 1958
		NO. PAGES	1
		REQUIREMENT NO.	RD
DATE OF INFO.	February 1958	REFERENCES	
PLACE & DATE ACQ.			

SOURCE EVALUATIONS ARE DEFINITIVE. APPRAISAL OF CONTENT IS TENTATIVE.

SOURCE:

> Dr. Ernesto GUEVARA Serna, an Argentine with Fidel CASTRO Ruz' forces in Cuba, is not a Communist Party member. Although he does not have deep Communist convictions, he is a Communist-sympathizer.

Headquarters Comment.

... According to a source GUEVARA joined the CASTRO forces in the Sierra Maestra Mountains in February 1957.

7. 1958: CIA report noting that Che Guevara is not a Communist Party member although "he is a Communist-sympathizer."

NTRY   Cuba   REPORT NO.   CS-3/350,670

ECT   Biographical Data on Ernesto   DATE DISTR.   2 April 1958
            GUEVARA Serna, Cuban Revolutionary
            Leader   NO. PAGES   3

                                                   REQUIREMENT
                                                   NO.

                                                   REFERENCES
ATE OF
FO.   November 1957—Late February 1958

ACE &
ATE ACQ.

            SOURCE EVALUATIONS ARE DEFINITIVE.   APPRAISAL OF CONTENT IS TENTATIVE.

URCE:

1. Ernesto GUEVARA Serna, commander of one of Fidel CASTRO's detachments
    in the Sierra Maestra Mountains, an Argentine national, is about 29
    years of age, is married, and has a two-year-old daughter. His wife
    and child are presumed to be living in Buenos Aires at the present
    time. Although GUEVARA pursued medical studies, he is not interested
    in physical healing in general; he is sympathetic only to victims of
    asthma, because he himself has suffered from persistent and chronic
    asthma since infancy. Frequently during marches with the CASTRO
    forces, GUEVARA suffers asthmatic attacks and has to treat himself
    with medicines and an inhaler which he always carries with him.

2. GUEVARA belongs to a middle-class family. He has pleasing manners,
    speaks French fluently, and has a good cultural background. He is
    familiar with such writers as Malaparte[1] and Koestler.[2] His life-
    long ambition has been to become a revolutionary fighter. He has
    never been to the United States, although he has traveled extensively
    in Central America and South America. On occasion he has described
    his experiences on the Bolivian plateau and in Mexico. From his
    references to Guatemala it is apparent that GUEVARA was in that
    country at the time Carlos CASTILLO Armas overthrew the regime of
    Jacobo Arbenz and assumed power. GUEVARA was apparently on the
    side of the Arbenz forces, since he criticizes the United States
    bitterly for helping to oust Arbenz. GUEVARA claims that the late
    John Peurifoy, then United States Ambassador to Guatemala, told
    Arbenz he could remain in power if he rounded up and killed his
    Communist followers. According to GUEVARA, when Arbenz refused to
    do this the United States sent warplanes into Guatemala to help
    overthrow him, and Arbenz' own chief of staff was bribed to turn
    against him. GUEVARA claims that CASTILLO Armas was then able to
    seize control of the country with American weapons. When CASTILLO
    Armas came into power GUEVARA's wife was taken to the border by
    Guatemalan police; she was given the equivalent of five dollars in
    United States currency and expelled from the country.

8. 1958 Three-page CIA biographical report on Che Guevara.
(a): Discusses Che's "chronic" asthma, his literary interests, his desire "to become a
revolutionary fighter" and his support for Arbenz in Guatemala.

One of GUEVARA's principal and most emotional preoccupations is the subject of what he considers United States interference in Latin American affairs and the resultant anti-democratic proceedings against nationalist or leftist public figures, i.e. SANDINO in Nicaragua, Jose MENENDEZ (sic), and others. GUEVARA is keenly aware of Latin America's inferior position in the world. He feels that the Latin Americans have made no contribution to the world. He resents bitterly the resultant handicaps of Latins trying to compete with advanced Westerners, and he resents the fact that at any job the American always has to be the boss. He feels that in social and political matters the role of Latin America has been one of neglect. As an example of this, he remarked on one occasion, "Five thousand workers are shot down on the Bolivian highlands, and maybe there is one line in the New York papers, which mentions that there is labor unrest in Bolivia." He wonders if the United States so-called international labor unions would take an interest in the South American worker and if it might help to raise the living standards of the Latin Americans to a level which might come closer to that of the North Americans.

4. GUEVARA's thinking does not appear to follow any fixed economic or sociological pattern. He has denied vehemently that he is, or that he ever was, a Communist. In fact, his thinking seems to be far removed from the orthodox Marxist pattern. GUEVARA would be described more accurately as a Latino populist, with a touch of the intellectual's self-focused searching and an intense degree of ultra-nationalistic Latin pride. GUEVARA, like Malraux's 3revolutionaries, seeks a meaning for his own life before anything else.

5. In his present role as commander of Fidel CASTRO's No. 2 column, GUEVARA seems to have found deep fulfillment. He does not appear to be troubled with such frequent asthma. Except for a scar on his neck directly under his jaw, the result of a nearly-fatal bullet wound sustained in fighting at Alegria in December 1956, he is unscathed and in high spirits.[4] He watches over his troops with paternal concern, and his men worship him. In the evening they gather around him like children, and he reads adventure stories to them. The rebel soldiers call him muy valiente (very brave fellow), which is about the highest term of approbation in the Sierra Maestra Mountains. His popularity is second only to that of Fidel CASTRO. He appears to be much more popular than Raul CASTRO, who is somewhat a martinet, is harsh, impatient, and self-righteous.

6. GUEVARA disclaims all political ambitions beyond helping CASTRO to achieve victory. He plans to settle in Cuba when the fighting is over; however, he does not seem to be the type of person to settle permanently in one place. GUEVARA sometimes talks about organizing an expedition in the future to explore the upper reaches of the Amazon and the Orinoco Valleys.[5]

Headquarters Comments

1. Presumed to be a reference to Curzio Malaparte, Italian leftist writer who died recently. Malaparte, one of the founding members of the Italian Fascist Party in 1919, wrote, among other books, The Skin and Caputt. Malaparte claimed to be strongly opposed to any form of totalitarianism.

---

8 (b). 1958: Describes Che Guevara's views of U.S. interference in Latin American affairs. Che's thinking is considered "far removed from the orthodox Marxist pattern"; he is described as more of a "Latino" populist. He is the commander of Fidel Castro's second guerrilla column and his men "worship him."

2. Presumed to be a reference to Arthur Koestler, who was born in Budapest in 1905 and joined the Communist Party of Hungary in 1931. Koestler left the Party at the time of the Moscow trials in 1938. He has lived in the United States, England, and France. He is the author of many novels, among them, Darkness at Noon, Spanish Testament, Scum of the Earth, Arrow in the Blue, and Invisible Writing. The two latter books are an autobiography of the author: Arrow in the Blue describes Koestler's life to his 27th year, and Invisible Writing is a detailed account of his seven years in the Communist Party of Hungary.

3. Presumed to be a reference to Andre Malraux, a Frenchman by birth, who went to Indo-China at an early age. He became involved in politics there and also wrote several books based on life in Indo-China. He was acting as associate secretary-general of the Kuomintang in China in 1925, at a time when the Kuomintang had a number of members who admired the Soviet Union. Malraux played a leading role in the National Liberation Movement of China. One of his books, Man's Fate, dramatizes the Chinese Revolution of 1924, in which he participated. Another one of his books, Days of Wrath, depicts the heroism of Communists under the regime of Adolph Hitler in Germany.

███ Comments

4. During late November or early December 1957 GUEVARA was wounded in the leg. This wound was serious enough to warrant his evacuation from the Sierra Maestra Mountains to Manzanillo.

5. In January 1958 ████████████████████████████████████ said that GUEVARA was no longer an Argentine citizen. He claimed that a ceremony conferring Cuban citizenship on GUEVARA had been performed by Fidel CASTRO Ruz in the Sierra Maestra Mountains. Although this act has no validity, it is possibly intended to provide an acceptable basis for the formal granting of citizenship when and if the revolution is successful.

8 (c). 1958: Mentions a wound Che Guevara had and that Fidel had conferred citizenship on him.

CENTRAL INTELLIGENCE AGENCY
TELETYPED INFORMATION REPORT

This material contains information effecting the National Defense of the United States within the meaning of the Espionage Laws, Title U.S.C. Secs 793 and 794, the transmission or revelation of which in any manner to an unauthorized person is prohibited by law

TO: STATE, ARMY, NAVY, AIR, JCS, SECDEF, FBI,
NSA, CIA, OCI

CLASSIFICATION		DISSEMINATION CONTROLS
TDCS 3/350,959	DATE DISTR. 3 April 1958	PRECEDENCE ☒ ROUTINE

COUNTRY
Cuba

PLACE ACQUIRED

SUBJECT
Ernesto GUEVARA Serna, Lieutenant of Fidel CASTRO Ruz

DEPARTMENT OF STATE
RECEIVED APR 7 1958

DATE OF INFORMATION
2 April 1958

REFERENCES

APPRAISAL OF CONTENT (TENTATIVE)

SOURCE (EVALUATION DEFINITIVE)

Ernesto GUEVARA Serna, Commander of Column No. 4 of the CASTRO forces, claims that the campaign of the Sierra Maestra is based on Regional Clandestine Committee Acts (sic), a Soviet post-war publication which has been translated and is published in Mexico. GUEVARA is anti-American. He is not a Marxist, but he follows blindly the Communist Party line in all issues. Although he may not be a registered Communist Party member, he is an easy target for the Communists.

Comment. GUEVARA has a police record in Miami, Florida, where he was arrested and interrogated during the Korean War. He was once employed by a news agency sponsored by Juan PERON, former Argentine President. Gilda GADES, his wife, formerly worked in Mexico for the United Nations as an economist).

Field Distribution None

End of Message.

9. 1958: CIA report stating that Che Guevara commands Column No. 4 of the Castro forces, that he is "anti-American," and that he has a police record in Miami where he was arrested and interrogated during the Korean war. (If this is so, it must have been during his 1952 visit.)

COUNTRY	Cuba	REPORT NO.	CS-3/351,466

SUBJECT	Biographical Data on Ernesto GUEVARA Serna, Commander of Column No. 4 of the Fidel CASTRO Forces	DATE DISTR.	15 April 19
		NO. PAGES	3
		REQUIREMENT NO.	

| DATE OF INFO. | 11 - 30 March 1958 | REFERENCES | |

CE & DATE ACQ.

SOURCE EVALUATIONS ARE DEFINITIVE.   APPRAISAL OF CONTENT IS TENTATIVE.

SOURCE:

1. Ernesto GUEVARA Serna ("Che") was born in Rosario, Province of Santa Fe, Argentina, on 6 June 1928. His parents still live in Rosario. He is Commander of Column No. 4 of the 26 of July Revolutionary Movement forces in the Sierra Maestra, the largest of the five columns under the command of Fidel CASTRO Ruz. GUEVARA studied medicine at the University of Buenos Aires. While at the University of Buenos Aires he expressed his opposition to Juan PERON, then dictator of Argentina, and later voted against him. In 1953, when GUEVARA was called for his compulsory military service, he refused to serve under PERON and for that reason left Argentina. He visited Bolivia, Peru, Ecuador, Panama, Costa Rica, Nicaragua, Honduras, Guatemala, Mexico, and Cuba.

2. GUEVARA specialized in allergies and for that reason has done a great deal of physiological research. When he graduated from medical school he did some work in this field with a doctor in Buenos Aires. Later in Mexico he apparently tried to resume this research. He never established a medical practice. In Mexico he married a Peruvian exile who was an Aprista and they have a two-year-old daughter. It is rumored that GUEVARA and his wife are separated. He has mentioned on occasion that she may have returned to Peru since the change of administration in that country.

3. GUEVARA was in Guatemala during the last days of the regime of Jacobo Arbenz and defended the latter in the Guatemalan press. After the fall of Arbenz GUEVARA went to Mexico where he joined the 26 of July Revolutionary Movement of Fidel CASTRO Ruz. While in Mexico he received training in mountain warfare. GUEVARA was to serve the CASTRO Movement in the capacity of combat surgeon. He is one of the twelve survivors of the GRAMA expedition led by CASTRO which landed in Cuba on 2 December 1956. During the sixteen months in the Sierra Maestra with the forces of Fidel CASTRO, GUEVARA abandoned his post as combat surgeon to assume command of one of CASTRO's columns.

10. 1958 Three pages of CIA biographical data on Che Guevara.
(a): Che voted against Perón, refused to serve in the Argentine military and left Argentina for that reason. Che was one of the 12 survivors of the *Granma* expedition.

GUEVARA claims emphatically that he is not now, nor has he ever been a Communist. He is a self-acclaimed individualist, a non-conformist, and an ultra-nationalist in the Latin American sense. He resents accusations that he is a Communist and blames the United States and the United Press for such charges. GUEVARA claims that he defended the regime of Arbenz in Guatemala because he believed in the rise of an American republic which could defend itself against exploitation by foreign capital, for example, by the United Fruit Company. He refuses to believe that there was a Soviet penetration in Guatemala during the regime of Arbenz, and he said that all Latin Americans resented United States interference in the affairs of Guatemala.

GUEVARA said he became interested in Cuba during his university days when he read several books on Jose MARTI, the Cuban patriot. Later he met several Cuban exiles in Guatemala who were members of the 26 of July Revolutionary Movement. The aims and the ideals of the Movement appealed to GUEVARA, so he joined the organization.

GUEVARA is well-mannered, soft-spoken, and hesitant in conversation. He is extremely popular throughout the 26 of July Movement, both among the civilian and military components of the organization. In spite of his gentle nature he seems to have better military command than most of the leaders of the Movement. He is energetic, athletic, participates in any type of activity about the camp no matter whether it is softball, general recreation, or caring for pets. His men respect him because he is daring in combat and never passes up an opportunity for an encounter. He is the only commander in the Movement who has ever been observed to stand a man at attention and discipline him for inefficiency.

GUEVARA is about 5'11" tall, weighs about 170 lbs, and has a medium build. He is very tanned, but normally his complexion is very fair. He has crudely cut, dark brown hair, brown eyes, a rather high forehead, and a sparse brown beard. He generally wears olive-drab combat dungarees and a black turtle-neck wool sweater. His dungaree and vest pockets are used as files for messages, and are always stuffed with papers.

GUEVARA suffers from chronic asthma and must use his inhaler at night and during marches. Fidel CASTRO has ordered him to ride whenever possible during marches.

GUEVARA's sense of humor seemed to overcome his vexation when asked about Communism during a recent United Press interview. He answered that he was not a Communist, but that such questions from the press and indirectly from the United States Government were inducive to becoming a Communist. Later, when asked why he had abandoned his country, his profession, his wife and child for a distant ideological cause, he answered with mirth that this could have been a result of two factors: 1) that he read MARTI as a boy, or 2) because of the rubles he had hidden in his headquarters. In the same interview he was questioned concerning the duration and hardship of the struggle in the mountains and how long morale of the Movement would hold up. He answered that they have all the time in the world; that they are constantly growing; that only 12 men survived the landing 15 months previously but that there were now 1,200 men in the Sierra Maestra fighting forces.

10 (b). 1958: Guevara says he defended Arbenz so that Guatemala could defend itself against "exploitation by foreign capital," particularly the United Fruit Company. He became interested in Cuba during his university days when he read books by José Martí.

CS-3/351,466

- 3 -

GUEVARA spends most of this time on combat missions. During his absence from his headquarters Ramiro VALDES, his second-in-command, takes over. When GUEVARA is in camp his typical day begins at 7 a.m. He has early coffee, plays with a dog or cat, and then wanders out for his morning tea. Messages and visitors begin to arrive about 8:30 a.m. Headquarters business may range from cases of military discipline to logistics, or to arbitration in cases of military transaction involving the property of farmers. Since his command is a base installation, the paper work is relatively heavy for a guerrilla movement. In the afternoon he may be needed at a civilian or military trial. Offenses involved may range from something as light as property liability to something as serious as treason. By evening he is ready to listen to news broadcasts or chat with camp visitors. He retires at 9 p.m., when he lights his carbide lamp, and a huge cigar, and brings out his book on Jose MARTI.

Headquarters' Comment.   CS-3/350,670

GUEVARA. Seria.   contain additional information on Ernesto

10 (c). 1958: Describes a typical day in Che Guevara's life as a guerrilla. He spends "most of his time on combat missions" and at night smokes a "huge cigar" and reads José Martí.

2

1959-1961

The First Years
of the
Revolution

★ ★ ★

On January 1, 1959, Che Guevara and his column liberated Santa Clara and a day later entered Havana. They occupied La Cabaña fortress, an important military post in Cuba of which Che was made commander. It was at La Cabaña where trials and executions of the most notorious Batista supporters were carried out. In October 1959, Che is appointed chief of the Department of Industry of the National Institute of Agrarian Reform. In November he is appointed president of the National Bank. In 1961 Washington breaks diplomatic relations with Cuba and bans travel by U.S. citizens to Cuba. Che becomes Minister of Industry. He spends a lot of time traveling throughout the world, particularly to socialist countries, in a largely successful effort to open trade relations with countries other than the United States. On April 17, 1961, the U.S.-sponsored Bay of Pigs invasion began; Che commanded troops at Pinar del Río. The U.S. mercenaries were defeated in a major victory for Cuba.

U.S. spy agencies have many more documents on this period and Che than we have been given. However, the following documents demonstrate their continued interest in Che, especially as to whether or not he was a communist. The United States also had informants in Cuba who probably reported to Embassy personnel; some of their reports appear to be the rankest, self-serving rumors — sure to please the United States — such as stories of distrust between Fidel Castro, Che Guevara and Raúl Castro. Included among the papers are transcripts of Che's live speeches taken off the radio or from tape recordings made by informants on location. These are probably the only extant copies of the speeches and contain Che's thoughts on the United States, nationalization, economics, and the Soviet Union and China.

★ ★ ★

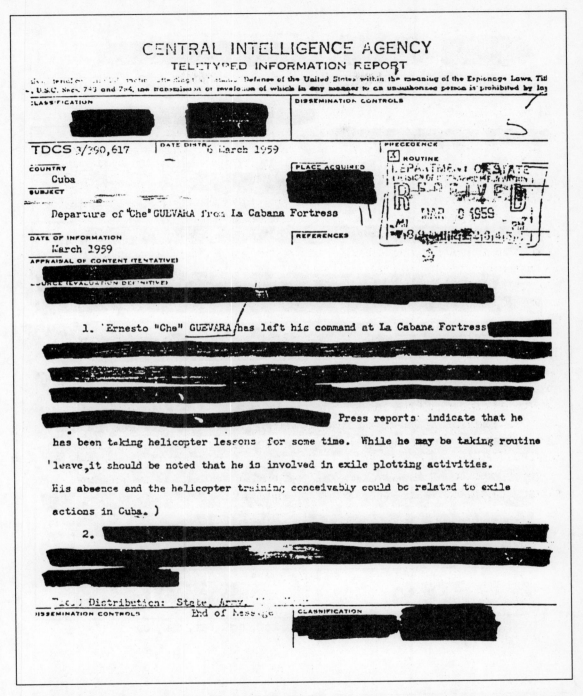

CENTRAL INTELLIGENCE AGENCY
TELETYPED INFORMATION REPORT

This material contains information affecting the National Defense of the United States within the meaning of the Espionage Laws, Title , U.S.C. Secs 793 and 794, the transmission or revelation of which in any manner to an unauthorized person is prohibited by law.

CLASSIFICATION		DISSEMINATION CONTROLS

TDCS 3/390,617   DATE DISTR: 6 March 1959   PRECEDENCE: ROUTINE

COUNTRY   Cuba

SUBJECT

Departure of "Che" GUEVARA from La Cabana Fortress

DATE OF INFORMATION   March 1959   REFERENCES

APPRAISAL OF CONTENT (TENTATIVE)

SOURCE (EVALUATION DEFINITIVE)

1. Ernesto "Che" GUEVARA has left his command at La Cabana Fortress

Press reports indicate that he has been taking helicopter lessons for some time. While he may be taking routine leave, it should be noted that he is involved in exile plotting activities. His absence and the helicopter training conceivably could be related to exile actions in Cuba.)

2.

Field Distribution: State, Army,

End of Message

DISSEMINATION CONTROLS   CLASSIFICATION

---

11. 1959: CIA report on Che Guevara's change in jobs from commander of La Cabaña Fortress and speculating that he "is involved in exile plotting activities" (activities relating to the elimination of U.S. sponsored attacks on Cuba). La Cabaña was the most important military post in Cuba and where opponents of the revolution were tried and executed. Che had a meeting with Salvador Allende of Chile at La Cabaña in January 1959.

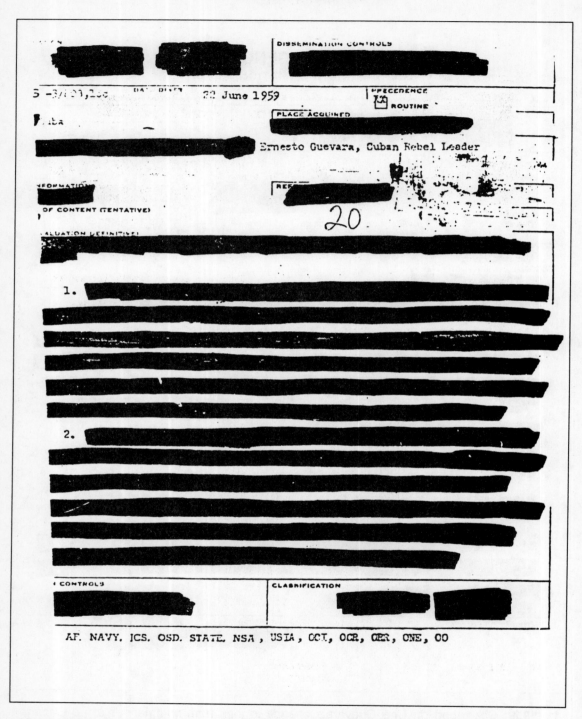

12 (a). 1959: CIA report on Che Guevara, "Cuban Rebel Leader," almost entirely deleted. Confirms Che as commander of La Cabaña and that he "follows the Communist line consistently." Note the wide dissemination of this document indicated by initials of U.S. agencies at the bottom of the two pages.

ASSIFICATION

DISSEMINATION CONTROLS

DCS-3/4.198

PAGE NO. **3.**

(Headquarters Comment. Guevara was a native of Argentina, and was given Cuban
citizenship and recognition for his part played in the Cuban revolution under
Castro. He is now Commander of the La Cabana Military Fortress in Havana.
He follows the Communist line consistently.)

Field Dissem: State , CINCSOUTH (Personal)
END OF MESSAGE

CENTRAL INTELLIGENCE AGENCY
TELETYPED INFORMATION REPORT

material containing information affecting the National Defense of the United States within the meaning of the Espionage Laws, Tit ..S.C. Secs 793 and 794, the transmission or revelation of which in any manner to an unauthorized person is prohibited by la...

...ASSIFICATION		DISSEMINATION CONTROLS	
DCS 3/405,195	DATE DISTR. 10 July 1959		PRECEDENCE [X] ROUTINE

...UNTRY ...ba

...BJECT
...iews of Ernesto 'Che' GUEVARA Serna
... Cuban Foreign Policy

PLACE ACQUIRED

...E OF INFORMATION

...RAISAL OF CONTENT (TENTATIVE)

REFERENCES

...RCE (EVALUATION DEFINITIVE)

Ernesto

...GUEVARA Serna,   was

...sked if the foreign policy of the new Cuban Government would consist of non-align-

ent   GUEVARA replied that, for the present,

...ba's hands are tied by the presence of a United States Naval Base in Cuba, i.e.

...namo, the agreement for which was signed by the previous regime under Fulgencio

...ISTA. GUEVARA added that the new Cuban regime gradually would find a way, as

...mal 'Abd-al-Nasir did with the Suez Canal, to force the U.S. base out of Cuba, and

...en the new regime would be able to show its true foreign-policy colors.

...eld Distribution: State, Army, Navy

(End of message)

...EMINATION CONTROLS	CLASSIFICATION

13 (a). 1959: CIA information report on "Views of Ernesto 'Che' Guevara Serna on Cuban Foreign Policy."

_UNTRY	Cuba/Latin America	REPORT NO.	CS -3/406,916
_BJECT	Views of Ernesto "Che" GUEVARA, Cuban Revolutionary Leader	DATE DISTR.	28 July 1959
		NO. PAGES	2
		REFERENCES	RD

TE OF
O.

CE &
TE ACQ.   FIELD REPORT NO.

SOURCE EVALUATIONS ARE DEFINITIVE.   APPRAISAL OF CONTENT IS TENTATIVE.

_RCE:

1. The policy of the United States in Latin America is wrong and will have to change, in the interest of the U.S. Whatever the intentions of the American people may be, the U.S. Government and U.S. business firms have, in fact, supported dictators from one end of Latin America to the other, notably BATISTA, TRUJILLO, and PEREZ Jimenez. In Cuba the revolutionary movement was opposed by BATISTA forces using U.S. planes, which dropped U.S. napalm. The CASTRO government has letters and documentary proof showing improper collaboration between the former U.S. Ambassador and the BATISTA regime. The U.S. military mission gave tactical advice to the BATISTA forces in their attempted suppression of the revolution. The U.S. sent spies into the CASTRO camp in the guise of journalists or others, whose information was then relayed to the BATISTA regime.

2. GUEVARA still remains suspicious of U.S. intentions toward Cuba. He said that there has been a build-up at Guantanamo Bay since the CASTRO victory which is not justified by any local unrest. The precedent of U.S. intervention in Guatemala is not forgotten. CASTRO's remark that, "if the Marines landed, there would be 200,000 dead gringos" was not intended for public consumption and was most unfortunate. However, it did contain a moral: everyone acknowledged the overwhelming power of the U.S., but the Cuban revolutionaries were willing to die to the last man if need be.

3. GUEVARA feels he is unfairly treated by the U.S. press. Reports that there were two Russian advisors with CASTRO, that Marxist indoctrination centers had been established, and that GUEVARA is himself a Communist are untrue. The U.S. press is prone to brand people as Communists who are fighting for freedom from tyranny, from economic domination by foreign companies, and from interference by such companies in local politics, which are legitimate aims. Rightly or wrongly, the U.S. is viewed throughout Latin America as the enemy of popular and reform movements.

4. The U.S. made a great mistake in Guatemala. Although Arbens and some others were Communists, the movement in Guatemala was essentially a popular one, the people versus United Fruit Company. GUEVARA feels more strongly about this than about U.S. aid to BATISTA. His then wife was dragged through the streets by the forces of CASTILLO Armas. Guatemala

- 2 -

was in the end a victory, perhaps, for United Fruit, but it alienated a whole generation of Latin Americans.

5. The coming year will see popular upheavals throughout Latin America— Nicaragua, the Dominican Republic, Colombia, Paraguay. In Argentina Frondizi has no power of his own but retains power by acting as a balance-wheel between the Army and the people. The editor of La Prensa had said that Frondizi had achieved the miracle of alienating both the Communists and the free press at the same time. Brazil had much poverty and distress but had achieved a certain political stability.

6. With respect to the future of U. S. business in Cuba, the U. S. note accepting the principles of agrarian reform and the right of nationalization was gratifying. The difficulty would lie in the valuation of properties. It was not Cuba's intention to drive out U. S. business or force it to the wall, but Cuba did insist on controlling foreign business within its borders to prevent injustices of the past and interference in local politics.

7. Whatever the respective motives might be, the fact is that U. S. influence or equipment was being used to suppress popular movement in Latin America, whereas the Communist bloc was supporting such popular movements around the world. In Cuba the Communists at first had hoped to take over the revolutionary movement, but, when they realized that the people were behind CASTRO, they fell into line, which was a prudent thing for them to do.

8. The United States has achieved social justice and liberty for its own people, but it objects when small Latin American countries struggle for the same things for themselves. This policy is inconsistent and doomed to failure.

CUBA SEEKS CLOSER TIES WITH YUGOSLAVIA

Belgrade, TANYUG, Radioteletype in English to Europe, Aug. 13, 1959,
2012 GMT--L (UNCLASSIFIED)

(Text) The head of the Cuban good-will mission on a visit to Yugoslavia,
Ernesto Guevara Serna, declared Aug. 13 to correspondents of BORBA and
POLITIKA that Cuba wanted to develop friendly relations with Yugoslavia
and to apply those Yugoslav experiences which might prove useful to
Cuba.

Guevara, a close associate of Fidel Castro, stressed in his interview with
BORBA's correspondent that Cuba desired the development of diplomatic
relations and trade, cultural, and other cooperation with Yugoslavia.
He dealt extensively with the policy of the revolutionary Cuban government which was fighting against the influence of foreign companies on key
positions in the entire Cuba economy. He said land reform was the
first step toward the general economic development of Cuba and its
industrialization.

In a special interview with POLITIKA's correspondent, the head of the
Cuban good-will mission pointed out that in Cuba lively interest is
shown in Yugoslavia as well as in other countries which are pursuing
a policy of independence and nonattachment to blocs, such as the
United Arab Republic, India, and Indonesia. He remarked that he
satisfied himself that in Yugoslavia there was also lively interest
in Cuba and in the events connected with her struggle, independence,
and progress.

Cuba wishes to insure its independence, said Guevara, and strives for
the cause of peace in the world. Cuba wishes good relations with all
countries on the basis of complete quality and noninterference. He
added that the principles of the Bandung policy and Panch Shila, that is,
the policy of coexistence, are very close to Cuba.

He said that the Fidel Castro government considers it indispensable
that a way should be found to ban nuclear weapons in general within
the framework of the agreement on disarmaments. During the visit to
Japan, he said we saw Hiroshima and grasped even more strongly what an
atomic world war would mean today.

Referring to the situation in his country, the Cuban leader said that
attempts are still being made there by the "forces of exploitation,
subordinated to foreigners" to put back the clock of history, but
they will not succeed since the unity and strength of the Cuban people
would never permit this.

14. 1959: Summary of Che Guevara's remarks on his visit to Yugoslavia. Che made a
three-month trip to Asia, Africa and Yugoslavia to build solidarity for Cuba and sell sugar.
Che stresses Cuba's interest in "pursuing a policy of nonattachment to blocs," and a ban on
nuclear weapons. This is typical of many documents covering Che's remarks and speeches
on his travels. The United States apparently kept tabs on his every move.

63 ~~OFFICIAL USE ONLY~~ 26 *uuy*

CUBAN ACCUSATIONS

BEIRUT ANA IN ARABIC CODE TO THE NEAR EAST 1945 8/26 M

(SUMMARY) KHARTOUM—ERNESTO GUEVARA, HEAD OF THE CUBAN
GOOD WILL MISSION NOW VISITING SUDAN, ACCUSED THE UNITED STATES
OF INTERFERENCE IN THE INTERNAL AFFAIRS OF CUBA, AT A PRESS
CONFERENCE IN KHARTOUM TODAY. HE SAID THAT THE AMERICAN AND
DOMINICAN GOVERNMENTS ARE HELPING CUBAN WAR CRIMINALS BY
SUPPLYING THEM WITH ARMS AND WITH LEAFLETS ATTACKING CUBA.

HE ADDED THAT THE CUBAN GOVERNMENT IS DETERMINED TO
STRENGTHEN ITS FRIENDLY RELATIONS WITH THE AFRO-ASIAN STATES,
PARTICULARLY COMMERCIAL RELATIONS. THE MISSION HAS ASKED SUDAN
TO PURCHASE CUBAN SUGAR, AND HAS HELD MEETINGS WITH THE
SUDANESE AGRICULTURE, FOREIGN, TRADE, AND INFORMATION
MINISTERS.

THE MISSION WILL LEAVE FOR MOROCCO ON AUG. 27 EN ROUTE TO CAIRO.

FBIS 8/26 1032P LF

15. 1959: A summary of Che Guevara's statement in Sudan stating that the U.S. and
Dominican governments are aiding Cuban "war criminals" with arms and leaflets.

C U B A

Sept. 9, 1959

GUEVARA HOME FROM TOUR, MEETS PRESS

Havana, PRENSA LATINA, In Spanish Morse to Authorized Recipients, Sept. 8, 1959, 2130 GMT--E

(Text) Havana--"A violent campaign against Cuba has been unleashed in Europe, Asia, and Africa in order to limit the sale of its sugar," Ernesto "Che" Guevara stated at a press conference one hour after his return on Sept. 8 from a three-month trip abroad. "In spite of this," he continued, "there is a chance of selling Cuban sugar to the countries I visited, on condition that we do not request total payment in dollars."

The young Argentine doctor, whom the Cuban Government made a Cuban citizen because of his contribution to the cause of national liberation, arrived at Rancho Boyeros and was met by a large crowd, including more than 400 members of the rebel army. Also present were Raul Castro, Juan Almeida, head of the air force, and high-ranking officers of the new Cuban army.

At the press conference Guevara said that a museum of the peoples' fight for freedom will be constructed in Havana. He also stressed the need of transferring part of the diplomatic corps now stationed in Europe to vital Afro-Asian countries and bitterly criticized the American TIME and NEWSWEEK and the international press agencies.

As for the impressions he gathered on his trip, "Che" Guevara said the following:

"1--The vigorous united Arab nation impressed us. It is developing its industry with astonishing rapidity and soon will be self-sufficient in steel, which it may even export.

"2--We were impressed by Japan, although industry there is not in the process of developing but is fully developed.

"3--People of India were sympathetic toward the Cuban people and we saw that they are trying to solve the problems of too little cultivable land and the large estates. While talking with Krishna, the learned Indian, we became aware of the evils of the means of mass destruction and when saw the frightful truth at Hiroshima we felt ashamed for having been glad at times when the atomic bomb was dropped on that city by the democratic powers during World War II.

16 (a). 1959: Che Guevara's press statement on his return home from his trip in September 1959. When met at the airport by 400 members of the Rebel Army, in reference to whether he will head the Ministry of Industry, Che states "I shall go wherever I am needed."

OFFICIAL USE ONLY

- 2 2 -   CUBA
                   Sept. 9, 1959

"4--Indonesia, aside from her domestic difficulties, must overcome
the colonial conditions imposed by the Dutch. In spite of this,
popular culture is being developed, especially in painting and sculpture.

"5--We concluded a payments agreement in (Ceylon?) and an agreement on
technical exchange in Pakistan. Under the latter agreement, Pakistan
can send cotton experts to Cuba and we can send sugar experts to Pakistan.

"6--As a revolutionary I must point out the progress made in Yugoslavia.
Great freedom of discussion exists there. We can exchange sugar for
electric generators, boats, and trolleys.

"7--We left lists of our products in Sudan and Morocco where possibilities
for exchange exist. We were forced to cancel our visit to Iraq and Ghana
because the trip had become too lengthy.

"8--When the international press agencies painted a terrible picture of
Cuba, mentioning three alleged invasions and the death or wounding of
Fidel Castro, I decided to return because I could not communicate directly
with Havana. Everything became clear to me, however, when I learned
the truth. I was to return only on Fidel's personal request."

"Che" Guevara finally said that he did not know whether he would head
the new Ministry of Industry. "I shall go wherever I am needed,"
he said.

- O -

CENTRAL INTELLIGENCE AGENCY

This material contains information affecting the National Defense of the United States within the meaning of the Espionage Laws, 10, U.S.C. Secs. 793 and 794, the transmission or revelation of which in any manner to an unauthorized person is prohibited by law.

COUNTRY	Cuba	REPORT NO.	CS -3/416,788
SUBJECT	Communist Activity of Major Ernesto "Che" GUEVARA Serna During Revolution	DATE DISTR.	28 October 1959
		NO. PAGES	
		REFERENCES	
DATE OF INFO.	1958		
PLACE & DATE ACQ			

DEPARTMENT OF STATE
DIVISION OF BIOGRAPHIC INFORMATION
RECEIVED
NOV -6 1959
A.M. 7 8 9 10 11 12 1 2 3 4 5 6 P.M.

8

SOURCE EVALUATIONS ARE DEFINITIVE.   APPRAISAL OF CONTENT IS TENTATIVE.

SOURCE:

During the revolution led by Fidel CASTRO Ruz for the purposes of overthrowing the dictatorship of Fulgencio BATISTA, Ernesto "Che" GUEVARA Serna refused to allow any Cuban to join his forces unless such person could prove that he was a Communist. If he could not prove that he was a Communist GUEVARA would send him off to join other anti-BATISTA troops elsewhere.

17. 1959: CIA document indicating the continuing interest in whether or not Che Guevara was a communist.

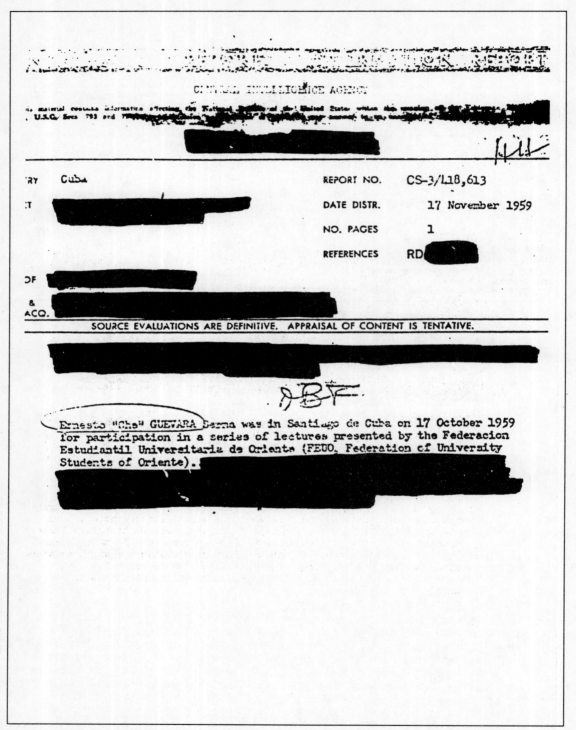

REPORT INFORMATION REPORT

CENTRAL INTELLIGENCE AGENCY

RY Cuba

REPORT NO. CS-3/418,613

DATE DISTR. 17 November 1959

NO. PAGES 1

REFERENCES RD

SOURCE EVALUATIONS ARE DEFINITIVE. APPRAISAL OF CONTENT IS TENTATIVE.

Ernesto "Che" GUEVARA Serna was in Santiago de Cuba on 17 October 1959 for participation in a series of lectures presented by the Federacion Estudiantil Universitaria de Oriente (FEUO, Federation of University Students of Oriente).

18. 1959: CIA document demonstrating the surveillance of Che Guevara in Cuba. Clearly many more such documents exist, but they have not yet been released.

COUNTRY	Cuba	REPORT NO.	CS	-3/452,715
SUBJECT	Plans of Ernesto "Che" GUEVARA to Leave National Bank to Assume Direction of Latin American Affairs	DATE DISTR.		12 October 1960
		NO. PAGES		1
		REFERENCES	RD	

DATE OF INFO.

PLACE & DATE ACQ.   FIELD REPORT NO.

THIS IS UNEVALUATED INFORMATION. SOURCE GRADINGS ARE DEFINITIVE. APPRAISAL OF CONTENT IS TENTATIVE.

SOURCE:

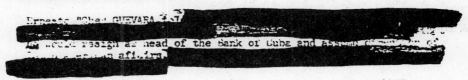

Ernesto "Che" GUEVARA ██████████ ████████████ ██ would resign as head of the Bank of Cuba and assume ██████████ of ██████████ affairs.

Headquarters Comment. While this is the first reference to any plans he may have for removing himself as head of the National Bank, there has been evidence of late which probably indicates that GUEVARA no longer regards his stewardship of the bank as essential to its operations. On 9 September 1960 the Habana press reported that he was on temporary leave of absence from the bank. (It was subsequently rumored that this absence was due to GUEVARA's attempt to direct military operations against counter-revolutionary forces operating in central Cuba.) More recently it has been overtly reported that GUEVARA would travel to the Soviet Union during mid-October.

19. 1960: CIA report that Che Guevara may have plans "for removing himself" as head of the National Bank and that he may be fighting counterrevolutionaries in central Cuba.

GUEVARA, Ernesto "Che"   CUBA
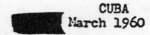   March 1960

Che Guevara is the most intellectual member of the group. He
creates fear because of his reserve, giving the impression of
holding back more than he is saying. While he does not cause the
antagonism that Raul does, the fadt that he is a foreigner is a
major factor preventing his ever being the leader. He knows
that he cannot force matters to a showdown. He tried to avoid
the foreign visits but had to give in to Fidel. He is not really
the "gray eminence"behind Castro, who gets out to the people too
much and is too individualistic to be so contbolled. Of course,
Che does present his point of view well and strongly, but his
position is not so important as reported in the US press. This is
more of a legend because of his inaccessibility than the true
picture. He is certainly a Marxist, a great admirer of the USSR,
but a party-liner would hardly praise such a deviationist as Tito.
I am not actually sure that he is a communist party member and do
not think that he is directed by Moscow.

CIA 00-B-3,155,060, 6 April 1960, CUBA,

20. 1960: CIA document that is most likely from an informant inside Cuba. States he is a
Marxist, but probably not a "party-liner" as evidenced by his praise of President Tito of
Yugoslavia.

HAVAN UNION RADIO IN SPANISH TO CUBA AT 0330 GMT 3/5
PRESENTED ERNESTO "CHE" GUEVARA ON "MEET THE PRESS." POOR
RECTION MAKES IT IMPOSSIBLE TO GET A FULL TEXT OF THE
INTERVIEW, AND THE OPENING STATEMENTS WERE MISSED. SOME OF
THE HIGHLIGHTS IN STATEMENTS MADE BY GUEVARA FOLLOW.

DISCUSSING PRIVATE ENTERPRISE VERSUS A CONTROLLED
ECONOMY, GUEVARA DECLARED THAT FREE ENTERPRISE FLOURISHED
UNDER BATISTA AND ON A RESTRICTED BASIS UNTIL THE MIDDLE OF
1959. AS A RESULT, CUBA'S RESERVES DROPPED FROM 251
MILLION PESOS IN 1957 TO 49 MILLION AT THE END OF 1959. DURING
THE PAST SEVEN YEARS, GUEVARA SAID, THE NATION LOST 450
MILLION DOLLARS IN RESERVES, AND NOW A POLICY OF RESTRICTION
IS "ABSOLUTELY NECESSARY." IN THE PAST, HE ASSERTED, CUBA
PAID OUT ITS RESERVES FOR THE "PRIVILEGE OF HAVING SO-CALLED
FREE ENTERPRISE."

SINGLING OUT THE PAPER DIARIO DE LA MARINA AS AN ADVOCATE OF
FREE ENTERPRISE, GUEVARA REFERRED SEVERAL TIMES TO THIS PAPER
IN DENOUNCING THE SYSTEM. DIARIO DE LA MARINA, HE DECLARED,
ALSO MAINTAINS THAT THE NATION MUST HAVE AN OPEN ECONOMY TO
ENJOY THE BENEFITS OF ITS TRADITIONAL EXPORT WEALTH. THE PAPER,
HE SAID, WOULD HAVE CUBA CONTINUE WITH A TYPE OF COLONIAL
ECONOMY, BUT THIS CUBA WILL NOT DO. THE UNITED STATES, GEVARA
STATED, ADVOCATES FREE ECONOMY, BUT WANTS IT APPLIED IN CUBA,
NOT AT HOME. "WHAT A CATASTROPHE IT WOULD BE," HE SAID,
"FOR THE UNITED STATES, IF OUR SUGAR COMPETED WITH THE AMERICAN
SUGAR BEET." U.S. ACTION, GUEVARA MAINTAINED, IN ARTIFICIALLY
RAISING THE PRICE OF CUBAN SUGAR, IS NOT IN ORDER TO MAKE A
GIFT TO CUBA, AS AMERICANS CLAIM, BUT TO PROTECT U.S.
INTERESTS.

CONCERNING NICKEL MINING IN CUBA, GUEVARA ASSERTED THAT CUBAN
NICKEL WILL COST THE CUBAN GOVERNMENT SOME 20 MILLION PESOS,
WHILE PRIVATE INVESTMENTS WERE ONLY 400,000 PESOS. NO ONE
CAN SAY, HE DECLARED, THAT THE NICARO NICKEL COMPANY WAS OF
ANY VALUE TO CUBA. THE ARTICLES OF THE LAW SETTING UP THE
COMPANY WERE "WRITTEN IN THE U.S. EMBASSY," AND THE COMPANY
TOOK ITS NICKEL OUT OF CUBA, LEAVING BEHIND "AN OX AS A SOUVENIR."
THE MONEY SPENT ON NICARO NICKEL, GIVING EMPLOYMENT TO 3,000
CUBANS, WILL PROVIDE A SOURCE OF INCOME FOR 100,000 WHEN SPENT
ON LAND REFORM.

WHEN ASKED ABOUT THE ADVISABILITY OF CUBA'S JOINING THE
INTER-AMERICAN BANK, GUEVARA REPLIED THAT THE BANK IS ORGANIZED
IN SUCH A WAY AS TO GIVE THE UNITED STATES CONTROL BECAUSE OF
ITS 60 PERCENT INVESTMENT. LOANS GRANTED BY THE BANK, HE
CHARGED, WOULD BENEFIT AMERICAN COMPANIES, NOT CUBA.
ALTHOUGH ADMITTING THAT CUBA IS THE ONLY AMERICAN STATE REFUSING
TO JOIN, GUEVARA STATED IT AS HIS "PERSONAL OPINION" THAT CUBA
SHOULD REMAIN ALOOF.

21. 1960: FBIS report of a radio interview with Che Guevara in March 1960 regarding free
enterprise and the U.S. exploitation of Cuba. Che criticizes the Nicaro Nickel Company, the
laws for which were "written in the U.S. Embassy," the nickel being removed from Cuba
leaving only "an ox as a souvenir" for the Cubans.

CUBA
July 29, 1960

GUEVARA COMPARES REVOLUTION WITH MARXISM

Havana, Radio Progreso, in Spanish to Cuba, July 29, 1960, 0320 GMT--E

(Live speech by Ernesto Guevara to the Latin American youth congress in Havana)

(Summary) Comrades of America and the world! Our country greets each of you and each of the countries you represent. We particularly salute the representative of Chile, Clotario Blest, (applause) who represents a country stricken by one of the worst earthquakes of history. We also want to salute particularly Jacobo Arbenz (prolonged applause, foot-stamping), president of the first Latin American nation which raised its voice fearlessly against imperialism.

We should also like to salute the delegates from countries still struggling to gain a free government.

We salute the Puerto Rican delegates. We salute Pedro Albizu Campos. (Applause) As free men, we salute a man who is free, although he is in a dungeon of the so-called North American democracy.

I also want to salute today, however paradoxical it may seem, the delegation which represents the best of the North American people. (Applause) I want to salute it because the North American people are not responsible for the barbarity of their rulers.

Cuba's arms are open here, ready to receive you all and to show you what is good here and what is bad, what has been done and what remains to be done by the Cuban revolution.

Many of you, of various political affiliations, will ask: What is the Cuban revolution? What is its ideology? Is it communist? Some will answer hopefully yes it is, or that it is moving in that direction. Others, perhaps disappointed, will also say yes. And there will be others, disappointed, who think no, and others who hopefully also think no. And if they should ask me whether this revolution is a communist revolution, I would say: Putting aside the charges brought forth by imperialism and the colonial powers which confuse everything, we should conclude that, if this revolution is Marxist, it is Marxist because it also has discovered, by its own methods, the road pointed out by Marx. (Applause)

22. 1960: Transcript of Che Guevara's speech to the Latin American Youth Congress in which he discusses whether or not Cuba is communist.
(a): Che salutes Jacobo Arbenz, who is present, as well as the Puerto Rican patriot, Albizu Campos, "a man who is free, although he is in a dungeon of the so-called North American democracy."

Recently Soviet Deputy Premier Mikoyan (applause) recognized that the Cuban revolution was a phenomenon which Marx had not foreseen. But this revolution, regardless of any labels applied to it, advanced, and the eyes of the continent were turned upon it, including the eyes of the monopolies.

When we were still in the Sierra Maestra the imperialist forces began to see that we were more than a group of bandits. Their bombs, bullets, planes, and tanks were generously given to the dictatorship to be used against us. But, nevertheless, we won. And we say to you today that if we were appear Marxist, it is because we discovered Marxism here. It was only after the fight in the Sierra Maestra was well advanced that a small pamphlet written by Mao Tse-tung fell into our hands. (Slight applause) This pamphlet dealt with the strategic problems of the revolutionary war in China and it appeared that, without knowing it, we had employed similar tactics. We did not know of the experience of the Chinese troops in their 20-year struggle on their territory, but here we knew our territory and our enemy and we used our heads as they did.

All of you must realize that there is no government in Latin America which can call itself revolutionary if it does not undertake agrarian reform as its first step. The system of land ownership has to be changed. All revolutionary governments must cope with this problem.

And after the agrarian reform there will come the great battle to industrialize the country. In this battle we have friends. The Soviet Union and China and all the socialist countries and also some colonial countries or semicolonial countries which have freed themselves are our friends. (Applause)

In the face of the aggression against us, perpetrated through sugar and petroleum, all the enormous faith, strength, and devotion of this people would have been needed to bear the blow inflicted upon us by the "North American democracy" if the Soviet Union had not been there to furnish us petroleum and to buy our sugar. Yet there are rulers in America who still advise us to take the hand of those who want to hit us and to turn away from those who want to defend us. (Applause)

We answer the rulers of these countries who advocate humiliation in the 20th Century as follows: In the first place, Cuba will not humiliate itself before anyone"; in the second place, Cuba knows the weaknesses and the faults of the government which advises this measure. Nevertheless, Cuba has not thought it permissible to advise the rulers of this country (not named—Ed.) to shoot all their traitorous officials, to nationalize all their monopolistic enterprises. (Applause, stamping of feet)

22 (b). 1960: Statement that "no government in Latin America [...] can call itself revolutionary if it does not undertake agrarian reform as its first step." Che Guevara defends the Soviet Union for supplying Cuba with petroleum and buying its sugar.

The Cuban people shot their murderers and dissolved the army of the dictatorship, but it does not tell any other government of America to shoot the murderers of the people. Yet Cuba knows that there are murderers in every country, and we have seen Cuban members of our own movement murdered in a friendly country by agents left over from the past dictatorship. (Applause, foot-stamping, shouts) Yet we do not ask that his murderer be treated as he would be here.

What we ask is this: Since we cannot be united in America, at least we should not be traitors to America. Let there be no repetition in America of a continental alliance with our (great exploiter?). ("Cuba yes, Yankees no" chanted) We do not admit intermediate terms. Either people are our friends or our enemies. We in Cuba do not ask any nation about its relations with the International Monetary Fund, for instance. But we do not permit them to give us advice.

We have stood alone, awaiting the direct aggression of the strongest power in the capitalist world, without asking aid from anyone. We were ready to accept the worst consequences of our rebellion. Therefore we speak, holding our heads high in all the congresses where our brothers meet.

When the Cuban revolution speaks, it may be mistaken, but it never lies.

We ~~areattackedrbehausearyare~~ demonstrating to each of the peoples of Americ attacked because we are demonstrating to each of the peoples of America what can be done. Therefore the agents of imperialism put roadblocks in our path whenever they can. And when they cannot place them in our path, unfortunately there are those in America who will do it for them.

Names are not important, because no one is guilty. We cannot say here that President Betancourt is responsible for the death of our compatriot. President Betancourt is simply a prisoner of a regime which claims to be democratic (applause) but which committed the mistake of not applying justice in time. And today the democratic Government of Venezuela is the prisoner of police agents (esbirros) like those who were once known to Cuba.

We cannot hold President Betancourt responsible for this death. We can simply say here that whenever President Betancourt feels himself so much a prisoner that he cannot go on and decides to ask for help from a sister nation, Cuba is here to teach Venezuela some of the experience it has gained in the revolutionary field.

Let President Betancourt know that it was not our diplomatic representative who initiated all this intrigue which resulted in a death. It was they, at the far end, the North Americans, or the North American government.

22 (c). 1960: Discussion of imperialism and aggression against Cuba. "Either people are our friends or our enemies." This speech includes Che Guevara's famous statement: "When the Cuban revolution speaks, it may be mistaken, but it never lies."

A little closer, the Batistianos. A little closer yet, all these who were the reserve of the North American government in that country and who paraded as anti-Batista men, but who actually wanted to defeat Batista and maintain the system--the Miros, the Quevedos, the Diaz Lanzes (shouts), the Huber Matos, and possibly the forces of reaction operating in Venezuela. Because, it is very sad to say, the Venezuelan ruler is at the mercy of his own troops.

The Venezuelan President at this moment is the prisoner of his forces of repression.

But a people which has achieved the political awareness and fighting faith of the Venezuelan people will not long be a prisoner of bayonets or bullets, because bullets and bayonets can change hands, and murderers can be killed.

But is is not my mission here to throw fuel on the fire of rebellion. In the first place, Cuba is not yet out of danger. It is still the foucus of the attention of the imperialists in this part of the world and needs the solidarity of all of you. It needs the support of Accion Democratica in Venezuela, just as that of the URD, or of the Communist, or of the COPEI or of any party. It needs the solidarity of all the people, of Colombia, of Brazil, and of each of the nations of America.

It is true that the colonialists are afraid too. They fear rockets and bombs like everyone else and they realize today, for the first time in their history, that rockets and bombs might fall on all they have built.

But this does not mean that they have in any way given up the idea of suppressing Cuban democracy. They are working laborously on their calculati machines to find out what is the best of the alternative methods available to attack the Cuban revolution. They have the Incaragua method, the Haitian method, and they also have that of the mercenaries now in Florida, or the OAS method. They have many methods and they have the forces to perfect these methods.

President Arbenz and his people know that they have many methods and many forces. (Applause) Unfortunately for Guatemala President Arbenz was not aware of their ability to ward off any aggression. This is a great strength--the force moving throughout the world, forgetting national political struggles, to defend the Cuban revolution at a given moment. Permit me to say that this is a duty of the youth of America. What we have here is something new, something worthy of study. I am not going to tell you what is good in it; you will see it. I know that it has much which is wrong. There is much disorganization. I know this. I know we lack experts. I know that our army is not yet fully ready and our militiamen are not sufficiently coordinated to become an army.

22 (d). 1960: Che Guevara discusses various ways the colonialists can attack the Cuban revolution: "They have the Incaragua [Nicaragua] method, the Haitian method, and they also have that of the mercenaries now in Florida, or the OAS method."

But each campesino and worker is behind the revolution, working and learning to handle a rifle to defend his revolution.

These people are absolutely united under the leadership of a man in whom they have the most absolute confidence. They would consider themselves completely happy and completely fulfilled if each of you, on arriving home, could say: We have been to the Sierra Maestra and we have seen the dawn. Our minds and our hands are filled with the seeds of dawn and are ready to sow them. Let freedom be won in very corner of America.

22 (e). 1960: Che Guevara acknowledges the revolution has problems, but says that "each campesino and worker is behind the revolution, working and learning to handle a rifle to defend his revolution."

We firmly believe that the current visit of the Cuban Revolutionary
Government's economic delegation headed by His Excellency Major
Guevara will undoubtedly strengthen further the friendly relations
and cooperation between our two countries and the militant friendship
between the Chinese and Cuban people. The Chinese people will always
remain together with the Cuban people, encourage and support each
other, and carry out to the end the struggle against U.S. imperialist
aggression and intervention and for defending world peace.

Long live the friendship between the Chinese and Cuban people! Long
live the Cuban people's revolution! Long live the people's national
and democratic movements in Asia, Africa, and Latin America! Long live
the great unity of the people of the world! Long live world peace!

Guevara Speech

Peking, NCNA, in Chinese Hellschreiber to the Press, Nov. 21, 1960,
1523 GMT--B

(Text of speech by Major Ernesto Guevara, president of the National
Bank of Cuba and head of the Cuban Revolutionary Government economic
delegation, at the Nov. 21 rally)

(Text). Dear comrades and friends: Today, we once again are warmly
welcomed with spontaneous enthusiasm by the Chinese people. We know
very clearly that this is by no means only a personal, warm welcome
to us alone, but rather highlights the feelings of the great Chinese
nation for the small island of Cuba. This expression of warm welcome
has been repeated several times in Peking, and in the many capitals
and cities of the socialist world. We have also warmly and cordially
been received by the masses of people in the various capitals, cities,
and rural areas of Latin America and in the colonial and semicolonial
countries in Africa and Asia.

In the past, Cuba as a small country almost had no history of international
activity of which to speak. In the short space of two years, however,
it has taken up an important position in the center of world friction.
To the imperialism situated on the opposite coast which endangers the
peace, well-being, and future of the world, Cuba has become a bad headache.
What historical conditions have caused this situation?

23 (a). 1960: FBIS report on Che Guevara's speech on his visit to China. He discusses
Cuba's nationalizations made necessary as a result of "imperialist aggression," and praises
the socialist countries for their material aid.

Cuba is an example of the education of the whole people by the people themselves. All members of its leadership are righteous persons. The movement led by Fidel Castro, the undoubted leader of the Cuban revolution, has adopted the correct line of keeping in constant contact with the people in order to know their needs. This forms the foundation of educating the masses by the masses themselves. In the course of studying and learning the views of the masses, even before we won the greatest victory in our revolution, we established the firm conviction that, under conditions of our island country, land reform must be carried out promptly. We knew this would incur the displeasure of imperialism, although at that time no one realized what would become of the relationship--and to what extent it would be strained--between the imperialist country and its erstwhile colony. This imperialist jackal, however, quickly bared its fangs and launched aggression against the Cuban people. In reply to each aggressive act, the Cuban people have taken a step forward and taken another countermeasure, which has intensified the revolution more and more.

At the beginning, we only reduced the electricity and telephone charges by imperialist companies, confiscated the property of elements of our own country who had spread corruption and committed theft, and carried out land reform. Then, imperialist aggression forced our people to adopt rapidly a series of countermeasures, such as the enactment of the mining law, the petroleum law, the takeover of enterprises which had suspended operations, the forcible expropriation of U.S. enterprises, the nationalization of all private banks and the basic means of production in our country, and the adoption of measures for the reform of cities. This was the first phase of our action.

This first phase, which started as early as July 26, 1953, has now been completed. The program of this phase of action was outlined in Fidel Castro's defense speech in court upon the thwarting of an attack launched by him against certain military camps. This speech, delivered in his defense, bore the title "History Will Pronounce That I Am Innocent," which happened to be the very last sentence of the speech. Now we have stepped on a new road along which we will quickly industrialize our country, carry the land reform further, completely wipe out unemployment and illiteracy, and institute a planned economy. All these tasks have been adopted by the Havana People's Assembly which denounced the exploitation of man by man.

23 (b). 1960

I am inviting the people's attention to this. What I have just said is not a promise because it is already true... and the leadership of our government... in the next few years to come. The road will be arduous, and there will be plenty of difficulties. However, we are not isolated. We are no longer the sardine which is defenseless before the U.S. shark, as a political fable has it.

The great peoples of the people's democratic and socialist countries, who have held their destiny in their own hands and who are united in combat spirit under the guidance of socialism, have built up a strong wall in the face of imperialism. They issued the most unequivocal warning in July 1960 through Nikita Khrushchev, premier of the Soviet Union.

The peoples of the socialist countries have shown that friendship can bridge oceans. This friendship is now no longer limited to issuing mass protests, oppositions, or helpless appeals against imperialism. This friendship has now taken the form of ICBM's and ocean-going steamships which can ship out our sugar, and ship in precious commodities and raw materials needed by us for consumption and production, as well as new factories craved by us which will contribute to the bright future of Cuba.

China, in conjunction with the other socialist countries headed by the Soviet Union, has opened a new historical era in extending generous aid. This shows that the people of the various American countries are no longer isolated in their economic struggles. By the same token, they will no longer be isolated in case of military aggression.

Ours is a country with only a little over 100,000 square kilometers and 6.5 million people. What sort of deep imperialist hatred, after all, has spurred the United States to risk its very national existence and, probably, its becoming no longer an inhabitable place? Is this hatred generated by the undoubted loss of investments of merely 1 billion U.S. dollars?

Today, Cuba has made imperialism lose 10 percent of its total investment in the Americas, and has dealt a crushing blow to it. Even more important, however, is the fact that Cuba has set forth the clear truth before the peoples of the Americas. We do not have to publicize this, because the truth that there is such a vigorous Cuba is eloquent enough.

23 (c). 1960

Cuba displays to all visitors from the Americas its present beautiful reality and the future of which it dreams. When asked by what means Cuba has obtained all this, it can only reply that it has achieved this neither by resorting to the method of the ballot box nor the method of establishing "his majesty's opposition party" through winning a number of seats in the skillfully manipulated parliaments of the so-called democratic countries in Latin America.

Cuba has won freedom and the fight to free development by her people's armed struggle face to face against the enemy clique and by defeating it and its imperialist masters who armed it. By smashing the troops which protected the wealth of the puppet dictatorship and replacing them by a people's army, the Cuban people eliminated the state organs of the former hypocritical government and laid in their stead the foundation for new organs which a people's government should have.

The army, the workers, and the peasants waged concreted struggles to defeat the enemy troops in decisive campaigns and seized cities from the country side. Those in the uprisings often conducted revolutionary propaganda agitation and, by incessantly attacking the lifelines of the enemy and the enemy troops with guerrillas, created the subjective and objective conditions for the seizure of state power.

Comrades, I hold that these are the factors which aroused the hatred of imperialism against Cuba. You are in a better position to talk on this subject than I. In your country wherein everything is calculated in millions and billions, you can talk about your experience in the past decades more eloquently. But Cuba is situated in the backyard of the U.S. colonial company. At the time of the birth, formation, and growth of the Cuban revolution and now when imperialism is seeing the eventual liberation of the people of various countries approach, a qualitative once has been taking place in America. Toward you, the people of China, and all the people of the socialist world, imperialism bears a frantic hatred, because you pose a threat of annihilation to militant imperialism. We have likewise incurred the hatred of imperialism. It is precisely because we have a common enemy who hates us and our common aspirations for a more beautiful world that our friendship will be everlasting like the snows of the Himalayas.

Long live the everlasting friendship between the people of China and Cuba! Long live the everlasting friendship between Cuba and all the socialist countries! Long live the unity of all the progressive forces in the world aiming at overthrowing imperialism and safeguarding peace!

23 (d). 1960

BANK SEIZURE, ECONOMIC AIMS JUSTIFIED

Havana, Radio Progreso, in Spanish to Cuba, Sept. 18, 1960,
0420 GMT--E

(Speech by Ernesto "Che" Guevara at a tobacco workers' meeting
in the CTC auditorium)

(Summary) The tobacco workers have finally achieved great gains, desired
by all of you, desired by us, desired by all the Cuban people. We
come full of enthusiasm and joy to speak, pausing in the daily struggle
in which events move so fast. As the imperialist forces acting from
without, and the regressive forces from within, increase their pressure
against the Cuban revolution, the latter becomes ever deeper,
responding to the people's will.

Today we expected merely to speak of the significance of this step
we have taken, when another event took place. Still fresh is ink of
the resolution nationalizing U.S. banks in Cuba.

And Fidel is preparing to go to New York, which is a battle post.
U.S. imperialists want to keep him from the right of every U.N. member--
to live where the U.N. has its site. Fidel is taking his hammock along,
and tomorrow we may see photographs of our delegation setting up
hammocks in Central Park. We set up our hammocks in the woods while
we were fighting for the freedom of Cuba; today we can set up our hammocks
in the midst of that barbaric civilization, and defend the right of
every nation to freely choose its own path.

The new measure will bring new economic problems. For many years
imperialism has based its power on money, on banking, which warp the
economy of nations until they become simply an appendage of the greater
economy of the empire. We developed the great sugar industry, not from
the goodness of North Americans, but because they dominated the entire
market. They paid us a preferential price because under it they could
introduce into our country all manufactured products under such conditions
that competition with other countries was impossible. The North Americans
would be the masters of Cuba.

24. 1960: FBIS transcript of Che Guevara's speech to tobacco workers.
(a): Che mentions Fidel's impending trip to the UN in New York and his difficulty in finding a
hotel. He says Fidel will bring a hammock and the delegation will set up its "hammocks in
[Central Park] the midst of that barbaric civilization...". Fidel eventually found lodgings at the
Hotel Theresa in Harlem.

- g 2 -

Liberation began when the first guerrilla group became strong in
Sierra Maestra. It will be completed when not an inch of foreign
intervention is left in our country.

But the North Americans needed accomplices. They needed a pro-consul
of a special sort. At times the pro-consul was an ambassador, at times
a military mission chief--but they all spoke English. Banks were
very important. During depressions, big monopolies see profits rise
and they expand their empire.

Finance, army, and, as a lesser brother, the government, are the
three branches on which U.S. power rests. Government and the army
represent U.S. finance but finance does not represent the U.S.
people. It represents a small group of financiers, owners of enterprises,
owners of the money. They exploit the U.S. people. Not to the same degree
that they exploit interior peoples of Latin America, Asia, or Africa,
but they exploit the U.S. people too. The U.S. people, too, are divided
into black and white, union and non-union, employed and unemployed.
In this structure, the U.S. Negro is no more unhappy than the Puerto
Rican or all our Latin American brothers who, impelled by poverty, go to
wash dishes in U.S. cities.

Here this disunity of discrimination has been overcome. The unity of
the laboring class marked the first step towards final liberation.
Economic empires depend on disunity among the people. Today we are all
together. We know where we are headed. We march united. There are
just a few who are against us. They are allies of the empires, the big
merchants, the industrialists, who used to get crumbs from the U.S.
empire. They will continue with the mentality of beggars. Today
they beg for intervention. When imperial powers get tired of feeding
them, they will come here to beg for a piece of bread. You will see
them desperately seeking work; then all of us will have the duty
of stretching out a hand to them and receiving them as one of us.
The allies of the empire, those who tried to wreck our economy at their
master's behest, used to profit from your work and take the money to
U.S. banks.

Now the step has been taken. A new horizon has opened, but with it
come serious obligations too. Again, today, we must change our mentality.
The old battles for minimal gains must disappear. Think of the past;
think of recent past, before Jan. 1, when wages were much lower,
when working conditions were worse, when there was no recourse. We
should remember the great gains made. These gains must be defended
every day with our sense of responsibility, with our work. The time
has past when the owner of a factory refused to obey laws, when the
worker was a pariah abandoned to his fate.

24 (b). 1960: In the United States, Guevara says power rests with "finance, army, and, as a lesser brother, the government." The U.S. people, too, are exploited and divided into "black and white, union and non-union, employed and unemployed."

Your task today must be concentrated on producing more. You must look on work with new eyes. You must save all possible, and organize. These steps will raise production and lower costs. You will be producing wealth. Everyone who has a task today must produce that wealth with more vigor than ever, but not yet for yourselves: for your comrades who still lack work. We must have capital to provide sources of work. In past all the wealth produced went to the few, for Cadillacs, trips abroad, servants in livery. Today the wealth must serve to develop agrarian reform, provide new sources of work. That is the great task we have ahead of us.

Fidel has said that next year will be the year of ending illiteracy, the year when we wipe out that shame. By the end of the next year, 1962, have the obligation of wiping out unemployment forever. But remember, this task is not one which calls for applause at one particular moment; it is a task that calls for every effort during these two years. Difficult conditions surround it. We must provide work for a nation which suffered from very serious chronic unemployment. We must carry out this task while we think about aggressions from abroad and from within. We must do this task while keeping a rifle at our side, with threat of a war that could destroy all that requires so much work to build. But if we are to face that, it is up to us to come out of it stronger and victorious. We are working for the future; the others are maneuvering to put us back in the past.

History is moving very fast, faster than the Pentagon or U.S. Senators like. Every day new cries of freedom rise in the world. Even when there is what appears to be defeat, as in the Congo, our progress continues. In America we have done something which already is history.

Today we can hold our heads high; today we can speak to you, because there is electricity provided by oil that is delivered by a friend of this small country so we can continue our fight for freedom. And remember this oil is furnished cheaper than the nearer oil of Venezuela, for example. This oil is delivered without demanding sovereignty or dignity in exchange.

Remember that all sugar which U.S. imperialists refuse to buy will be bought by this friend. Thanks to this we can keep our factories operating at a pace until recently undreamed of, providing employment, advancing agrarian reform, setting an example in Latin America.

Remember that many peoples with living conditions and freedom much inferior to ours are battling. Be ready to help others, like British Guiana, suffering from colonial oppression. Let us remember that the people of Puerto Rico are still under imperialism, that their island has been made an atomic base, that their leader Pedro Albizu Campos is condemned to slow death in a dungeon for the crime of fighting for freedom.

24 (c). 1960: Che Guevara states: "next year will be the year of ending illiteracy, the year when we wipe out that shame. By the end of the next year, 1962, we have the obligation of wiping out unemployment forever."

I remind you, of course this is so you will remember your duty of
solidarity with all peoples who suffer, with all peoples of America
who fight for freedom, with all men and women of this country whose
economic condition is worse than ours. The victory today is victory
for all Cuban people and the American Continent and all oppressed
peoples of the world. As we take another trench from the enemy, we
should remember that this battle is worldwide in scope; we have on
our shoulders the glorious task of being an outpost for America and for
liberation of the world.

Trying to smooth out all petty differences in our ranks, we must
begin the great task of reorganizing the tobacco industry. We have a
difficult task because of the great numbers of people employed in the
various branches of the industry. All places of employment must be
kept going; the living standard of every worker must be improved. Our
task is to mechanize in order to produce more, not to displace some
employed men. Therefore, we must seek new markets. There are many
markets, even though tobacco is not an item of vital necessity. In
many places of the world Cuban tobacco is not known. Formerly Cuban
smokes were just for a small stratum of society in wealthy countries;
Cuban cigars were luxury. As those groups become more and more
enemies of Cuba, gradually they become poorer. We must seek markets
elsewhere. That is the job of those of us who deal with foreign trade.
We need help from all of you, understanding and unity from all of you.

Now you make up the tobacco industry. We call on you to work for
improvement in the industry, you know that the voice of the Government
is the voice of the people. When the Government asks for cooperation,
it is because cooperation is needed. I am happy to congratulate you on
this new gain for the Cuban laboring mass.

(Editor's Note—W) Havana, Radio Progreso, in Spanish to Cuba, on
Sept. 19, at 0300 GMT, in an unscheduled broadcast, states that the
president of the National Bank of Cuba guarantees the accounts of all
depositors in the three nationalized U.S. banks. They are urged,
however, not to be frightened into withdrawing large sums of money at
once. He informs all employees of these banks that they have the
right to unionize and none of the posts of unionized personnel will be
abolished, and asks that the members of the union of bank employees
abstain from any extreme action which might cause alarm.

24 (d). 1960: "The victory today is victory for all Cuban people and the American Continent
and all oppressed peoples of the world." The next day in an unscheduled broadcast, Che
Guevara states that all deposits in nationalized banks are guaranteed and that all employees of the banks have the right to unionize.

GUEVARA, Ernesto ~~OFFICIAL USE ONLY~~ CUBA

Captain Hector SALINAS has died as a result of wounds received in the attempted assassination of Ernesto GUEVARA yesterday morning. The official newspaper Combate reports Salinas' death but makes no reference to the thwarted attempt against Guevara. Unofficial sources said there was an exchange of gun fire, including automatic rifle fire one block from Guevara's home in the residential Miramar. A 21-year old civilian named Pedro LELGADO Duarte from Las Villas Province was reported to have been shot through both hips.

FBIS, AFP, AP and The New York Times), 28 Feb 1961

FORM FS-438
4-23-57

25 (a). 1961: The year of the Bay of Pigs invasion. A group of five file cards containing information gleaned by FBIS (Foreign Broadcast Information Service). They make various claims of attempts on Che Guevara's life. The most bizarre of these is a report that Che was in a critical condition after a suicide attempt. Supposedly, after the Bay of Pigs landing, Che had said, "I have failed as a good Communist," and shot himself. Even the U.S. spy agency was skeptical of this report which was taken from Radio Swan, a Cuban exile station sponsored by the CIA.

GUEVARA Serna, Ernesto "Che"

reportedly hovers between life and death as a result of a wound he received recently.

FBIS (LA VOZ DOMINICANA) 19 Apr 61   rlb 4/20/61

FORM FS-438
4-23-57

CUBA   OFFICIAL USE ONLY   rpt 19 Apr 61

GUEVARA Serna, Ernesto "Che"

Radio Swan reports that a Cuban refugee, who arrived in Florida 18 Apr 61, said that "Che" Guevara is in a critical condition following an attempted suicide. The refugee, who has just escaped from Pinar del Rio, siad that Che Guevara met with the Government military leaders in Pinar del Rio regarding details of the armed rebellion and the landing of the liberation army and that when the meeting ended, Che said to one of his colleagues: "I have failed as a good Communist." He then want to an (adjoining) room and truned his own weapon on himself and was (seriously) wounded.

FBIS (FROM RADIO SWAN!! careful) 19 APR 61 rlb 4/20/61

FORM FS-438
4-23-57

CUBA ~~OFFICIAL USE ONLY~~ 23 Apr 61

GUEVARA Serna, Ernesto "Che"

The Cuban Embassy in Ric de Janeiro has received a communique saying that "Che" Guevara is not wounded as U.S. telegraph agencies have reported.

FBIS TKR 23 Apr 61   338A LEM/WG   rlb 4/29/61

CUBA ~~OFFICIAL USE ONLY~~ 23 May 61

Two persons were hurt the evening of 23 May 61 in Rio de Janeiro when unidentified persons in an auto, which fled, threw a bomb into a place where a meeting of supporters of Cuban Premier Fidel Castro was taking place. The attempt took place when

GUEVARA, Celia - mother (see Argentine files) of GUEVARA Serna, Ernesto "Che" - Cuban Minister of Industry, was making a speech. The explosion caused some panic among the participants of the meeting. The police are investigating and have arrested 2 suspects.

The Permanumbuco state legislative assembly has denied the request to permit Señora Guevara to speak before that body. She was the object of several hostile demonstrations in Recife.

FBIS 24 May 61

FORM FS-438
4-23-57

INFORMATION REPORT INFORMATION REP

CENTRAL INTELLIGENCE AGENCY

This material contains information affecting the National Defense of the United States within the meaning of the Espionage laws, 18, U.S.C. Secs. 793 and 794, the transmission or revelation of which in any manner to an unauthorized person is prohibited by

COUNTRY Cuba

SUBJECT Fidel Castro Nervousness/Conversations/ Replacement Rumors

REPORT NO. OO-K 3,202,844

DATE DISTR. 30 Nov 61

NO. PAGES Two

REFERENCES

DATE OF INFO.

PLACE & DATE ACQ

THIS IS UNEVALUATED INFORMATION

SOURCE:

1. Of recent weeks Fidel Castro has shown signs of extreme nervousness and fear. He is constantly surrounded by armed guards and now takes careful security measures whereas a while ago he was quite lax in this respect. When he travels he moves quickly from building to automobile and slumps down low on the car seat while traveling. His car is always preceded and followed by cars with heavily armed militia men, and there are always armed militia in the same car with him. Castro has always been erratic, but in recent weeks he has shown himself to be extremely jittery.

26 (a). 1961: CIA report in which an informant in Cuba states that Fidel Castro lives in fear, that he and Che Guevara "apparently suspect each other of trying to undermine the other" and that Raúl Castro "suspects both." This appears to be a fantasy of the informant, probably to please the United States.

2. ████████████████████████████ it has been apparent that for some time there has been great suspicion and distrust between the top officials of the Cuban Government. Fidel and "Che" Guevara apparently suspect each other of trying to undermine the other, and Raul Castro suspects both of trying to undermine him. On several occasions, Fidel, in his long ranting tirades on television, has blurted out statements regarding things that were supposed to be secret. He then has compounded the error by saying, "I shouldn't have said that, Ramiro Valdes will be angry with me for telling secrets."

3. The invasion alarm of 15-16-17 November appears to stem only from Fidel's nervousness. There appears to be no basis in fact for his belief that an invasion is imminent. The internal situation has not yet become acute enough that Fidel must divert people's attention from their troubles to an imaginary invasion. It is possible that the presence of US fleet units in the Caribbean could be the basis of Fidel's fears, but if so, he is the only one who is experiencing this fear.

4.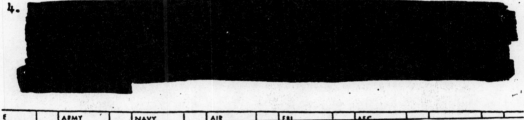

E	ARMY	NAVY	AIR	FBI	AEC			

26 (a). 1961: continued

OO-K 3,202,844

5.

6.

-end-

26 (b). 1961

3

1961

Richard Goodwin's Memos to President John F. Kennedy

★ ★ ★

When Richard Goodwin met Che Guevara at a party in Uruguay in August 1961, approximately four months after the Bay of Pigs invasion, it was unlikely that it was fortuitous. Goodwin suspected that Che wanted the meeting. Goodwin was then an aide to President John F. Kennedy. Goodwin had a discussion with Che and wrote three memos to JFK.

By 1961 the Cuban economy was in trouble; the United States was strangling it. Washington's policymakers, Goodwin and Kennedy in particular, regretted that they had allowed the Cuban revolution to take power. Their regrets echoed those of Winston Churchill when he reflected that, in retrospect, "we should have strangled the Bolshevik baby in its crib."

Che Guevara was the head of the Cuban delegation at the Punte del Este conference of the Organization of American States where the meeting between Che and Goodwin took place. Che made a major speech at the conference condemning the recently proclaimed Alliance for Progress, stating that Cuba guaranteed not to "export revolution," but "what we do guarantee this conference is that if urgent measures of social prevention are not taken, the example of Cuba will take root in the people" of the Americas.[1]

The conference marked a high point in the rising tensions between Washington and Havana. However, in his first memo, Goodwin informs Kennedy that Che approached him looking for a modus vivendi between Cuba and the United States. He heard Che out. He reports that Che was extremely personable and well informed. The second memo, in Goodwin's words, "is substantially a complete account of the entire conversation." Then, in his third and last memo on the meeting, Goodwin suggests policies of further isolation, and economic warfare and propaganda. He hopes these will succeed in reversing the Cuban revolution, again restoring the Caribbean as an American lake. Goodwin's reputation today remains as an American liberal intellectual.

★ ★ ★

---

[1] Che Guevara's speech at Punte del Este is published in *Che Guevara Reader* (Ocean Press, 1997).

THE WHITE HOUSE

WASHINGTON

NLK 79-175

#9

August 22, 1961

MEMORANDUM FOR THE PRESIDENT

The following is an extremely condensed statement of ~~recommenda~~ First Thoughts
~~tions~~ regarding some aspects of our Cuba policy.

The Conference at Punta del Este adds, I believe, two new factors
to our consideration of Cuba policy.

First, is the conversation with Che Guevara which is appended to this
paper. I believe this conversation -- coupled with other evidence which
has been accumulating -- indicates that Cuba is undergoing severe economic stress, that the Soviet Union is not prepared to undertake the
large effort necessary to get them on their feet (a Brazilian told me
"you don't feed the lamb in the mouth of the lion"), and that Cuba desires
an understanding with the U.S. It is worth remembering that Guevara
undoubtedly represents the most dedicated communist views of the Cuban
government -- and if there is room for any spectrum of viewpoint in
Cuba there may be other Cuban leaders even more anxious for an accomo-
dation within the U.S. This is only a speculative possibility but it is,
I believe, a reasonable speculation.

Second, is the emerging fact that any hope for OAS action -- along the
lines of the Colombian initiative -- is dead. It is my strong belief that
the big countries (Brazil and Mexico especially) are not prepared to buy
this, that they feel such action would be a meaningless gesture at great
internal political cost to them, and that there is no point on going ahead
without the support of the large countries. A numerical majority -- led
by Nicaragua and Peru -- would not be in our interest.

This being so I believe we should consider the following general lines of
action.

SECRET

SANITIZED

27 (a). 1961: Memorandum for the President, August 22, 1961

- 2 -

(A) Pay little public attention to Cuba. Do not allow them to appear as the victims of U. S. aggression. Do not create the impression we are obsessed with Castro -- an impression which only strengthens Castro's hand in Cuba and encourages anti-American and leftist forces in other countries to rally round the Cuban flag.

(B) Quietly intensify, wherever possible, the economic pressure. This means selectively discouraging those doing business with Castro, invoking the Trading with the Enemy Act upon the first apparent provocation, and focussing some expert attention on the problem of economic warfare.

(D) Step up propaganda aimed at:

1. Telling the Cuban people how their government is sacrificing their welfare to international communism.

2. Widely publicizing the economic failures of the Castro regime throughout Latin America.

(E) Form the Carribean Security pact strictly as a defensive measure. Aside from the substantive value of such an organization in dealing with the spread of revolution, it will have an adverse impact on the psychology of peaceful coexistence which Castro is now trying to create.

- 3 -

(F) Seek some way of continuing the below ground dialogue which Che has begun. We can thus make it clear that we want to help Cuba and would help Cuba if it would sever communist ties and begin democratization. In this way we can begin to probe for the split in top leadership which might exist.

Dick Goodwin

August 22, 1961

MEMORANDUM FOR

THE PRESIDENT

Subject: Conversation with Commandante Ernesto Guevara of Cuba

The conversation took place the evening of August 17 at 2 A. M. Several
members of the Brazilian and Argentine delegations had made efforts --
throughout the Punta del Este Conference to arrange a meeting between
me and Che. This was obviously done with Che's approval, if not his
urging. I had avoided such a meeting during the Conference. On Thurs-
day we arrived in Montevideo and I was invited to a birthday party for
the local Brazilian delegate to the Free Trade area. After I arrived,
and had been there for about an hour, one of the Argentines present
(who had been on the Argentine delegation) informed me they were inviting Che to the party. He arrived about 2 A. M. and told Edmundo
Barbosa DaSilva of Brazil and Horation Larretta of Argentine that he
had something to say to me. The four of us entered a room, and the
following is a summary of what took place. (The Argentine and Brazilian alternated as interpreters).

Che was wearing green fatigues, and his usual overgrown and scraggly
beard. Behind the beard his features are quite soft, almost feminine,
and his manner is intense. He has a good sense of humor, and there
was considerable joking back and forth during the meeting. He seemed
very ill at ease when we began to talk, but soon became relaxed and
spoke freely. Although he left no doubt of his personal and intense devotion to communism, his conversation was free of propaganda and
bombast. He spoke calmly, in a straightforward manner, and with the
appearance of detachment and objectivity. He left no doubt, at any time,
that he felt completely free to speak for his government and rarely dis-
tinguished between his personal observations and the official position of
the Cuban government. I had the definite impression that he had thought
out his remarks very carefully -- they were extremely well organized.

28 (a). 1961: Memorandum for the President, August 22, 1961.

- 2 -

I told him at the outset that I had no authority to negotiate my country's problems, but would report what he said to interested officials of our government. He said "good" and began.

Guevara began by saying that I must understand the Cuban revolution. They intend to build a socialist state, and the revolution which they have begun is irreversible. They are also now out of the U. S. sphere of influence, and that too is irreversible. They will establish a single-party system with Fidel as Secretary-General of the party. Their ties with the East stem from natural sympathies, and common beliefs in the proper structure of the social order. They feel that they have the support of the masses for their revolution, and that that support will grow as time passes.

He said that the United States must not act on the false assumptions that (a) we can rescue Cuba from the claws of communism (he meant by other than direct military action); (b) that Fidel is a moderate surrounded by a bunch of fanatic and aggressive men, and might be moved to the Western side; (c) that the Cuban revolution can be over-thrown from within -- there is, he said, diminishing support for such an effort and it will never be strong enough.

He spoke of the great strength of the Cuban revolution, and the impact it has had on liberal thought throughout Latin America. For example, he said, all the leftwing forces in Uruguay were joining forces under the banner of Cuba. He said civil war would break out in many coun-tries if Cuba were in danger -- and such war might break out in any event. He spoke with great intensity of the impact of Cuba on the con-tinent and the growing strength of its example.

He said that in building a communist state they had not repeated any of the aggressive moves of the East. They did not intend to construct an iron curtain around Cuba but to welcome technicians and visitors from all countries to come and work.

He touched on the matter of the plane thefts. He said he didn't know if I knew but they had not been responsible for any hijackings. The first plane was taken by a young fellow who was a good boy but a little wild and who is now in jail. They suspected that the last plane was taken by a provocateur (a CIA agent). He is afraid that if these thefts keep up it will be very dangerous.

28 (b). 1961

- 3 -

He began to discuss the difficulties of the Alliance for Progress. He asked me if I had heard his speech at the closing of the conference. I said I had listened to it closely. He said that it explained his viewpoint on the Alliance for Progress. (In this speech he said the idea of the Alianza was fine, but it would fail. He spoke also of the play of historical forces working on behalf of communism, etc. -- that there would be either leftist revolutions or rightist coups leading to leftist takeovers, and there was also a strong chance that the commies would get in through popular election.) He then said he wished to add that there was an intrinsic contradiction in the Alianza -- by encouraging the forces of change and the desires of the masses we might set loose forces which were beyond our control ending in a Cuba style revolution. Never once did he indicate that Cuba might play a more direct role in the march of history.

He then said, now that he had discussed our difficulties he would like to discuss his own problems -- and he would like to do so very frankly. There were in Cuba, he said, several basic problems.

    1. There was disturbing revolutionary sentiment, armed men and sabotage.

    2. The small bourgeoisie were hostile to the revolution or, at best, were lukewarm.

    3. The Catholic Church (here he shook his head in dismay).

    4. Their factories looked naturally to the U. S. for resources, especially spare parts and at times the shortages of these resources made things very critical.

    5. They had accelerated the process of development too rapidly and their hard currency reserves were very low. Thus they were unable to import consumer goods and meet basic needs of the people.

He then said that they didn't want an understanding with the U.S., because they know that was impossible. They would like a Modus vivendi -- at least an interim modus vivendi. Of course, he said, it was difficult to put forth a practical formula for such a modus vivendi -- he knew because he had spent a lot of time thinking about it. He thought we should

- 4 -

put forth such a formula because we had public opinion to worry about whereas he could accept anything without worrying about public opinion.

I said nothing, and he waited and then said that, in any event, there were some things he had in mind.

    1. That they could not give back the expropriated properties -- the factories and banks -- but they could pay for them in trade.

    2. They could agree not to make any political alliance with the East -- although this would not affect their natural sympathies.

    3. They would have free elections -- but only after a period of institutionalizing the revolution had been completed. In response to my question he said that this included the establishment of a one-party system.

    4. Of course, they would not attack Guantanamo. (At this point he laughed as if at the absurdly self-evident nature of such a sentiment).

    5. He indicated, very obliquely, and with evident reluctance because of the company in which we were talking, that they could also discuss the activities of the Cuban revolution in other countries.

He then went on to say that he wanted to thank us very much for the invasion -- that it had been a great political victory for them -- enabled them to consolidate -- and transformed them from an aggrieved little country to an equal.

Guevara said he knew it was difficult to discuss these things but we could open up some of these issues by beginning to discuss subordinate issues. He suggested discussion of the airplane issue. (Presumably, we would use the airplane issue as a cover for more serious conversation).

He said they could discuss no formula that would mean giving up the type of society to which they were dedicated.

At close he said that he would tell no one of the substance of this conversation except Fidel. I said I would not publicize it either.

- 5 -

* * * * * * * * *

After the conversation was terminated I left to record notes on what had been said.   He stayed at the party, and talked with the Brazilian and Argentine.

The Argentine fellow -- Larretta -- called me the next morning to say that Guevara had thought the conversation quite profitable, and had told him that it was much easier to talk to someone of the "newer generation."

The above is substantially a complete account of the entire conversation.

Richard N. Goodwin

28 (e). 1961

August 29, 1961

MEMORANDUM FOR
      THE PRESIDENT

A few additional details -- which did not seem important at the time
I wrote the original memorandum -- about the encounter with Che.

1. Throughout the Conference the Brazilians and, to a lesser extent,
the Argentines had tried to arrange a social confrontation with Che.
I had consistently refused such a pre-arranged meeting; the last re-
fusal being to attend a final party on the last night of the Conference.

2. On the night before we left I went to Montevideo (as did most of the
rest of the delegation). I had not planned to go to Montevideo and
decided to do so only at the last moment. I arrived at the hotel, and
had dinner with Dixon Donnelly (press man for the Treasury) and
Dillon's Secretary.

3. While we were finishing dinner a few acquaintances (a young member
of the Argentine delegation and a couple of Brazilian newspapermen,
along with a couple of blondes) asked me if I wanted to come along with
them to a near-by party for a friend of theirs. I said I would.
birthday

4. On leaving I remarked kiddingly to the Argentine, "you're sure Che
won't be there." He took this very seriously and said, "of course not,
I wouldn't do anything like that." He informed me that Che was at the
Brazilian embassy talking with his Brazilian pals.

5. There were about thirty people at the party -- drinking and dancing to
American music. I talked with several people and, after about an hour,
I was told that Che was coming. In a few minutes he arrived. I did not
go to talk to him; while all the women at the party swarmed around him.
One of the Brazilians said he (Che) had something important to say to me.
There then began the conversation as reported in the memo. Although there
were four of us present during most of the conversation there were as many
as seven present at some times and we were being interrupted by waiters
and autograph seekers.

6. I took the initiative in breaking up the conversation after 20-40 minutes.

       Dick Goodwin

29. 1961: Memorandum for the President, August 29, 1961.

4

1962

The Cuban Missile Crisis

★ ★ ★

This was the year that saw the world brought close to the brink of nuclear war in what is referred to in the United States as the Cuban Missile Crisis. The Soviet Union had placed missiles in Cuba as a means of defending it against aggression from the United States. The United States threatened to bomb Cuba with nuclear weapons unless those missiles were withdrawn. Eventually, the missiles were withdrawn, supposedly in exchange for Washington's pledge not to invade Cuba.

Carlos Lechuga, who was rushed to New York to take up the post of Cuba's Ambassador to the United Nations during the crisis, observed that "the roots of the conflict had been manifest ever since the triumph of the revolution in 1959.... The seeds of the climax already existed, nurtured by [Washington's] policy of extreme aggression that reached a critical point in 1962 and went beyond the limits of the arms race during the Cold War."

"Cuba," wrote Lechuga, "had thrown off its yoke as a U.S. protectorate and was standing up against U.S. hegemony in its immediate sphere of influence."[1]

Che Guevara's continued insistence that armed struggle was the only solution for freedom in Latin America caused consternation in Washington and was a factor in their negotiations with the Soviet Union. The United States kept open its option of destroying communism in Cuba.

★ ★ ★

---

[1] Carlos Lechuga, *In the Eye of the Storm: Castro, Khrushchev, Kennedy and the Missile Crisis* (Ocean Press, 1995).

C U B A

15 May 1962

GUEVARA ADDRESSES TECHNOLOGY STUDENTS

Havana CMBF Television Revolucion in Spanish 0240 GMT 12 May 1962--F

(Live speech by Industry Minister Ernesto Guevara at Havana University)

(Summary) Comrade professors and students of this department: While listening to the speaker who preceded me, I was thinking of the contacts that we have had in the last three years, and how circumstances have changed radically, including relations between the students of this university and the revolutionary government.

We are dealing today with students of a new technology department which responds to the demands of new times within a reformed university in a country which is changing rapidly and moving toward the building of a social system which would have been considered a fantasy only a few years ago. It is our fate today to be the vanguard and bulwark of new ideas that have come to these shores, giving to the people sufficient strength to resist the attacks of an enemy who is still very powerful.

There was a talk given here in regard to the role of the technology students within the framework of national industrialization. In fact, the topic goes much further than the industrialization and beyond the students of one or the other faculty. The topic today is that of the role of the students within the revolutionary process. The students do not represent a class, but they reflect the aspirations of the social class to which they belong. Therefore, the university changes its thinking and organization with the changes occurring in the makeup of the students. This happens here and at the other universities in Cuba.

There are here many comrade students who belong to a social class which has been destroyed as such in the battle that was waged in Cuba, students who are incapable of perceiving the changes in this country and unwilling to accept the new historical truth. But there are also those who, although coming from a social class which has been destroyed, are capable of understanding historical necessity and the absolute impossibility of changing what has occurred in Cuba--students who want to join the revolution. It is the task of the university to attract the greatest possible number of students and to convert them to the new mentality that has to exist and does in fact exist. This new mentality has to be made more perfect as we are improving our economy and getting into a position where we can give to the people more products and a better life--in other words, more material justice.

30 (a). 1962: FBIS transcript (first three pages) of Che Guevara address to students at Havana University in which he considers the revolutionary transition to a new society.

CUBA
15 May 1962

This is the road which we have undertaken, which the Cuban people have chosen. "It leads us toward a magic world which, nevertheless, is at the door of humanity. This road leads us to communism."

But before reaching that ideal stage of humanity in which everybody gives according to his capacity and receives according to his needs, this society must be built. First, we have to pass through an intermediate stage. This is the socialist society. We are now at the stage of building a socialist society which must entail the liquidation of exploitation of man by man, a more equitable distribution of the national revenue, and constantly increasing production for our people. We are, of course, still far from being able to say that we have built socialism. We are still further away from the moment in which we can start on preparations for the transition toward communism. Nevertheless, in the Soviet Union, they are already preparing for this transition. The utopias of the philosophers of the last century are about to be implemented for humanity.

This shows us merely that Marxism is a science. Whether the aspirations of a class are felt by those who belong to it or not, "it must be admitted that Marxism is a science and that, as a science, it has been able to foresee the future of humanity. It is in our hands to accelerate or delay the transition toward socialism. Evidently the counterrevolutionaries are doing everything in their power to delay this transition. In many cases they believe sincerely that they are fighting for a cause that has possibilities of victory.

"This belief in the possibility of victory and the usual characteristics of the class struggle have motivated the deep split of the Cuban people in recent times. It has brought to many homes—mainly those known as middle class—profound difficulties within the family. It has led to great differences and caused many comrades to receive the shock of their women leaving, of their parents going away at times, and of their brothers fighting in the counterrevolution. It has caused the struggle at this time to turn into a fight to the death. It means that brothers separated by ideological problems to the point of joining gangs and different classes are preparing to fight to the death."

This is, of course, a sad feature of revolutions. However, the people's revolutions are always generous. But they have to comply with a duty which takes precedence over any generosity: the duty of keeping alive and of progressing. The attacks of the reaction against the new society in the process on formation must be met with full force. Reaction also responds with all its might and the fighting ensues.

As the forces of reaction are becoming weaker in the process of the creation of the socialist society, the bitterness of the class struggle will be weakened and render the transition easier for all. But it is our duty

CUBA
15 May 1962

always to save what can be saved and to recover what can be recovered. "The one who at this time is rushing against all opposition is not a better revolutionary than the one who reasons and is trying to convince a comrade student, worker, or farmer of the fairness and justice of the revolution. On the contrary, he who knows how to do this well and who is doing it by giving an example himself, is a much better revolutionary. There is nothing that is more convincing than one's own example to express or defend an idea."

But the basic task of the young students of the university is to study and to study more in preparation for the new society. To this effect it is necessary to develop socialist awareness and to increase production.

What does development of revolutionary awareness mean? It means basically that theory and practice must always be joined. The development of a revolutionary consciousness must be closely related to the study of the social and economic phenomena which prevail in our times, and to revolutionary action. Revolutionary action among students is primarily study. Students must look for the reply to the problems of this time. They must go on changing their attitudes toward basic problems. In the first place, there is the attitude toward work. Physical labor during the capitalist period was considered a necessary evil symbolic of the lack of ability to reach higher levels--those of the exploiters or those of the aides of exploiters. The attitude of our technicians toward manual labor was vitiated by this kind of prejudice.

The middle class used to foster this prejudice. It was interested in splitting the exploited masses, because an engineer or technician working for an imperialist company was also an exploited individual. This attitude toward manual labor must be changed. It has already been changed. In talks with representatives of the students of the department of technology, we have reached a series of agreements for students to work in projects and industrial plants. Manual labor is part of the work of society--equal to other work. There must be no differentiation between manual and intellectual labor. Those who want to be useful in intellectual and technical work will be given an opportunity by the ministry.

"We must change our attitude toward development programs. We must learn more about planning. Planning is important at this time. We have sensed the need for it at this time with our own instincts. We have clashed with obstacles put into our way. We have realized that our lack of foresight had been responsible for such obstructions. We have learned the lesson well and are arranging things rapidly. Starting with this year of planning, planning will be not only a familiar term, but its real menaing will be well-known to the students and technicians of Cuba."

C U B A

28 May 1962

DR. GUEVARA ASKS ARGENTINE LIBERATION

Havana Reloj Nacional Network in Spanish 1700 GMT 26 May 1962--F

(Summary) Let us celebrate another 25 May--not any more in this generous country, but in Argentina. This statement was made by Maj. Ernesto Guevara in delivering the main address at the Argentine national holiday celebration. Major Guevara spoke before several hundred Argentineans residing in Cuba at a function organized by the Argentine-Cuban Friendship Institute. He said that Cuba has the glory of being the initiator of this new era of liberation in Latin America. The industry minister made reference also to the case of the Guatemalan revolution which was destroyed by Yankee imperialism.

"Guevara said that there is no victorious revolution which does not set out first to change the defeated army by replacing it with a new army and to establish the rule of the masses. This is what we have done, Guevara added. That is our merit. It is the experience which we can offer to the peoples of the world and which the peoples of the hemisphere may interpret with greater vigor, because we are speaking the same language and have had the same experiences."

Subsequently, Guevara said: We do not presume that this experience constitutes the only way for the independence of the Americas, but we do say that it is the most important way." In another part of his address, Guevara said that in order to achieve the revolution it is necessary to seize the arms that are available and to turn a small army into a great people's army. After referring to the deeds of 25 May 1810 in Argentina Guevara said that period of liberation is being repeated here today in this small Caribbean island where the experiences which occurred at one moment of Argentine history are actually being lived through."

At another point, Guevara said that "our revolution is one which needs to expand its ideas and that other people are helping and embracing us. Let other peoples of the hemisphere get angry and take up arms or seize power and aid us in this task which is the task of the entire hemisphere and of humanity," Guevara said in his address. He added that the "monopolist and imperialist enemy will not be defeated definitively until the last one of its magnates has at least been sent to jail or to the execution block." Guevara stressed that all the people of America must fight for the noble idea of destroying the monopolists and imperialists to rid themselves definitively of exploitation and hunger.

31. 1962: FBIS report on part of a speech by Che Guevara on the May 25 Argentine national holiday. He stresses that armed revolution is not the only way to achieve the independence of the Americas, "but the most important way."

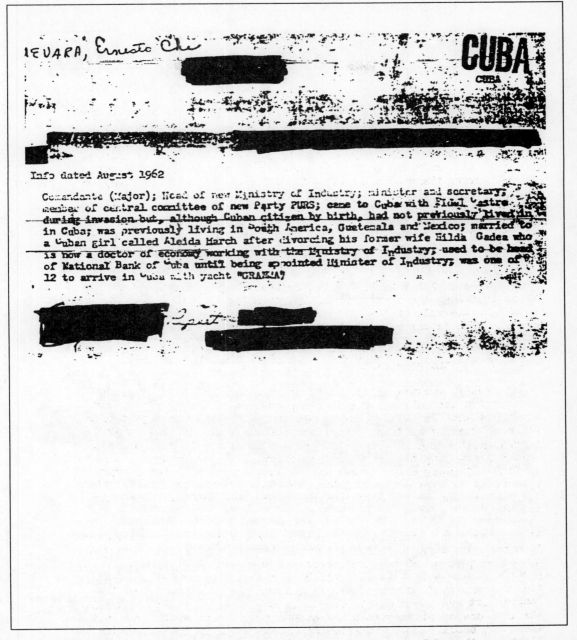

IEVARA, Ernesto 'Che

CUBA
CUBA

Info dated August 1962

Comandante (Major); Head of new Ministry of Industry; minister and secretary; member of central committee of new Party PURS; came to Cuba with Fidel Castro during invasion but, although Cuban citizen by birth, had not previously lived in in Cuba; was previously living in South America, Guatemala and Mexico; married to a Cuban girl called Aleida March after divorcing his former wife Hilda Gadea who is now a doctor of economy working with the Ministry of Industry; used to be head of National Bank of Cuba until being appointed Minister of Industry; was one of 12 to arrive in Cuba with yacht "GRANMA"

32. 1962: File card on Che Guevara mentioning that he became a member of the Central Committee of PURS, the United Party of the Socialist Revolution. Che "came to Cuba with Fidel Castro during the invasion but, although Cuban citizen by birth, had not previously lived in Cuba; was previously living in South America, Guatemala and Mexico; married to a Cuban girl called Aleida March after divorcing his former wife Hilda Gadea who is now a doctor of economy working with the Ministry of Industry." Errors in this file card include that Che was Cuban "by birth" and that he "was one of 12 to arrive in Cuba with yacht 'Granma'." (Che was one of 12 survivors.)

CUBA

Cuba	REPORT NO. CS –3/520,600
Possible Reassignment of Ernesto "Che" Guevara, Minister of Industries	DATE DISTR. 24 August 1962
	NO. PAGES 2
	REFERENCES RD

21–30 July 1962

IS IS UNEVALUATED INFORMATION. SOURCE GRADINGS ARE DEFINITIVE. APPRAISAL OF CONTENT IS TENTATIVE.

Major Ernesto "Che" Guevara Serna will change his post as Minister of Industries to become chief of the Junta Central de Planificacion (JUCEPLAN, Central Planning Board). His undersecretaries will be Lieutenant Francisco Garcia Valls and Enrique Oltuski, an engineer. Undersecretary Orlando Borrego Diaz will become the new Minister of Industries.

Guevara makes the political decisions for the Ministry of Industries, as well as for internal and foreign trade procedures, and, in general, for all of the national economy of Cuba. He is also a member of the Economic Committee of the Organizaciones Revolucionarias Integradas (ORI, Integrated Revolutionary Organizations).

Comments

1.   Francisco Garcia Valls was listed as the General Coordinator in 1960 of the Cuban National Institute of Agrarian Reform.

2.   Enrique Oltuski was Minister of Communications from January 1959 until June 1960.

33 (a). 1962: CIA document most likely based on an informant stating that Che Guevara is changing jobs and that he has responsibility for Cuba's economy. The ORI (Integrated Revolutionary Organizations) was made up of three groups: the July 26 Movement, Popular Socialist Party and Revolutionary Student Directory. It was the forerunner of PURS (the United Party of the Socialist Revolution).

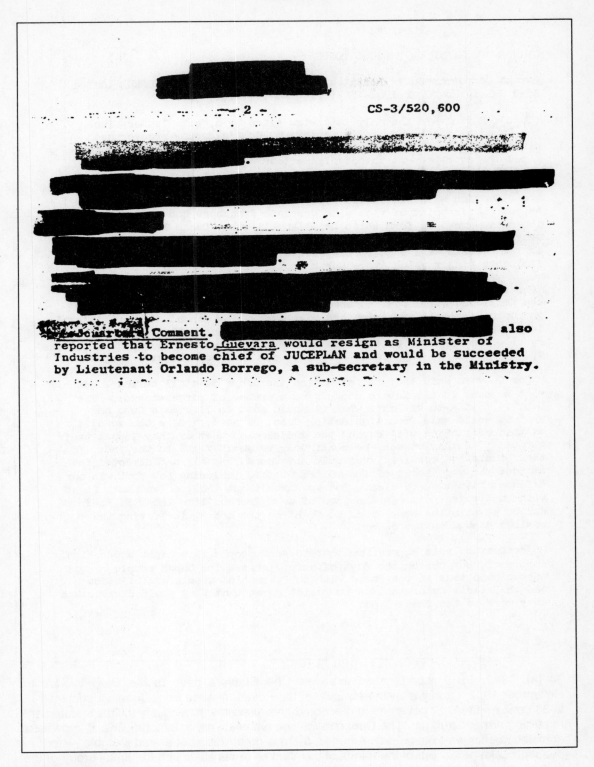

2 -   CS-3/520,600

Comment.   also
reported that Ernesto Guevara would resign as Minister of
Industries to become chief of JUCEPLAN and would be succeeded
by Lieutenant Orlando Borrego, a sub-secretary in the Ministry.

GUEVARA COMMENTS ON VARIOUS TOPICS

Havana Correspondent's Dispatch in English to the DAILY WORKER London
1540 GMT 29 November 1962--E (OFFICIAL USE ONLY)

(Text) Havana--In the only interview given by a Cuban leader since
the Cuban crisis began over a month ago, Cuba's deputy premier and
minister of industries, Commandant Che Guevara, on 28 November underlined the ever-present threat of American aggression against Cuba,
despite American attempts to lull the world into a false sense of
security. For over two hours--until well past midnight--I discussed
the situation with him in his office on Havana's Revolution Square as
he put Cuba's point of view with complete frankness and sincerity.
The olive-green uniform which he, like all other Cuban leaders, still
wears, the armed guards on the building and the men and women drilling
in the streets as I came to his office also underlined the sense of
imminente danger which every Cuban feels.

"The rockets have gone," he said, "and the Il-28 planes are going, but
the Americans still want to come here. They have still not given any
guarantee against aggression and make everything dependent on unilateral
inspection, which we will not accept. What is more, the Americans
reserve the right to be the sole arbiters as to when they should intervene
openly as well as the right to violate our airspace whenever they want."

Major Guevara said that the situation therefore is still serious, but
what happens in the future depends on a number of circumstances. The
U.S. is trying to estimate what it would cost to liquidate Cuba and
what it would gain from liquidating Cuba, he said, and on the results
of this estimation will depend the decision on whether they launch their
attack. "If they attack, he continued, we shall fight to the end. If
the rockets had remained, we would have used them all and directed them
against the very heart of the United States, including New York, in our
defense against aggression. But we haven't got them, so we shall fight
with what we've got. In the face of an aggressor like the U.S., there
can be no solution other than to fight to the death, inflicting the
maximum damage on the enemy."

Major Guevara said he realizes that to some people this might sound highly
emotional, but during the days of actute crisis the Cuban people
appreciated that it was faced with the threat of atomic annihilation
and that their determination to resist meant that they would die because
they were in the front line.

---

34 (a). 1962: FBIS report on an interview Che Guevara gave to the *Daily Worker* in
November 1962, shortly after the removal of the Soviet missiles from Cuba. Documents 35
to 37 concern the U.S. government reaction to this interview, particularly to Che's statement
regarding armed struggle: "The Cuban revolution has shown that in conditions of imperialist
domination such as exist in Latin America, there is no solution but armed struggle — for the
people to take power out of the hands of the Yankee imperialists and the small group of the
national bourgeois who work with them."

"Whether the Americans attack or not depends on their estimate of our internal situation and of the international situation. That is why the solidarity of the peoples of the world is of such importance to us. We are under no illusion. We know we cannot exist on our own. We depend on the solidarity of the socialist camp and of the whole world."

While not underestimating the importance of the solidarity movement that has developed in the world in support of Cuba, Major Guevara considered that the most effective form of help was the armed struggle already taking place in a number of Latin American countries where the peoples are in action to overthrow American imperialism. "We know," he continued, "that some people in Europe are saying that a great victory has been won. But we say that the danger is still here, and we say that while war may have been avoided, that does not mean that peace has been assured. And we ask whether in exchange for some slight gain we have only prolonged the agony. For so far, all that has happened is that a confrontation has been avoided."

I then asked Major Guevara what was the present state of relations between the Soviet Union and Cuba--especially in view of Premier Fidel Castro's statement on 1 November that certain misunderstandings or discrepancies had arisen. "During Comrade Mikoyan's visit," he said, "we went into a great number of questions with the Soviet Union. We discussed frankly and fully and each side put his point of view. "We know that the Soviet Union is the friend that can help us most, and we are convinced that it will continue to help us. All we have done is to use our right as an independent party within the framework of the principles of international proletarian solidarity. The discrepancies are past and will not be of importance in the future. We consider ourselves part of the socialist world and absolutely faithful to Marxism-Leninist ideas."

My next question was on the effects of the U.S. economic blockade of Cuba and how Cuba has dealt with the situation. Major Guevara pointed out that while President Kennedy had announced the end of the so-called quarantine, the economic blockade continues and that President Kennedy himself has declared that political, economic and other measures against Cuba will be intensified.

He pointed out too that the blockade had been imposed in a number of stages. The first stage was when the U.S. closed its ports to Cuban goods and stopped the export of goods Cuba needed. Then the United States asked its allies not to trade with Cuba. "And now," he continued, "the United States is preparing to impose sanctions on those ships, merchants and manufacturers who are trading with Cuba. This will hit Britain most of all.

"There could be further acts in this connection. But we can say that each time, we have found ways of overcoming the effects of this blockade policy."

Major Guevara said that it would be ridiculous to pretend that the blockade has not hit Cuba, for our factories and public services are equipped mostly with American and British machinery, which need spare parts for servicing. "But if we cannot get these spare parts," he added, "then we shall find other ways of overcoming our difficulties and we have achieved considerable success in this respect already.

"Of course, this will mean hardship for us, but today it is impossible to strangle a country economically. So we shall win out. Of course, it will mean that our development plans will have to be modified and be less ambitious."

On President Kennedy's threat to use, apart from political and economic pressure, "other measures" against Cuba, Major Guevara said that this covered the whole field of paramilitary action, including espionage, sabotage, the dropping of arms and agents by parachute along Cuba's long coastline—in fact, "everything short of open war, while reserving the right to resort to open attack. The violation of our airspace continues all the time, and we have not seen the end of this sort of thing by any means."

Major Guevara then gave me some interesting details about the way in which the Cuban people had strengthened their political organization in the past year in face of the growing American threat. The trade unions, the women's organization, the young communist league, and the mass organizations of the people in the defense committees which exist in every street and village have been drawn into the solution of a multitude of questions—including things like rationing, health measures, especially vaccination, immunizations of children—as well as ensuring round-the-clock vigilance to protect factories, fields, and homes against sabotage and espionage.

The past seven months, however, have been especially significant, for they have seen the beginning of the formation of the new United Party of the Socialist Revolution (PURS), following the removal of the former communist leader Anibal Escalante for sectarianism and his attempts to create an elite separated from the masses of the people.

At present the political organization of the Cuban people is the Integrated Revolutionary Organizations (ORI), which was formed from Premier Fidel Castro's 26 July movement, the old Popular Socialist Party, and the directoire, which was mainly a students' organization.

34 (c). 1962

The new party is being formed on the basis of mass meetings being held at all places of work. The workers are invited to choose model workers from among themselves. These are then invited to join the new party, while the fitness for membership of the new party of members of the present organizations is also discussed at mass meetings. This process is continuing at the present time all over the country, although it has been held up somewhat by the mobilization measures necessitated by the crisis of the past month. When completed by the beginning of next year, it is hoped to have the first nucleus of some 50,000 to 60,000 members and to hold the first congress of the new party built on the basis of men and women chosen by the people themselves to be the vanguard of Cuba's socialist revolution.

My final question to Major Guevara was on the contribution that the Cuban revolution has made to the development of Marxist thought and practice. His reply was typically modest, and he deliberately limited himself to the effects of the Cuban example in Latin America. "The Cuban revolution," he said, "has shown that in conditions of imperialist domination such as exist in Latin America, there is no solution but armed struggle--for the people to take power out of the hands of the Yankee imperialists and the small group of the national bourgeoisie who work with them." The question then was, he added, how this armed struggle could be most effectively carried through. While the bourgeoisie had their armed forces concentrated in the cities where they had the factory workers at their mercy. They were comparatively weak in the countryside, where the peasants are living mostly in a state of feudal oppression and are also very revolutionary.

"Cuba has shown," he continued, "that small guerrilla groups, well-led and located in key points, with strong links with the masses of the people, can act as a catalyst of the masses bringing them into mass struggle through action. "Such action, to be convincing, must be effective, and guerrilla action has shown how armed forces can be beaten and how guerrillas can be converted into an army which eventually can destroy the armed forces of the class enemy.

"We say," Major Guevara continued, "that this can be done in a large number of Latin American countries. But this is not to say that Cuba's example is to be followed mechanically, but rather adapted to the specific conditions in each of Latin America's 20 countries." He pointed out that in Venezuela, Guatemala, Paraguay, and Colombia, guerrillas are already active in armed struggle against the American imperialists and their henchmen, while there have been clashes in Nicaragua and Peru, and none of this had any physical connection with Cuba.

"There is no other solution possible in these countries except armed struggle. The objective conditions for this exist, and Cuba's example has shown these countries the way."

34 (d). 1962

UNCLASSIFIED ~~CONFIDENTIAL~~

DEPARTMENT OF STATE

THE DIRECTOR OF INTELLIGENCE AND RESEARCH

NOV 30 1962

```
TO      :  The Secretary
THROUGH :  S/S
FROM    :  INR - Allan Evans
```

INTELLIGENCE NOTE: "CHE" GUEVARA INTERVIEW SHOWS BITTERNESS

<u>Cuba left undefended.</u> In his only public statement since the outset of the missile crisis, "Che" Guevara (whose views usually parallel Fidel's) complained yesterday to a correspondent of the London Daily Worker that the withdrawal of the Soviet missiles had not removed the threat of US aggression. While he granted the immediate danger of war was avoided, he denied that a great victory had been achieved. Instead he feared that agony may only have been prolonged. Nevertheless, he said, Cuba will fight to the death with what weapons it has left.

<u>Early support for missiles in Cuba.</u> Guevara was probably an early advocate of bringing Soviet missiles into Cuba. It was during his visit to Moscow, while the build-up was in progress, that Soviet military aid to Cuba was first formally acknowledged. Soon afterward, Guevara called the Soviet aid a matter of historic importance before which the US would have no choice but to capitulate. The significance of his words only became clear as the extent of the build-up became known. "Che's" present bitterness is probably a reaction to his former enthusiasm.

<u>Focus shifted to Latin America.</u> Guevara notes the continued necessity of relying on the USSR, but he cites as more important the pro-Castro, anti-US activities in Latin America as the key to gaining independence of US "imperialism". In precisely the way that Mao Tse-tung might like, he called for armed struggle in the countryside to expand the revolutionary

35 (a). 1962: This Department of State document, addressed to the Secretary of State, comments on Che Guevara's *Daily Worker* interview in Document 34.

CONFIDENTIAL

- 2 -

base. While emphasizing the Cuban <u>example</u>, and denying direct Cuban
involvement in other Latin revolutionary movements, "Che" probably had
in mind a Fidel-lod native Marxist movement in this hemisphere, one
which Cuban activists could hardly keep their fingers out of.

December 3, 1962

Three indicators from Cuba that worry me are:

1.   This
would suggest that we soon would face the prospect of operational SAM
sites manned by Soviets.

2. Che Guevara's statement to the London Daily Worker that
peace has been assured and that Cuba will pursue the arms struggle
already xx taking place in a number of Latin American countries such as
Venezuela, Guatemalam Paraguay and Colombia. This would indicate no intention
to halt Castro sub version in Latin America.

3. Mikoyan's public statement in Moscow that he had achieved Soviet
objective of maintaining a Communist regime in the Western hemisphere.

These three statements would prompt extreme caution on the part
of the United States in any agreement which might give Castro and the
Communists a sanctuary.

John A. McCone
Director

SANITIZED COPY

36. 1962: Document from John A. McCone, Director of the CIA, possibly to the Secretary of State or the President concerning an agreement with the Soviet Union regarding Cuba. Specifically mentions as one of three negative "indicators" Che Guevara's *Daily Worker* interview (Document 34) on armed struggle. McCone says "Cuba will pursue the arms [sic] struggle already taking place in a number of Latin American countries...".

OUTGOING TELEGRAM Department of State

Brinkley 38

INDICATE: ☐ COLLECT
☐ CHARGE TO

~~CONFIDENTIAL~~

Origin **ACTION:** USUN NEW YORK   PRIORITY   1531 **ADVANCE COPY**

Info.   FOR STEVENSON AND McCLOY

With reference to current negotiations with Kuznetzov, White House wants to be positive that you are aware of following excerpt from XXX Che Guevara interview with Havana correspondent of London Daily Worker contained in FBIS No. 70, November 29:

QUOTE My final question to Major Guevara was on the contribution that the Cuban revolution has made to the development of Marxist thought and practice. His reply was typically modest, and he deliberately limited himself to the effects of the Cuban example in Latin America. "The Cuban revolution," he said, "has shown that in conditions of imperialist domination such as exist in Latin America, there is no solution but armed struggle--for the people to take power out of the hands of the Yankee imperialists and the small group of the national bourgeoisie who work with them." The question then was, he added, how this armed struggle could be most effectively carried through. While the bourgeoisie had their armed forces concentrated in the cities where they had

Drafted by:	Telegraphic transmission and classification approved by:	
S/S-Mr. Little: amp 12/7/62		:/S-ESLittle
Clearances:		
IO-Mr. Handyside		
White House - Bromley Smith		

DECLASSIFIED
E.O. 11652, Sec. 3(E) and 5(D) or (E)
By _____ NARS, Date 2/22/74

~~CONFIDENTIAL~~

REPRODUCTION FROM THIS COPY IS PROHIBITED UNLESS "UNCLASSIFIED".

FORM DS-322
8-61

37 (a). 1962: Telegram from State Department to the U.S. Ambassador to the United Nations, Adlai Stevenson, regarding negotiations with the Soviet Union. Once again, it warns them about Che Guevara's comments on armed struggle in the *Daily Worker* interview and quotes the pertinent sections.

CONFIDENTIAL

the factory workers at their mercy. They were comparatively weak in the countryside, where the peasants are living mostly in a state of feudal oppression and are also very revolutionary.

"Cuba has shown," he continued, "that small guerrilla groups, well-led and located in key points, with strong links with the masses of the people, can act as a catalyst of the masses bringing them into mass struggle through action. "Such action, to be convincing, must be effective, and guerrilla action has shown how armed forces can be beaten and how guerrillas can be converted into an army which eventually can destroy the armed forces of the class enemy.

"We say," Major Guevara continued, "that this can be done in a large number of Latin American countries. But this is not to say that Cuba's example is to be followed mechanically, but rather adapted to the specific conditions in each of Latin America's 20 odd countries." He pointed out that in Venezuela, Guatemala, Paraguay, and Colombia, guerrillas are already active in armed struggle against the American imperialists and their henchmen, while there have been clashes in Nicaragua and Peru, and none of this had any physical connection with Cuba.

"There is no other solution possible in these countries except armed struggle. The objective conditions for this exist, and Cuba's example has shown these countries the way."

UNQUOTE

END

37 (b). 1962

Б.U.B A

10 December 1962

GUEVARA, HART MARK MACEO ANNIVERSARY

Guevara Speech

Havana in Spanish to the Americas 2535 GMT 7 December 1962--E

(Live speech by Ernesto Guevara commemorating 66th anniversary of death of Antonio Maceo)

(Summary) On this 66th anniversary of the death of Antonio Maceo in the fight for the liberation of Cuba, the people of Cuba, as they do every year, render tribute to his memory. The people pass before his monument as in the past, but today when we are engaged in the task of building socialism in Cuba, the memory of Antonio Maceo takes on a new light. All the history of his life, his marvelous struggle and his heroic death take on new meaning.

After his death, leaders capable of carrying the revolutionary war in Cuba through to complete liberation from all the colonial powers were not yet emerging on the horizon and his heirs "did not have sufficient penetration to understand the scope of the Yankee plans and all the malignant maneuvers buried in the Maine and what followed." The struggle was not over. "But, unfortunately, the task of the liberation of Cuba is not completed even today. So long as the imperialist enemy maintains its claws, its appetite, its desire to destroy our revolution, we must continue on a war footing."

Now we have passed the harshest test any people can pass through. We have faced atomic destruction. We have watched the enemy prepare his immense resources in rockets, arms of destruction of all kinds. We have seen all of this arsenal pointed toward Cuba. We have heard his threats. We have been his planes streaking over our territory, through our air space. And this people, worthy of Maceo, of Maceo's lineage, of Marti, and of Maximo Gomez, did not tremble, nor did they vacillate, and the modern world saw the extraordinary spectacle of a whole people preparing for the worst of catastrophes with incredible morale. All of the history of the great heroic struggles of humanity could be summed up without exaggeration, without excessive chauvinism, in this moment of the history of Cuba. All of our people are Maceos."

38 (a). 1962: Che Guevara's speech commemorating the 66th anniversary of Antonio Maceo who died fighting for Cuban freedom in the war against Spain. Che says that all Cuban people are "Maceos" for having "passed the harshest test any people can pass through. We have faced atomic destruction." He urges that the Cuban people "cannot be indifferent to any injustice any place on earth."

EXHIBIT 2   CUBA
                            10 December 1962

All of our people fought to be in the front line in a battle
in which they would be attacked from air, sea, and land "fulfilling
our function as the advance guard of the socialist world in this
moment and this specific place in the struggle."

Therefore the beloved words of Maceo resound in the heart of the Cuban
people and we point to the words on the side of his monument: "Anyone
who attempts to seize Cuba will gather the dust of its soil drowned
in blood if he does not perish in the struggle." This was the spirit
of Maceo and this is the spirit of our people. We have been worthy
of him in these recent difficult moments. "In this confrontation we
have been perhaps only millimeters away from atomic disaster."

With Maceo's faith "In the future of humanity, in the future of all
that is noble in humanity, in the socialist future of humanity" we
repeat "perhaps slightly changing his words, that so long as there
remains in America, or perhaps so long as there remains in the world a
wrong to be righted, an injustice to be corrected, the Cuban revolution
cannot stop. It must continue forward and feel within itself all the
wrongs of this oppressed world in which it is our fate to live. It
must make its own the sufferings of peoples which, like ours a few
years ago, are raising the banner of freedom and see themselves massacred,
destroyed by colonial power. Not only here to America where we have
so many ties, but to Africa, to Asia, wherever a people in arms
raises any weapon which may be the symbol of the machete of Maceo
or the machete of Maximo Gomez, wherever the national leaders of these
peoples raise their voices, which may symbolize the voice of Marti,
there our people must take their affection, their immense understanding.

"A people emerging from a test such as ours has emerged from cannot
be indifferent to any injustice in any place on earth. This people
would cease to be a follower of Marti if it should remain indifferent
when somewhere in the the world the repressive powers massacre the
people."

Today we commemorate our heroes of the past, because their struggle
was but "a phase of the same struggle of humanity to free itself of
exploitation; because all the words of Antonio Maceo, Marti, and Gomez
are applicable today in this state of the fight against imperialism."
They followed the same road of liberation of the peoples, the road
of tireless struggle against colonial power.

38 (b). 1962

HHHH 3

CUBA
10 December 1962

This same road is being followed by many peoples of the world and daily on various parts of various continents they rise to tell imperialism that "when reason is not enough there is also the strength of the people, to teach imperialism that when the people unite there is no force of arms which can stop them." Imperialism may take advantage of a moment of weakness of the people, of its credulity sometimes, as in the case of the unfortunate hero of the Congo, Patrice Lumumba, but never can it stop the advance of the peoples.

"And against its bestial arrogance, its desire to annihilate everything which is pure in the world, men rise, men led by people who raise the banners of Marti, Maceo, and Gomez. Anywhere in the world where these flags flutter we must turn our eyes and our salute against imperialism which threatens us today with as much fury as yesterday, with as great a desire to destroy us as yesterday, which is preparing in silence a new underhand attack, we bring forth the arsenal of all our strength, all our faith. We point to the slogans of all our great fighters, who represent the will of the people, and we add the newest, the latest, which our people have made in this latest stage of their history, to hurl it again and again into the face of imperialism: Homeland or death, we shall win!" (Applause)

5

1963–1964

Solidarity with the Third World

★ ★ ★

Che Guevara is appointed a member of the Politburo of the Central Committee of the United Party of the Socialist Revolution. He travels to Algeria to celebrate the first anniversary of independence, attends a UN Conference on Trade and Development, travels to Moscow for the 47th anniversary of the Russian Revolution and in December 1964 heads the Cuban delegation to the UN General Assembly.

The documents contain the usual rumors about rifts between Che Guevara and Fidel Castro. Fidel is described as "ill," of "sloppy appearance" and as "an alcoholic," and Che is said to be "in disgrace." There is also a request for a more recent copy of Che's fingerprints. In a five-page CIA biography Che is described as a "dry calculating man," familiar with "Western culture," with "an acute aversion to bathing." Cuba is considered to have shortcomings from a "Communist standpoint" as Cubans "prefer to idle in the sun or dance to their native rhythms."

A number of important speeches by Che Guevara are contained in these documents in which he lauds the heroism of Vietnam, calls the Organization of American States the "ministry of colonies," and describes elections in the United States as North Americans simply having the "power to elect their jailer for four years."

★ ★ ★

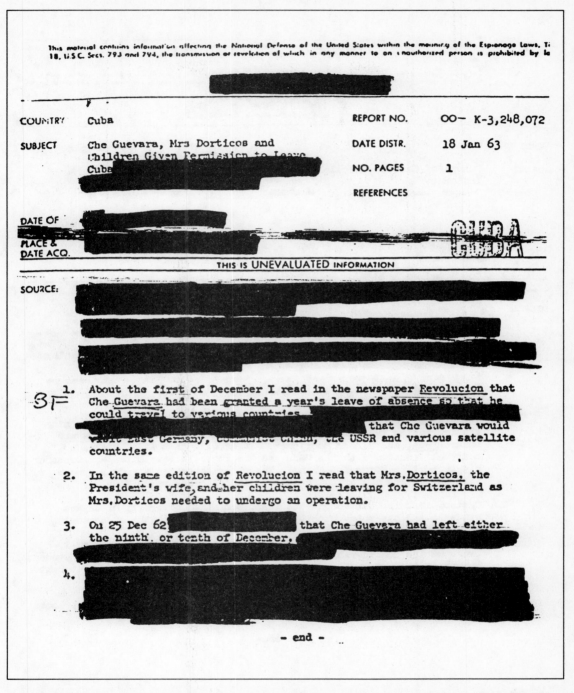

COUNTRY	Cuba	REPORT NO.	OO— K-3,248,072
SUBJECT	Che Guevara, Mrs Dorticos and Children Given Permission to Leave Cuba	DATE DISTR.	18 Jan 63
		NO. PAGES	1
		REFERENCES	

DATE OF

PLACE & DATE ACQ.

THIS IS UNEVALUATED INFORMATION

SOURCE:

1. About the first of December I read in the newspaper Revolucion that Che Guevara had been granted a year's leave of absence so that he could travel to various countries ▓▓▓▓ that Che Guevara would visit East Germany, communist China, the USSR and various satellite countries.

2. In the same edition of Revolucion I read that Mrs. Dorticos, the President's wife, and her children were leaving for Switzerland as Mrs. Dorticos needed to undergo an operation.

3. On 25 Dec 62 ▓▓▓▓ that Che Guevara had left either the ninth or tenth of December.

4. ▓▓▓▓

- end -

39. 1963: Documents 39–41 contain reports from informants in Cuba. Although the information is "unevaluated," it does give a sense of the self-serving nature of the reports from those opposed to the Cuban revolution. Document 39 reports what an informant read in a newspaper, although the title of the document implies that Che Guevara needed permission even to take a trip out of Cuba. Substantial information is deleted.

CENTRAL INTELLIGENCE AGENCY

This material contains information affecting the National Defense of the United States within the meaning of the Espionage Laws. T. 18, USC Secs 793 and 794, the transmission or revelation of which in any manner to an unauthorized person is prohibited by lc

COUNTRY	Cuba	REPORT NO. 00-K-3,248,377
SUBJECT	Rumors of Castro's Declining Influence	DATE DISTR. 21 Jan 63
		NO. PAGES 2
		REFERENCES

DATE OF
INFO.
PLACE &
DATE ACQ.

THIS IS UNEVALUATED INFORMATION

SOURCE:

1. Very strong rumors have been circulating recently in Havana concerning the increasing friction between Castro and his henchmen, Che Guevara, Lazaro Pena, and Rafael Rodriguez. It is said that Fidel wishes to cease all contact with the USSR and the European Satellites and transfer his support to Communist China. The other three men strongly oppose this switch and are bringing much political pressure on Fidel.

2. Castro, in turn, has sought the support of the University of Havana students and has spent much time recently talking to the students.

3. It is also rumored that he is mingling with the students in order to overcome the considerable disaffection which has developed within student groups at the University. There was some talk of an attempt by students to assassinate Castro.

4. Those who have seen Fidel recently report that he has lost weight, looks ill, maintains a sloppy appearance and has been drinking heavily.

-end-

40. 1963: CIA report on "increasing friction" between Che Guevara and Fidel Castro and other substantially inaccurate information.

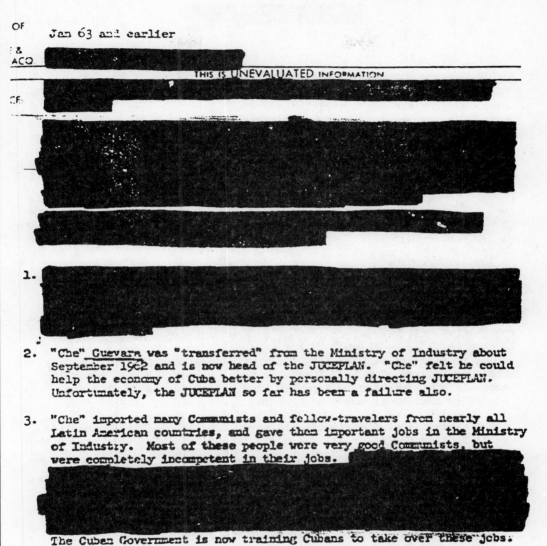

OF

& ACQ

Jan 63 and earlier

CF

1.

2. "Che" Guevara was "transferred" from the Ministry of Industry about September 1962 and is now head of the JUCEPLAN. "Che" felt he could help the economy of Cuba better by personally directing JUCEPLAN. Unfortunately, the JUCEPLAN so far has been a failure also.

3. "Che" imported many Communists and fellow-travelers from nearly all Latin American countries, and gave them important jobs in the Ministry of Industry. Most of these people were very good Communists, but were completely incompetent in their jobs.

The Cuban Government is now training Cubans to take over these jobs. The main problem in this respect is that they are selecting young Cuban boys for these jobs who have "graduated" from Castro-Communist indoctrination schools. Many are barely literate. Most of these boys come from farms and know nothing about economics.

4. The latest and newest trend, however, is to "recruit" well qualified Cuban persons whom the government knows are anti-Communist. These

41 (a). 1963: CIA report regarding Che Guevara's change of assignment and supposed failure of his economic plan. Claims that Che is "in disgrace."

00-K-3,253,82?

- 2 -

persons are being told that if they will do a good job they will not
be required to join the militia, attend Communist meetings, or any
other meeting they do not wish to attend. They are promising these
people very important positions with high salaries. There have been a
few people that have accepted these positions, but most of the people
have turned the jobs down because they do not want to be "tainted" as
Communists, and even if they get high salaries they cannot buy anything
with the money.

5.

6. "Che" Guevara has not appeared in public lately and has not made a
single major speech since the crisis. "Che" Guevara appears
to be in disgrace because he is primarily credited with the great
economic failure of Cuba. "Che", in turn, blames all his "expert"
economic advisors that he imported from all of the Latin American
countries that he is now sending home.

7. Fidel Castro is also attempting to purge all the old line Communists.
He is in fact replacing all these old time Communists with "new Castro-
type Socialists." The only old-type Communist that Fidel
Castro now trusts is Carlos Rafael Rodriguez. All the other old-type
Communists will be purged as soon as the "proper native can be manu-
factured."

8. Fidel is also trying to woo all former "26 July" personnel, and
university students. He has delivered many lectures lately at the
University of Havana and has also talked personally to many of the
university students asking for their support. Fidel is also trying
to get the support of veterans of Playa Giron, the "becados" (kids
attending Communist indoctrination schools) and other young students
now attending secondary schools. Fidel has been 'politicking' nearly
full time lately, telling young people confidentially that the USSR
cannot be trusted, that they must have a great "Socialist Revolution"
of their own.

—end—

41 (b). 1963

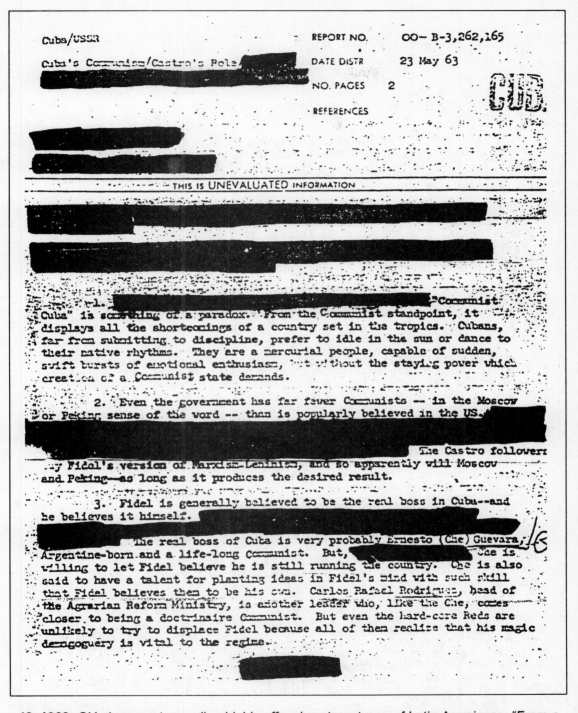

Cuba/USSR

Cuba's Communism/Castro's Role

REPORT NO. OO— B-3,262,165

DATE DISTR 23 May 63

NO. PAGES 2

REFERENCES

CIA

— THIS IS UNEVALUATED INFORMATION

.... "Communist Cuba" is something of a paradox. From the Communist standpoint, it displays all the shortcomings of a country set in the tropics. Cubans, far from submitting to discipline, prefer to idle in the sun or dance to their native rhythms. They are a mercurial people, capable of sudden, swift bursts of emotional enthusiasm, but without the staying power which creation of a Communist state demands.

2. Even the government has far fewer Communists -- in the Moscow or Peking sense of the word -- than is popularly believed in the US. The Castro followers by Fidel's version of Marxism-Leninism, and so apparently will Moscow and Peking—as long as it produces the desired result.

3. Fidel is generally believed to be the real boss in Cuba—and he believes it himself.

The real boss of Cuba is very probably Ernesto (Che) Guevara, Argentine-born and a life-long Communist. But, Che is willing to let Fidel believe he is still running the country. Che is also said to have a talent for planting ideas in Fidel's mind with such skill that Fidel believes them to be his own. Carlos Rafael Rodríguez, head of the Agrarian Reform Ministry, is another leader who, like the Che, comes closer to being a doctrinaire Communist. But even the hard-core Reds are unlikely to try to displace Fidel because all of them realize that his magic demagoguery is vital to the regime.

42. 1963: CIA document revealing highly offensive stereotypes of Latin Americans: "From a Communist standpoint" Cuba has shortcomings as the Cuban people "prefer to idle in the sun or dance to their native rhythms." Asserts erroneously that the "real boss of Cuba is very probably" Che Guevara.

(FYI) GUEVARRA RECALLED THE GENEVA AGREEMENT WHICH DIVIDED
VIETNAM INTO TWO PARTS BUT PROVIDED FOR ELECTIONS IN WHICH THE
VIETNAMESE PEOPLE WOULDBE ALLOWED
TO DECIDE THEIR OWN DESTINY. BUT AS SOON AS THE FRENCH
IMPERIALISTS LEFT, THE U.S. IMPERIALISTS ARRIVED, GUEVARA SAID.
THE AMERICANS BEGAN A WAR OF EXTERMINATION AGAINST THE SOUTH
VIETNAMESE PEOPLE AND THE VIETNAMESE HAD NO CHOICE BUT TO TAKE
UP ARMS.

GUEVARA NOTED THAT GUERRILLA WARFARE IS BEING WAGED IN ANGOLA,
PORTUGUESE GUINEA, NICARAGUA, HONDURAS, GUATEMALA, THE DOMINICAN
REPUBLIC, COLOMBIA, AND PARAGUAY. IN ALL THESE COUNTRIES, HE
DECLARED, THE ARMIES WHICH ARE TRYING TO PUT AN END TO THE PEOPLES'
ASPIRATIONS FOR FREEDOM ARE REVEALING THEIR IMPOTENCE.

GUEVARA SAID THAT IN THE LATTER PART OF THIS YEAR GREAT VICTORIES
HAVE BEEN WON BY THE VENEZUELANS AND THE SOUTH VIETNAMESE. HE
OBSERVED THAT THE STRUGGLE IN VIETNAM IS IMPORTANT FOR THE
FUTURE OF AMERICA, AS IMPERIALISM IS THERE TESTING THE WEAPONS
AND THE METHODS WHICH IT WILL LATER USE IN THE AMERICAS.
SOUTH VIETNAM IS IIMPERIALISM'S LABORATORY, HE SAID.

NEVERTHELESS, GUEVARA WENT ON, THE SOUTH VIETNAMESE LIBERATION
FORCES ARE AN EXAMPLE TO ALL. OUR MISSION HERE IN CUBA, GUEVARA
SAID, IS TO FOLLOW THEIR EXAMPLE: OUR TASK IS TO SHOW THE PEOPLE
OF LATIN AMERICA THAT WHEN REACTIONARY POWERS DECEIVE THE PEOPLE,
THE FLAG OF REVOLUTION MUST BE RAISED.

GUEVARA CONTINUED: "THE SITUATION IN SOUTH VIETNAM SHOWS THAT
IN SPITE OF CHEMICAL WARFARE, IN SPITE OF ALL THE NEW METHODS OF
DESTRUCTION WHICH THE YANKEES TEST EVERY DAY, THE WAR CAN BE
WAGED. IF WE SEE THE MAP OF SOUTH VIETNAM, AND SEE HOW SMALL IT
IS, AND THEN LOOK AT THE 20 MILLION SQUARE KILOMETERS OF OUR
IMMENSE AMERICA, WE WILL SEE THAT THE STRUGGLE CAN BE WAGED EASILY.
MANY NATIONS OF LATIN AMERICA ARE RIPE FOR REVOLUTION, AND
NOT ONLY THOSE WHICH HAVE STARTED THEIR STRUGGLE. THERE
ARE SOME THAT HAVE NOT STARTED IT YET. BUT ARE PATIENTLY
SHARPENING THEIR MACHETES BECAUSE THEY KNOW THAT HOUR APPROACHES.
THEY KNOW THAT U.S. IMPERIALISM WILL INTERVENE IN AMERICA. THEY
ALSO KNOW THAT THE MORE FRONTS ARE OPENED SIMULTANEOUSLY,
THE MORE DIFFICULT THE FIGHT WILL BE."

GUEVARA WENT ON: "TODAY WE ARE NOT DEALING WITH NATIONS,
FOR CUBA IS NOT A NATION IN THIS REGION OF THE WORLD; IT IS ONE
PART OF ONE SINGLE NATION AND IS, FURTHERMORE, A SYMBOL
FOR ALL AMERICA. THUS, EACH NATION THAT BEGINS ITS STRUGGLE
ALSO BEGINS TO DIG THE GRAVE OF IMPERIALISM AND SHOULD WARRANT
ALL OUR SUPPORT AND ALL OUR PRAISE."

GUEVARA CONTINUED: "FOR THIS REASON THE STRUGGLE SHOULD BE WELL
PLANNED; AFTER IT HAS BEGUN IT SHOULD BE CONTINUED UNTIL THE END.
THERE CAN BE NO DEALS; THERE CAN BE NO MIDDLE TERMS; THERE CAN
BE NO PEACE AGREEMENTS THAT GUARANTEE THE STABILITY OF A NATION
HALFWAY. VICTORY MUST BE COMPLETE. THINKING IN THIS VEIN, OUR
PEOPLE ARE ON A WAR FOOTING. THINKING ALONG THE SAME LINE
THE ALGERIAN PEOPLE WERE ON A WAR FOOTING FOR SEVEN LONG YEARS. WITH
THAT SAME CONVICTION, THE SOUTH VIETNAMESE PEOPLE ARE TODAY
ON A WAR FOOTING."

43. 1963: FBIS report of Che Guevara's broadcast to the Americas on the struggle in Vietnam and its importance to Latin America.

Headquarters
14 JAN 1964

MEMORANDUM FOR :   Special Agent in Charge

SUBJECT   :   GUEVARA de la Serna, Ernesto
                        aka Che
                        #261 746   F   SD/4

1.

2.   As Office of Origin, you are requested to obtain a copy of Subject's fingerprints subsequent to August 1952.

3.   Attached is the biographic information available on Subject.

4.   A deadline of 28 January 1964 has been established in this case.

Attachment
  Control Cards
  Bio Data

Approved for Release
Date

jh
14 Jan 64
PENDING

E. 82

---

44. 1964: Request from FBI headquarters for a more recent copy of Che Guevara's fingerprints. What is the reason for the request at this particular time? Did they suspect Che of a crime? Of traveling as a guerrilla fighter? Of using a disguise? Did they have a plot to kill him and wanted to make sure they got the right guy?

CENTRAL INTELLIGENCE AGENCY

Material contains information affecting the National Defense of the United States within the meaning of the Espionage Laws, Title U.S.C. Secs. 793 and 794, the transmission or revelation of which in any manner to an unauthorized person is prohibited by law.

INTRY		REPORT NO.	CS LT-3/717,334
ECT		DATE DISTR.	30 June 1964
Booklet on Guerrilla Warfare Written by Ernesto "Che" Guevara		NO. PAGES	1
		REFERENCES	

E OF
O.   May 1964
CE &
E ACQ.

THIS IS UNEVALUATED INFORMATION. SOURCE GRADINGS ARE DEFINITIVE.   CONTENT IS TENTATIVE.

JRCE:

1. Available in the CIA Library is a 16-page booklet in Spanish entitled Guerra de Guerrillas: Un Metodo, by Ernesto "Che" Guevara.

2. The booklet, dated 1964, appears to be one of a series. Primarily a propaganda work apparently designed to create the atmosphere for the future organization of guerrilla groups, it does not deal comprehensively with guerrilla activity as such but offers a justification for the method and includes some basic suggestions for the formation of a "people's army."

Attachment available in CIA Library

(Distribution of Attachment: CCR)

45. 1964: Document notifying CIA staff that Che Guevara's new book *Guerra de Guerrillas: Un Método* is available in the CIA library.

CUBA   Ernesto "Che" GUEVARA de la Serna

Minister of Industries

OFFICE OF
CENTRAL REFERENCE

BIOGRAPHIC
REGISTER

Economic-czar Ernesto Guevara presently
serves the Cuban Government as Minister of
Industries, as secretary of JUCEPLAN (the board of
economic planning and coordination), as a national
director of PURS (the developing monolithic Cuban
party), and as the unofficial but powerful political
advisor to Fidel Castro. An original member of the
Granma expedition in 1956, he rose to become one
of the most prominent military commanders in the
mountains and later became one of the major voices
in the Cuban economy. An advocate of rapid industrialization despite the cost, Guevara recently
has been forced to reverse his position to one of concentration on
consumer goods. He maintains that Cuba's economic future lies in
industrialization and, consequently, is frequently at odds with Carlos
Rafael Rodríguez, Minister-President of the Institute for Agrarian
Reform (INRA), who feels that Cuba must develop her agricultural
resources. Rodríguez seems to have won the argument for the moment
and Cuba presently appears to be concentrating on agricultural
development. A prime mover in the drive for nationalization and
centralization of various facets of the economy, Guevara is extremely
anti-United States and was one of the main instigators in antagonizing
US economic interests and in forcing Cuban reliance on the Soviet bloc
early in the Castro regime. Moreover, he has traveled to the Soviet
bloc many times to negotiate trade agreements and also has gone to
various Afro-Asian and European countries to establish new trade patterns
for Cuba.

Despite his reliance on the USSR for economic aid, Guevara seems
to follow the Chinese Communist Party line ideologically. One indication
of his militancy and disdain for Soviet policy was his threat, however
empty, during the October 1962 crisis to launch rockets against the
United States. An admirer of Mao Tse-tung, he has persistently agitated
for expansion of the Cuban revolution throughout Latin America. His
manual on guerrilla warfare has been circulated clandestinely throughout
Latin America and he is regarded as the principal Cuban official supporting
the revolution movements of various hemispheric exile groups seeking
refuge in Cuba. Notably, he was a prominent figure in assisting the
proposed invasions of the Dominican Republic and Haiti (March 1959),
Nicaragua (June 1959) and Guatemala (November 1959). He has tenaciously
encouraged revolution in Uruguay, Brazil and Argentina.

46. 1964: Five-page CIA biography of Che Guevara.
(a): "Guevara is extremely anti-United States." He "seems" to follow the "Chinese
Communist Party line." He is described as "the principal Cuban official supporting the
revolution movements" throughout Latin America.

Accused of being a Communist since his university days, Guevara claims that he was never affiliated with the Communist Party either in Argentina, Guatemala or Cuba. His reply to a 1959 accusation was: "If it appears to you that what we do is Communist, then we are Communists." No evidence is available to the effect that he was ever affiliated with any Communist Party, although he seems to have had many contacts with party members and associates in Argentina, Guatemala and Mexico. On any count, Guevara plainly has a strong, emotional anti-US bias and a sympathetic outlook toward Communism. He especially condemns the US role in replacing the pro-Communist Arbenz government in Guatemala with a military junta in 1954.

Because he is so steadfast in his opinions, Guevara has, from time to time, reportedly been somewhat out of favor with Fidel Castro. One issue of contention between them was a variation of the usual "guns or butter" problem. Guevara, arguing for the latter, considered the maintenance of a large standing army to be wasteful when the personnel could be better used in domestic industrial production. He was also concerned about the fact that the money going into the armed forces was providing no return for the national economy. In a television speech in January 1961 Guevara criticized Castro openly on this issue. However, Castro reportedly is influenced by and relies on Guevara to such a degree that Guevara is the only leader who can offer any opposition to Castro with impunity.

Ernesto Guevara de la Serna was born in Rosario, Argentina, on 6 June 1928, the eldest of five children of a comfortable, middle-class family. His parents have been separated since his university days. Guevara's father, Ernesto R. Guevara Lynch, is an architect and surveyor of Spanish-Irish descent who reportedly approved of the Castro movement at its inception. His mother, Celia de la Serna, claims not to be a Communist but has been active in the Latin American Woman's Congresses and in speaking in support of the Cuban revolution. Suffering from asthma since childhood, "Che" (the Argentine equivalent of "hey you" or "bud") underwent a program of rigorous physical exercise--hunting, fishing and other mountain activities--to counteract this deficiency, under the direction of his father. (Nevertheless, he still carries an oxygen inhaler with him at all times.)

In 1947 Guevara entered the University of Buenos Aires to study medicine, reportedly receiving his medical degree in 1952. Politically active during his student days, he participated in several incipient revolutionary movements against the Perón regime. In his final year at medical school Guevara and a friend left on a "study" tour of loprosariums and allergy clinics. It has also been reported that he made the trip to escape his military obligations in Argentina. In any case, indicative of his adventurous nature, he made the trip by motorcycle across the Andes, through Chile and Peru, and by canoe along a portion of the upper Amazon to Colombia and Venezuela. His travels

46 (b). 1964: The report states that there is no evidence that Che Guevara was ever affiliated with a Communist party. From "time to time, [he has] reportedly been somewhat out of favor with Fidel Castro."

finally carried him to Miami, where he was turned back by US immigration authorities. After graduation from medical school Guevara left on a similar tour which ended in Guatemala, where he became involved in that country's domestic politics.

Guevara's role in the pro-Communist regime of former President Jacobo Arbenz Guzmán (1951-54) has been the subject of much controversy and has never been satisfactorily resolved. ▓▓ Guevara himself maintains that he never knew Arbenz personally, that he was having financial difficulties while in Guatemala, and that his sole employment by the Guatemalan Government was as a medical orderly during Arbenz's last days (June 1954). Whatever may have been his true role in Guatemalan politics, he has consistently defended the Arbenz regime while bitterly criticizing the United States for effecting its overthrow.

After the Arbenz government fell, Guevara moved to Mexico, where he allegedly made contact with Vicente Lombardo Toledano, leader of Mexico's Marxist Popular Socialist Party (PPS) and prominent leader in hemispheric pro-Communist agitation. An unsubstantiated report alleged that Lombardo obtained two sinecures for Guevara in Mexico City, one as a doctor at the General Hospital and another as a teacher on the Medical Faculty of the National University. In the summer of 1956, Fidel Castro reportedly met Guevara by chance at the home of a mutual friend in Mexico, and in the ensuing discussion Castro outlined his political ideas and a general plan for invading Cuba with the 26th-of-July group then forming in Mexico. Apparently attracted by the prospect of a guerrilla war, Guevara agreed to join in a medical capacity and underwent guerrilla training under the supervision of Spanish Republican General Alberto Bayo Giroud.

In July 1956 Castro's fellow conspirators, including Guevara, who even then was considered to be one of the most important, were rounded up by the Mexican security police for conspiring to overthrow the Cuban Government. They were released on 25 July and in December 1956 embarked on the Granma expedition which set the revolt in motion. When the 82-man force landed in Cuba all but 12 of the group were either killed or captured. Guevara was among the survivors, wounded but still active. As the Sierra Maestra-based movement gained strength, Guevara proved to be a capable fighter and military leader and, consequently, stepped up to a high position in the rebel military organization. He practiced medicine infrequently and only when absolutely necessary. Commander of one of the largest of the five rebel columns (Column 4), he gained a reputation for bravery and military prowess second only to Fidel Castro himself. Further, he led the march from Oriente Province through government lines to central Las Villas Province in November 1958 which eventually culminated in the surrender of the provincial capital of Santa Clara.

46 (c). 1964: Says Che Guevara was turned back by U.S. immigration at Miami [in 1952]. Details his move to Mexico, his arrest, landing in Cuba and military leadership in the Sierra Maestra.

Ernesto "Che" GUEVARA de la Serna   (cont)

After the success of the revolution in January 1959, Guevara elected to remain in Cuba and was awarded "naturalized citizenship" by a special decree which was tailor-made to make him eligible for the presidency. Guevara's first position in the new government was that of commander of La Cabaña Fortress in Havana. There he had jurisdiction over the notorious "war criminals" trials, which allegedly resulted in the execution of 600 civilian and military officials. Able to arrest, try and execute anyone at all under the Revolutionary Code of Justice, he took a personal interest in the prosecution of former members of Batista's Bureau for the Repression of Communist Activities (BRAC), gaining possession of the BRAC files. Guevara also assisted Raúl Castro in purging and reorganizing the national army to make it the "principal political arm of the people's revolution." As head of the armed forces' Department of Instruction he was conspicuous in promoting political indoctrination courses which reportedly followed the Communist line. Guevara is also credited with the development of Cuba's civilian militia.

Guevara's first position of non-military nature was that of head of the industrial department of INRA. Although he had an intensive interest in land reform, he remained at the post only two months (September-November 1959). He publicly espoused the principle of ownership of land by the farmer who worked it, but he is alleged to have privately favored a system of national collectives. Appointed president of the National Bank in November 1959, Guevara, lacking formal qualifications for the post, surrounded himself with able advisors and soon demonstrated a quick grasp of technical matters. As bank president, he led the drive for nationalization and centralization of various facets of the economy. His solution for paying the cost of the revolution was to increase the amount of money in circulation by 62 per cent, while curbing inflation by other means.

In February 1961 Guevara became Minister of Industries and continued his efforts to submit the nation's economic activities to government control. He fixed prices for staples, reduced rents, and introduced measures prohibitive to the accumulation of private capital. He set up a strict licensing system to reduce imports and cut down on the outflow of dollars. His austerity program rigorously taxed the upper and middle income sectors while attempting to placate the working classes, but his policies furnished Castro with the necessary currency to carry on his ambitious development program while minimizing inflation.

Guevara's influence in Cuban economic affairs increased steadily thereafter. In late 1960 he led an economic mission to Europe and the Soviet bloc, where he succeeded in negotiating trade agreements for capital goods for Cuba. Since then, he has led many other trade missions to bloc and non-bloc countries and has headed several delegations to international conferences, including the Punta del Este meeting in August 1961 and the April 1964 UN Conference on Trade and Development.

46 (d). 1964: As commander of La Cabaña Fortress in 1959 Che Guevara had jurisdiction over the "war criminals" trials. Details Che's role in the economy and that he "demonstrated a quick grasp of technical matters."

Ernesto "Che" GUEVARA de la Serna   (cont)

Appointed a member of the executive committee of JUCEPLAN in August 1961, Guevara, by July 1962, was reportedly already engaged in a power struggle with Regino Boti (the board's technical secretary) for control of the organization. Guevara was appointed a JUCEPLAN secretary at that time.

Although he still wears an army uniform, Guevara has no official military position. However, according to one source of undetermined reliability, as of December 1963 Guevara was to command the forces in Pinar del Rio Province in case of an invasion. In March 1964 he was identified as a member of the General Staff.

A dry, calculating man who affects an old world hauteur, Guevara has more than a passing acquaintance with Western culture. During the Sierra Maestra days he reportedly read to his troops from the works of Charles Dickens, French author Alphonse Daudet, Cuban poet and revolutionary José Martí, and Chilean Communist poet Pablo Neruda. He fancies himself something of a bon vivant with a connoisseur's appreciation for fine foods, brandies and cigars. He frequently displays a cultured, soft-spoken manner. Despite this aura of culture, however, Guevara has an acute aversion to bathing and presents an unkempt and neglected appearance.

Guevara's first marriage to a Peruvian, Hilda Gadea Acosta, ended in divorce. One child of that marriage remains with the mother, who is employed by INRA. On 3 June 1959 Guevara married Aleida March de la Torre after the two had apparently been living together for some time. She spent a considerable amount of time in the Sierra Maestra during the revolution and in September 1959 became a member of the sponsoring committee for the Communist-dominated Latin American Women's Congress. She has lent her name to other leftist organizations as well. A daughter was born of this marriage in 1960. Guevara speaks French and some English.

August 1964

46 (e). 1964: "A dry, calculating man who affects an old world hauteur, Guevara has more than a passing acquaintance with Western culture." This document repeats earlier "information" regarding the books Che Guevara read to his troops and that he has "an acute aversion to bathing and presents an unkempt and neglected appearance."

6

1965

Che's Farewell

★ ★ ★

During the first three months of 1965 Che Guevara traveled to a number of countries in Africa. In late February he took part in the Second Economic Seminar of Afro-American Solidarity. It was at this conference that Che, in addressing trade issues, said the socialist countries "have the moral duty to liquidate their tacit complicity with Western countries."[1] Some commentators have claimed that this speech angered Fidel Castro as Cuba was relying for aid on some of these socialist countries and was therefore a factor in Che's leaving Cuba. However, these commentators have taken this sentence out of context. Che went on to say that the Soviet Union and China were "the most generous toward the Third World." Other evidence demonstrates that Che was preparing to leave Cuba long before this speech and for reasons unrelated to any supposed disagreements with Fidel.

Che clearly left Cuba to fight in and lead liberation struggles. In almost every speech he gave, he exhorted people to fight against imperialism and to do so with armed struggle; he saw the fight as a worldwide necessity and that Cuba was an example to be emulated. He was not willing to stay in Cuba and deepen the revolution — as important as that was. It is known that he was planning a Bolivian and Latin American guerrilla strategy since at least as early as 1962 and probably before. Tania (Tamara Bunke), the revolutionary who was with him in Bolivia, was trained in Cuba. She met with Che in March 1964 and in that meeting Che explained that her mission was to go to Bolivia.

After the Africa trip Che arrived back in Cuba on March 14 and dropped out of public sight towards the end of March. His whereabouts during the next year and a half were open to speculation. He reportedly went to the Congo to evaluate the Kinshasa rebellion and returned to Cuba to train Cubans to fight. He took this force to the Congo where he supported the anti-Mobutu forces, one of whose leaders was Laurent Kabila. (Kabila finally led an insurrectionary force that toppled Mobutu in 1997.) Sometime in December 1965, in secret, Che returned from the Congo to Cuba.

The documents below concern Che's trip to Africa, excerpts from his speech in Algeria and a long U.S. government (probably CIA) analysis of his trip. The analysis is particularly interesting because, contrary to much of the speculation, it concludes that Che's absence from public events in Cuba was not motivated by problems with Fidel. Also, reprinted here is the text of the monitored October broadcast of Fidel reading Che's farewell letter.

---

[1] Che Guevara's speech in Algiers is published in *Che Guevara Reader* (Ocean Press, 1997).

GUEVARA ON U.N., AFRICAN FREEDOM STRUGGLE

Havana PRENSA LATINA in Spanish 1228 GMT 28 January 1965--E (NOT OFFICIAL NOT ONLY)

(Excerpts) Algiers--In an exclusive statement for the international programs
department of the Algerian Radio and Television, Cuban Minister of Industry Maj.
Ernesto Guevara said that "new measures are necessary to save the United Nations."
Commenting on the current U.N. crisis, the Cuban leader pointed out that the
international organization is today suffering an extremely grave financial crisis
as the result of maneuvers conducted by the colonialists in an attempt to make the
U.N. members pay for their adventure and their aggressions.

Referring to Indonesia's withdrawal from the United Nations, Major Guevara said
that this has presented a new situation. He expressed the opinion that it is
necessary to save the United Nations: "The United Nations must be saved," he
said, "but it must be saved with a new and different criterion so that it will serve
the majority interests of the peoples of the world."

The Cuban minister of industry expressed his admiration for the way in which the
African peoples are becoming aware of the dangers presented by U.S. imperialism and
the conviction with which they are fighting it. "We have brought these peoples,
sometimes through their rulers and sometimes through direct contact with the
masses--since I had an opportunity to give lectures--the support of the Cuban
Revolution for the just causes of these peoples."

Major Guevara said that the Cuban revolution has always made clear its support
"for the Congolese patriots fighting valiantly and stubbornly against U.S. imperialism
and the second class imperialisms which are trying to continue to exploit and
pillage the resources of the Congo."

Finally, after condemning racial segregation and "apartheid" in South Africa, he
said that Cuba also reaffirms its support for the peoples struggling to free
themselves from the colonial yoke, as in the cases of Angola, Mozambique, and
so-called Portuguese Guinea, "and also, although this is of principal importance
for the Arab peoples, for the people of Palestine and their fight for their claims."

47. 1965: Excerpt from Che Guevara's statement on Algerian radio and TV stating that
"new measures are necessary to save the U.N." Stresses Cuban support "for the
Congolese patriots fighting valiantly and stubbornly against U.S. imperialism."

(TEXT) ALGIERS, 28 FEBRUARY--CUBAN INDUSTRIES MINISTER ERNESTO CHE GUEVARA TODAY CALLED ON NATIONS OF THE THIRD WORLD TO FORM A UNITED FRONT AGAINST IMPERIALISM.

GUEVARA, WHO IS HERE TO ATTEND THE CURRENT AFRO-ASIAN SEMINAR, TOLD AFP IN AN INTERVIEW THAT AN ORGANIZATION OF THIRD WORLD STATES SIMILAR TO THE GROUP OF 77 COUNTRIES AT LAST YEAR'S WORLD TRADE CONFERENCE IN GENEVA WOULD NOT HELP THE FIGHT AGAINST IMPERIALISM.

THE CUBAN MINISTER SAID: SUCH AN ORGANIZATION WOULD BE A BATTLEFIELD IN WHICH CERTAIN GOVERNMENTS WOULD HAVE TO STRUGGLE AGAINST OTHERS TO DEFEAT IMPERIALISM. WHAT IS NEEDED IS SOMETHING ELSE--NAMELY, A UNITED BLOCK AGAINST IMPERIALISM, HE SAID. GUEVARA, IN ANSWER TO A QUESTION ON THE PROSPECTS FOR THE ADHESION OF SOUTH AMERICAN LIBERATION MOVEMENTS AND POLITICAL PARTIES TO THE AFRO-ASIAN PEOPLES SOLIDARITY ORGANIZATION SAID: THE DECISION IN PRINCIPAL TO ENLARGE THE ORGANIZATION HAS BEEN TAKEN, BUT ITS REALIZATION DEPENDS ON MANY FACTORS. FOR THE TIME BEING, IT IS NOT POSSIBLE TO FORECAST THE NEXT MOVES. . . BUT THESE CERTAINLY WILL BE MADE.

ON THE QUESTION OF CUBA'S RELATIONS WITH THE UNITED STATES GUEVARA SAID: THE UNITED STATES IS ENTANGLED IN A WEB WHICH IT SPUN ITSELF. THAT COUNTRY HAS MADE CUBA IN ELECTION FOOTBALL, AN INTERNAL PROBLEM.

CUBA REPRESENTS AN EXAMPLE AND A HOPE FOR SOUTH AMERICAN COUNTRIES, AND THE UNITED STATES CANNOT ACCEPT THE IDEA OF LOSING ITS LATIN AMERICAN ECONOMIC COLONIES, HE SAID. THE UNITED STATES WOULD ONLY ACCEPT PEACEFUL COEXISTENCE WITH CUBA IF WE RENOUNCED OUR REVOLUTION, WHICH IS UNTHINKABLE, THE MINISTER ADDED.

ASKED WHETHER HE THOUGHT BRITISH GUIANA AND GUATEMALA COULD BECOME SECOND CUBA'S GUEVARA REPLIED: IT IS DIFFICULT TO KNOW WHETHER ANOTHER COUNTRY COULD, BY ITSELF, TAKE THE PATH WHICH CUBA CHOSE. IN ANY CASE, THE UNITED STATES WOULD INTERVENE TO PREVENT IT. THE STRUGGLE WOULD DEPEND NOTABLY ON THE PRICE THE UNITED STATES DECIDED TO PAY TO MAINTAIN ITS DOMINATION AND ON THE SUPPORT FOR THE REVOLUTIONARY MOVEMENT IN THE POPULAR MASSES, HE SAID.

BUT THE CUBAN MINISTER FELT THAT WHEN A PEOPLE IN ARMS IS CONFRONTED BY A FOREIGN ARMY, IT IS LOGICAL THAT IN THE LONG RUN VICTORY WILL BE WON BY THE PEOPLE.

ON RELATIONS BETWEEN THIRD WORLD COUNTRIES AND SOCIALIST NATIONS GUEVARA SAID: I HAVE SAID THAT SOCIALIST COUNTRIES HAVE THE MORAL DUTY TO LIQUIDATE THEIR TACIT COMPLICITY WITH WESTERN COUNTRIES WHICH EXPLOIT OTHERS. THEY MUST ABSTAIN IN THEIR TRADE DEALINGS WITH THE THIRD WORLD FROM PRACTICING THE SYSTEM USED BY CAPITALIST POWERS WHICH BUY RAW MATERIALS AT A LOW PRICE FROM UNDERDEVELOPED COUNTRIES AND SELL THEM THE FINISHED PRODUCTS.

GUEVARA CONCLUDED: THERE IS NO QUESTION OF ASKING SMALL SOCIALIST COUNTRIES SUCH AS ALBANIA, NORTH KOREA, OR NORTH VIETNAM TO CONFER ON US THE SAME ADVANTAGES AS SOVIET RUSSIA OR PEOPLE'S CHINA FOR THE PURCHASE OF OUR SUGAR. THE USSR AND CHINA ARE THE MOST POWERFUL NATIONS IN THE SOCIALIST CAMP, AND THEY ARE THE MOST GENEROUS TOWARD THE THIRD WORLD.

48. 1965: Excerpt from a speech that Western commentators falsely claimed angered Fidel because of Che Guevara's remarks on socialist countries.

FROM: [deleted]   1 Jun 65
SUBJECT: Major Ernesto GUEVARA de la Serna, Minister of Industries
  and member of the Secretariat of the PURS National Directorate

SOURCE: Cuban newspapers and radio news from 1 Dec 64 to 31 May 65.
  Attached herewith is an analysis of Major Ernesto GUEVARA de la
  Serna's trip from 9 Dec 64 to 14 Mar 65.

Also included are currents of opinion about Major Guevara's absence
from public and official events during the last 72 days.

Major Ernesto GUEVARA de la Serna joined the 26th of July Movement
in Mexico City, Mexico, in late 1955 or early 1956. He was one of
the expeditionaries on the yacht 'Granma' who landed in Cuba on 2
December 1956 under the command of Fidel CASTRO Ruz.
   During his stay in the Sierra Maestra mountains, Oriente
province, he became one of the top leaders of the guerrilla
movement and finally was given command of the 'Ciro Redondo' Column
#8 which he led from the Sierra Maestra to the Escambray mountains
in Las Villas province.
   Upon his arrival in Las Villas province on 16 October 1958, he
was designated as Provincial Chief of the 26th of July Movement in
that province. He fought important battles in Las Villas province.
   At the victory of the revolution on 1 January 1959, he was
appointed as Chief of the Military Regiment at La Cabaña Fortress,
City of Havana. Later, on 21 November 1959, he was made Chief of
the Industrialization Department of the National Institute of
Agrarian Reform (INRA), and held this position until 26 November
1959 when he was appointed as President of the National Bank of
Cuba.
   On 23 February 1961 he abandoned the position as President of
the National Bank of Cuba and was made the Minister of Industries,
a newly created organism.
   In September 1961, he was appointed as Minister of Labor due to
the temporary absence of the current Minister of Labor, and held
this position for the duration of the absence of the current
Minister.
   On 22 March 1962, when the list of the members of the National
Directorate of the Integrated Revolutionary Organizations (ORI) was

49 (a). 1965: This document excerpts a 17-page analysis of Che Guevara's trip, possibly prepared by the Foreign Broadcast Information Service or the CIA using primarily information from radio and newspapers. It includes biographical data and documents Che's trip abroad from December 9, 1964 to March 14, 1965. The report states categorically that his absence from public events was not "motivated by problems with Fidel," concluding that either Che is in North Vietnam, Algeria or Latin America or that he is sick with a lung ailment that could become tuberculosis. This document has been retyped from the original.

made public, Major GUEVARA appeared as the number 3 among the members of the Secretariat of the ORI.

When the ORI became the United Party of Socialist Revolution (PURS), Major GUEVARA kept his position in the Secretariat of the PURS National Directorate.

Since early 1959, observers have considered Major GUEVARA as the number three man in the hierarchy of the Cuban Government. On 8 December 1964, Major GUEVARA was temporarily appointed as President of the Cuban Delegation to the XIX period of sessions of the U.N. General Assembly.

[The document continues with a detailed account of Che Guevara's trip to the United States, Africa, Europe and Asia from December 9,1964, to March 14, 1965.]

* * *

Cuba

14 March: Arrived in Havana and was met at the airport by Fidel CASTRO Ruz, Dr. Osvaldo DORTICOS Torrado, President of the Republic, Aleida MARCH de Guevara, member of the National Directorate of the Cuban Women's Federation, Carlos Rafael RODRIGUEZ Rodriguez, member of the PURS National Directorate, [illegible] Major Jesus MONTANE Oropesa, Minister of Communications, and Lt. Orlando BORREGO Diaz, Minister of the Sugar Industry.

Captain Osmany CIENFUEGOS Gorriarán and Arnold RODRIGUEZ [illegible] returned to Havana in the same aircraft.

20 March 1965: Speech in an event organized by the UJC (Union of Young Communists)of the Ministry of Industries in connection with the IX Youth and Students Festival to be held in Algeria. In his speech, he talked about his recent visit to different African countries and about the II Afro-Asian Economic Seminar held in Algiers. (Source: HOY newspaper, 23 Mar 65, page 3.)

Comments:

Major GUEVARA's last public appearance in Cuba was on 20 March 1965 in an event held in the Ministry of Industries in the City of Havana. The fact that he has not appeared in any public event in 72 days has motivated various comments about his present whereabouts.

After making a detailed analysis of Cuban newspapers and radio from 1 December 1964 to 31 May 1965, we have not found any indication that Major GUEVARA has had problems with the leaders of the GOC [Government of Cuba] or with Major Fidel CASTRO Ruz.

[What follows are reports on Che Guevara which appeared in the Cuban press and radio as monitored by FBIS.]

Conclusions:

After making an analysis of the Cuban press and radio, we have eliminated the possibility that Major GUEVARA's absence from the different public events held during the last 72 days was motivated by problems with Major Fidel CASTRO Ruz, and the possibility that he might have been set aside in the leading cadres of the Government.

The two current opinions which seem to be more reasonable are:

1. Refugees who have recently arrived from Cuba have said that the rumor they had heard in Cuba about the disappearance of Major GUEVARA was that he was outside Cuba on an official GOC mission, and that he was in one of the following places:
  (a) North Viet Nam, (b) Algeria, (c) Latin America

2. During the last 15 years, Major GUEVARA has had an irregular and agitated life. This, together with his weak physical condition has brought about a lung ailment which came to a crisis during his 23-month stay in the Sierra Maestra (December 1956–August 1958), he had more than [illegible] asthma attacks which forced him to rest. In mid-1959, he was examined in the City of Havana by Dr. Gustavo [illegible], a respiratory specialist and old PSP militant, who recommended that he have absolute rest because, due to the bad living conditions in the Sierra Maestra, it was logical to suppose that his lung ailment was aggravated and could become tuberculosis. As result of this advice, Major GUEVARA spend about 2 months at Playa [illegible], Havana province, in absolute rest.

On various occasions during the last few years, it has been rumored in Havana that Major GUEVARA has been forced to stop his activities and take absolute rest as a result of his lung ailment.

In view of the fact that Major GUEVARA had just made a long 96-day tour of Afro-Asian countries, leading an irregular life during that trip, it is logical to suppose that his lung ailment got worse and that, when he returned to Havana, the top GOC leaders ordered that he take a new rest period.

It is possible that Major GUEVARA's disappearance might have been motivated by bad health.

49 (c). 1965

EVARA, ERNESTO

22 March 1965

3F

CUBA CU

INTERVIEW WITH CHE GUEVARA IN JEUNE AFRIQUE

Algiers Correspondent's Dispatch in French to PRENSA LATINA Havana 0138 GMT
19 March 1965--E (FOR OFFICIAL USE ONLY)

(Excerpts) Algiers, 18 March--Question: Africans are eager to know of experiences
like Cuba's. Can a Cuban tell us what Cuba really is?

Answer: The most important characteristic of Cuba is that of being a country
experiencing a revolution that is constantly in motion and constantly being renewed.
While carrying on its revolution, the country thinks and ponders. There is an
"action" aspect and a "reflection" aspect.

For us, communism not only is not a dogma, but is almost a discovery. We have
conducted a socialist experiment and have found that our experience jibes with the
great socialist experiences, particularly in regard to their scientific content.

Today Cuba is seeking new elements for socialism. It is necessary to conduct a
deeper study of political economy in transition periods, something that has not
been sufficiently analyzed. There is also--and I should even say first of all--
the very important problem of the significance of the new revolutionary institutions.

Question: Are you socialists from conviction or from necessity?

Answer: We are socialists both from conviction and from necessity.

Question: Beyond the struggle it is waging today, Cuba, already a symbol, wants to
become an example. What is the example you wish to offer?

Answer: What you call a symbol is for me the example. Cuba can be the example
of struggle. That example could even be compared to a biblical form of battle, the
one between David and Goliath. Cuba could also be a showcase for socialism, and
that might be a good example for the people. What to me is much more important is
the example of struggle. The people must not hope to be happy because socialism
has come; they must begin to build socialism and realize that this can be done only
when they are freed. They must realize, too, that they can free themselves, but
that this requires struggle.

Question: The socialist world is divided into two camps today. Is reconciliation
between the two possible?

Answer: The socialist world is experiencing violent differences. This is no secret.
We believe much greater unity is possible. The factors of unity are much more
important than the factors of division. We are striving to have the stress laid on
the factors of unity and to impart a different tone to discussion of elements of
division.

Question: You have been in Africa two months. What have you discovered here as
a revolutionary and as an economist?

50. 1965: Interview with Che Guevara in Algeria published in *Jeune Afrique*.
(a): Che discusses Cuba's revolutionary example.

Answer: I have discovered a continent. We have always been divided by imperialism and colonialism. They tried to have some of us believe they were superior to the rest. Hence, as regards America, we had the pride of being the best educated of the illiterates, and we were satified. During that time, Africa was for us a continent far removed, not just by distance but by prejudices as well-- those curtains the colonialists hang.

As Cubans, we might say we have discovered a very close relative. I am speaking of Black Africa in particular. We ourselves have a population that is 30 percent black or mixed.

I wish to speak of politics from an economic angle. There are deep differences in the economic field, even among the progressive countries. To my knowledge, no serious effort is being made to unite the efforts of the countries that have the same political line and are fighting for true economic liberation. It is necessary to study the possibility of making a division of labor and strengthening ties with the socialist countries. The thing is to find means for joint action between the various African countries and the socialist countries, while at the same time conducting the battle against neocolonialism, which is an economic battle.

Question: What do you mean by "division of labor"?

Answer: A harmonious use of specialization in production. For example, Algeria has oil, Guinea has aluminum, and Tanzania sisal. For each of these resources, the main center should be the country best situated for the purpose. These countries would supply the other African countries and would export. Competition among African countries must be avoided. This competition could only reduce prices and help the capitalists capture the market.

I have found here in Africa not only great leaders of nations, but also complete teams of men well trained for action. I have found entire nations under pressure, as is, if you permit the comparison, water just below the boiling point . . . . I have found great natural resources and I have found leaders who are aware of the importance of the struggle against colonialism and neocolonialism.

Question: You spoke of teams well trained for action. It is generally conceded that Africa lacks cadres.

Answer: When I speak of people well trained for action, I mean leaders in the middle echelons, and that is very important. They are the seed . . . . But along with all these factors, which are positive, there are also the threats--the lesser threat of colonialism and the greater threat of neocolonialism. There are often two aspects of colonialism: the brutal aspect, as in the Congo, and the subtle aspect, which is more dangerous.

Question: The Congo is an example of an African country which has no cadres. If it alerted Its economic structure, do you think that it would be capable of operating its industries, such as L'Union Miniere?

Answer: Certainly. Look at Guinea's nickel factories. Look at the Suez Canal. What is necessary is freedom.

Question: Are there any points of comparision between Africa and Cuba?

50 (b). 1965: Che Guevara emphasizes the importance of his two-month trip to Africa and says "we have discovered a close relative... black Africa in particular."

Answer: Cuba is a country and Africa is a continent. Cuba is a victorious revolution, a violent revolution carried out with weapons against a capitalistic structure which developed under neocolonialism. From this viewpoint, there exists an extraordinary similarity between the Cuban Revolution and the African revolution. There also exist similarities between the neocolonialist countries of Africa and those of Latin America, but Latin America is moving, too. This evolution is perhaps slow, because in the countries where it settles, neocolonialism may bring improvements compared with the former colonialism; but as time goes on, it has less and less to offer.

Question: What do you think of Africa's struggle for freedom, particularly after your contact with the leaders of the liberation movements in Dar es Salaam?

Answer: Cuba's national hero Marti said: "One must speak of goals, but not of means." All I can say is that we agree with those who are waging this struggle and we will assist them with the slight means at our disposal.

Question: Is Cuba's example valid for a struggling Africa, or do there exist conditions peculiar to our continent which require other methods?

Answer: Cuba is an example of a victorious struggle. The rest is secondary. All the countries which are fighting have something to teach, but liberation is the product of the struggle of a country's own forces.

Question: But you are a theoretician in guerrilla warfare . . . .

Answer: There are theoreticians who are greater than I. I am only one of Fidel Castro's soldiers. I learned everything at his side. As for guerrilla warfare theoreticians, there are the Chinese, the Vietnamese, the Koreans, and the Algerians. I believe that the importance of all that is to realize that liberation is possible, and that to attain it, it is necessary to fight.

Question: What do you think of the African forms of socialism?

Answer: I define socialism as a transitional state between developed capitalism and communism, that is, a transformational stage of the revolution. All forms of African socialism are in this stage. We ourselves are not complete socialists. We are building a socialist society.

The methods which each nation believes useful can be employed. The results must be the abolition of the exploitation of man by man and an improvement in the people's living standard. Outside these objectives, there is no socialism.

Question: How do you see Africa's future?

Answer: Africa's future is socialism, and the more distant future is communism. But it is often hazardous to prophecy. There are problems to be solved. We shall solve them by working together, not by prophecying.

50 (c). 1965: Che Guevara credits Castro for who he is: "I am only one of Fidel Castro's soldiers. I learned everything at his side." When asked about how he sees Africa's future, Che responds: "Africa's future is socialism, and the more distant future is communism. But it is often hazardous to prophecy [sic]. There are problems to be solved. We shall solve them by working together, not by prophecying [sic]."

CASTRO SPEECH HIGHLIGHTS

FOR YOUR INFORMATION E/X

1965

HAVANA DOMESTIC SERVICE IN SPANISH AT 0250 GMT ON 17 JUNE BEGAN
BROADCASTING A SPEECH BY PREMIER FIDEL CASTRO ON THE OCCASION OF THE
ANNIVERSARY OF THE FOUNDATION OF THE MINISTRY OF INTERIOR. THE
GREATER PART OF THE SPEECH, MADE IN HAVANA AND LASTING ONE HOUR 46
MINUTES, DEALT WITH DOMESTIC TOPICS, PARTICULARLY THE NEED TO COMBAT
COUNTERREVOLUTIONARY ACTIVITIES.

SPEAKING ON INTERNATIONAL AFFAIRS, CASTRO SAID THE UNITED STATES
WAS REAPING DEFEATS ALL OVER THE WORLD AND PARTICULARLY IN SANTA
DOMINGO AND VIETNAM. THE UNITED STATES, IN FOLLOWING ITS BELLICOSE
POLICY, HE DECLARED, IS NOW USING LATIN-AMERICANS AS CANNON FODDER
IN SANTA DOMINGO. IT WAS THE UNITED STATES IN ATTEMPTING TO EXTEND
THE OCCUPATION ZONE, WHICH BROKE THE CEASE-FIRE YESTERDAY, CASTRO
CHARGED. THIS ACT, HE ADDED, HAS STRENGTHENED THE SPIRIT OF
THE CAAMANO GROUP.

ON THE SUBJECT OF CHE GUEVARA, CASTRO HAD THE FOLLOWING TO SAY:
"YOU PROBABLY HAVE HEARD THE RUMORS CIRCULATED BY THE IMPERIALISTS
THAT COMRADE ERNESTO GUEVARA HAS NOT APPEARED IN PUBLIC RECENTLY;
THAT HE WAS NOT PRESENT ON MAY DAY AND THAT HE WAS NOT PRESENT DURING TH
WEEK WHEN THE CANE WAS CUT. THEY ARE REALLY VERY CURIOUS. THERE
ARE VERSIONS OF THIS AND THAT, OF QUARRELS, OF PROBLEMS. THEY ARE
REALLY VERY CURIOUS.

"WELL, WE ARE GOING TO ANSWER THEM. WHAT BUSINESS IS IT OF YOURS?
(APPLAUSE) WE ARE NOT OBLIGED TO ACCOUNT OR TO REPORT TO YOU. THEY ARE
CURIOUS. THEY CAN KEEP ON BEING CURIOUS. AND THEY ARE WORRIED,
AND THEY CAN KEEP ON BEING WORRIED. THEY ARE NERVOUS. LET THEM TAKE
A TRANQUILZER OR A SEDATIVE. OUR PEOPLE ARE NOT WORRIED.
THEY KNOW THEIR REVOLUTION. THEY KNOW THEIR MEN. (APPLAUSE) WHEN
COMRADE GUEVARA DOES NOT APPEAR AT A PUBLIC MEETING, COMRADE GUEVARA
HAS HIS REASONS FOR NOT APPEARING AT A PUBLIC MEETINGS. HE HAS NEVER
BEEN A MAN TO COURT OR ATTRACT NOTORIEY. COMRADE GUEVARA (WORDS
INDISTINCT).

"THE IMPERIALISTS SAY THAT HIS HEALTH IS POOR. THEIR CONCERN ABOUT
MAJOR GUEVARA, (APPLAUSE) INDICATES THAT THEY VALUE HIM; IT IS A
SIGN THAT HE WORRIES THEM. WHEN WILL THE PEOPLE KNOW ABOUT MAJOR
GUEVARA: WHEN MAJOR GUEVARA WANTS THEM TO. THEY WILL KNOW WHAT THEY
WILL KNOW. WHAT DO WE KNOW? NOTHING. WHAT DO WE THINK? YES, WE THINK.
MAJOR GUEVARA HAS ALWAYS DONE, AND WILL ALWAYS DO REVOLUTIONARY THINGS.

"I CANNOT UNDERSTAND THIS IGNORANCE ON THE PART OF THE
IMPERIALISTS. WHY DON'T THEY TAKE A PICTURE WITH THE U-2? LET THEM
LOOK FOR HIM, AND TAKE A PICTURE OF HIM. WE BELIEVE THAT IT IS MORE
DIFFICULT TO TAKE A PICTURE OF A MAN, REGARDLESS OF HOW GREAT HE IS,
THAN OF A (WORDS INDISTINCT). MEANWHILE, ALL OF US ARE QUIET AND
SATISFIED. NO ONE IS (WORRIED HERE)."

CASTRO'S LAST SENTENCE ON THE SUBJECT OF GUEVARA WAS INDISTINCT.

51. 1965: FBIS excerpt from Fidel Castro's speech of June 17 dealing primarily with
domestic topics, in which he addresses the rumors about Che Guevara's disappearance
from public view. Note the two slightly different versions. Fidel says it is none of the
imperialists' business where Che is and if they are worried they should "take a tranquilizer
or a sedative." Fidel comments: "What do we know? Nothing. What do we think? Yes, we
think Major Guevara has always done, and will always do revolutionary things."

SIXTH AND LAST ADD 113 OF 17 JUN (CASTRO SPEECH)

X X X BEING WORRIED. (APPLAUSE)

(EXCERPTS) IF THEY ARE NERVOUS, LET THEM TAKE A SEDATIVE. OUR PEOPLE, HOWEVER, ARE NOT CONCERNED. THEY ARE ACQUAINTED WITH THEIR OWN REVOLUTION AND THEY KNOW THEIR MEN. (APPLAUSE) SO COMRADE GUEVARA DOES NOT SHOW UP AT A PUBLIC MEETING (APPLAUSE). SO HE IS GIVEN NO PUBLICITY? HE HAS NEVER BEEN A MAN WHO SEEKS PUBLICITY? COMRADE GUEVARA HAS ALWAYS BEEN ALLERGIC TO PUBLICITY. HE IS ALLERGIC. (LAUGHTER)

THEY SAY THAT HE IS ILL. THAT IS WHAT THE IMPERIALISTS WOULD LIKE TO SEE. HOWEVER, WHEN THEY ARE PREOCCUPIED WITH COMRADE GUEVARA, THIS IS A SIGN THAT THEY RESPECT HIM. (LAUGHTER AND APPLAUSE) THIS IS AN INDICATION THAT THEY ASSESS HIM HIGHLY AND DENOTES THAT HE BOTHERS THEM. WHEN WILL MAJOR GUEVARA'S PEOPLE KNOW ABOUT MAJOR GUEVARA? WHEN MAJOR GUEVARA WISHES. (APPLAUSE)

WILL THEY KNOW? YES, THEY WILL KNOW. WHAT DO WE KNOW ABOUT (HIM)? NOTHING. (LAUGHTER AND APPLAUSE). WHAT DO WE THINK? (AUDIENCE ANSWERS: "NOTHING!") YES, WE KNOW THAT MAJOR GUEVARA HAS ALWAYS DONE AND WILL ALWAYS DO REVOLUTIONARY THINGS. (APPLAUSE)

I CANNOT UNDERSTAND THIS IGNORANCE OF THE NEWSMEN. WHY DO THEY NOT TAKE A PICTURE OF HIM WITH THE U-2'S? (LAUGHTER) LET THEM LOOK FOR HIM AND LET THEM PHOTOGRAPH HIM. IT IS HARDER TO TAKE A PICTURE OF A MAN, REGARDLESS OF HOW BIG HE IS THAN TO PHOTOGRAPH A MISSILE. (LAUGHTER) SO LET THEM PUT THE ELECTRONIC BRAINS TO WORK (MORE LAUGHTER) AND LET THEM SOLVE THAT PROBLEM.

MEANWHILE, ALL OF US ARE CALM AND WE ARE SATISFIED. NO ONE IS INTRIGUED HERE. NO ONE. AND PEOPLE DO NOT EVEN ASK. (LAUGHTER) THEY CAN ASK AND THEY WILL GET AN ANSWER AND NOTHING MORE. (APPLAUSE) VERY WELL--(AN AUDIENCE VOICE PIPES UP--ED.) DID YOU HEAR THAT? (LAUGHTER) THE FELLOW WHO COULD NOT HEAR HEARD. (MORE LAUGHTER) (HE WAS) ASLEEP. HE WAS NOT LISTENING. HE HAS NOT MISSED ANYTHING (CASTRO CHUCKLES--ED.)

VERY WELL. WE HAVE ARRIVED AT THE FOURTH ANNIVERSARY. THIS CHILD IS ALREADY WALKING AND IT WALKS WELL AND MARCHES VIGOROUSLY. IT IS STRONG. THE SPIRIT OF THE PEOPLE IS IN IT--THE MEN AND WOMEN OF OUR NATION.

MANY HAVE BEEN CHOSEN BY THE PARTY FOR THIS WORK. I HOPE THAT MANY, MANY WILL BECOME EXEMPLARY, AND THAT MANY--BETTER STILL--THAT ALL WILL ASPIRE TO THE HONOR OF BECOMING A MILITANT MEMBER OF THE PARTY. (APPLAUSE)

ALL GOOD WISHES TO ALL OF YOU, LADIES AND GENTLEMEN. FATHERLAND OR DEATH, WE WILL WIN!

(ENDALL) 1445

52. 1965: Second, slightly different FBIS version of Fidel's June 17 speech.

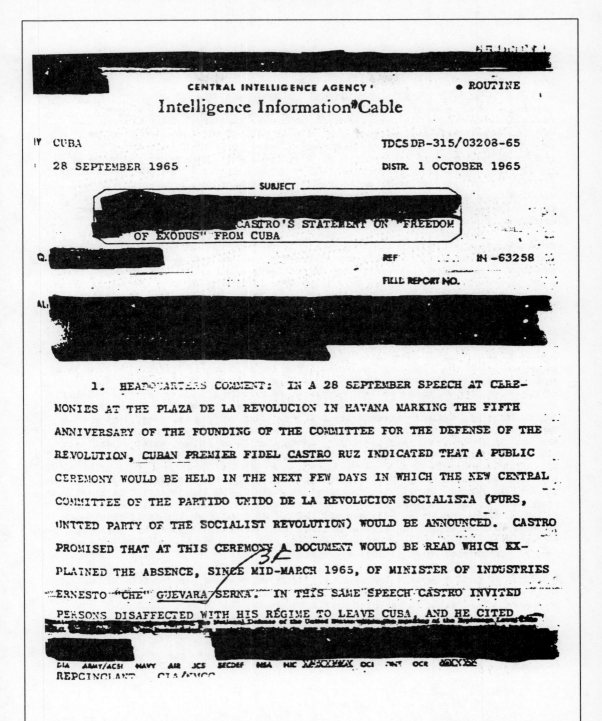

CENTRAL INTELLIGENCE AGENCY • ROUTINE

Intelligence Information Cable

CUBA   TDCS DB-315/03208-65

28 SEPTEMBER 1965   DISTR. 1 OCTOBER 1965

SUBJECT

CASTRO'S STATEMENT ON "FREEDOM OF EXODUS" FROM CUBA

Q.   REF   IN -63258

                                        FIELD REPORT NO.

AL.

1. HEADQUARTERS COMMENT: IN A 28 SEPTEMBER SPEECH AT CERE-
MONIES AT THE PLAZA DE LA REVOLUCION IN HAVANA MARKING THE FIFTH
ANNIVERSARY OF THE FOUNDING OF THE COMMITTEE FOR THE DEFENSE OF THE
REVOLUTION, CUBAN PREMIER FIDEL CASTRO RUZ INDICATED THAT A PUBLIC
CEREMONY WOULD BE HELD IN THE NEXT FEW DAYS IN WHICH THE NEW CENTRAL
COMMITTEE OF THE PARTIDO UNIDO DE LA REVOLUCION SOCIALISTA (PURS,
UNITED PARTY OF THE SOCIALIST REVOLUTION) WOULD BE ANNOUNCED. CASTRO
PROMISED THAT AT THIS CEREMONY A DOCUMENT WOULD BE READ WHICH EX-
PLAINED THE ABSENCE, SINCE MID-MARCH 1965, OF MINISTER OF INDUSTRIES
ERNESTO "CHE" GUEVARA SERNA. IN THIS SAME SPEECH CASTRO INVITED
PERSONS DISAFFECTED WITH HIS RÉGIME TO LEAVE CUBA, AND HE CITED

CIA   ARMY/ACSI   NAVY   AIR   JCS   SECDEF   NSA   NIC   XXXXXXX   OCI   INT   OCR   XXXXXXX
REPCINCLANT   CIA/NMCC

53. 1965: CIA report noting that Fidel Castro says he will read a statement at a forthcoming public ceremony which will explain Che Guevara's absence.

GUARA, ERNESTO

4 October 1965   BF   HHHH 9   CUBA

CASTRO REFERS TO GUEVARA IN SPEECH AT PRESENTATION OF PURSC CENTRAL COMM
Havana Domestic Radio & Television Services in Spanish 0150 GMT 4 Oct 65

You will never hear a lie from the mouth of a revolutionary. These are weapons
which do not benefit any revolutionary, and no serious revolutionary needs to
resort to lies--ever. His weapon is reason, (word indistinct), the truth, the
ability to have an idea, a purpose, a position; in short, the moral spectacle of
our adversaries is truly lamentable. And thus, the diviners, the interpreters, the
specialists in Cuban affairs, and the electronic brains have been working incessantly
to solve this mystery, whether Ernesto Guevara has been purged, (applause) whether
Ernesto Guevara was ill, whether Ernesto Guevara had had differences, and other
questions of the same ilk.

Naturally, the people have confidence. The people have faith, but enemies will say
these things, especially abroad, to slander him and the communist regime, dark,
terrible things: men disappear; they do not leave a trace; they do not leave prints;
there is no explanation; and we told the people at this time, when the people began
to note this absence, that in due time we would talk. We would have some reasons
to wait, we are developing surrounded by the forces of imperialism.

The world is not living in normal conditions. As long as the criminal (?bombs) of
Yankee imperialists are falling on the people in Vietnam, we cannot say that we are
living under normal conditions. When more than 100,000 Yankee soldiers land there
to try to smash the liberation movement, when the soldiers of imperialism land in a
republic which has equality of rights, juridically, as do all the rest of the
republics of the world, as in Santo Domingo, to trample its sovereignty, (applause)
the world is not living under normal conditions. When around our country, the
imperialists are training mercenaries and organizing vandalic attacks, in the most
unpunished manner, as in the case of (few words indistinct), when the imperialists
threaten to intervene in any country of Latin America or of the world, we are not
living under normal conditions.

And when we were fighting in clandestine conditions against the Batista tyranny,
we revolutionaries did not live in normal conditions. We had to adjust to the
struggle. In the same way, although the revolutionary power exists in our country,
in regard to the realities of the world, we do not live in normal conditions, and
we shall have to adjust to this situation. And to explain this, we are going to
read a letter, here, in handwriting, here copied by typewriter, from Comrade Ernesto
Guevara, (applause) which is self-explanatory.

I thought of coming to tell the story of our friendship and our comradeship, how it
began and under what conditions it began and how it developed, but it is not
necessary. I am going to restrict myself to reading the letter. It says:

Havana--The date was not written down because this letter was to be read at the
moment we felt it most convenient, but keeping to strict reality, it was delivered
on 1 April of this year, exactly six months and two days ago, and it says the
following:

54 (a). 1965: Fidel Castro's introduction and reading of Che Guevara's farewell letter as
taken off radio by FBIS.

GUEVARA LETTER

Havana, year of agriculture; Fidel: At this moment I recall many things, of when I met you in the home of Maria Antonia, of when you proposed that I come, of all the tension of the preparations. One day they came to ask whom should be informed in case of death, and the real possibility of the fact was a blow to all of us. Later

we learned that it was true, that in a revolution one triumphs or dies if it is a real one. Many comrades fell along the road to victory. Today everything has a less dramatic tone because we are more mature, but the event repeats itself.

I feel that I have done my duty, which tied me to the Cuban revolution in its territory, and I take leave of you, of the comrades, of your country, which is already mine. I formally resign from my posts in the leadership of the party, of my ministerial post, of my rank of major, of my condition as a Cuban. Nothing legal binds me to Cuba, only ties of another kind, which cannot be broken like appointments.

Reviewing my past life, I believe I have worked with sufficient honesty and dedication to consolidate the revolutionary triumph. My only shortcoming of some gravity is not having confided in you more from the first moments in the Sierra Maestra and not having realized with sufficient celerity your qualities as a leader and a revolutionary. I have lived magnificent days and I felt at your side the pride of belonging to our country during the luminous and (word indistinct) days of the Caribbean crisis. Few times has a statesman shined more brilliantly than on those days. I am also proud of having followed you without hesitation, identified with your way of thinking, seeing, and of estimating dangers and principles.

Other lands of the world demand the aid of my modest efforts. I can do what is denied you by your responsibility at the head of Cuba, and the time has come for us to separate. Let it be known that I do so with a mixture of happiness and pain. Here I leave the purest of my hopes as a builder and the dearest of my dear ones, and I leave a people who accepted me as a son. That wounds a part of my spirit.

In the new fields of battles, I will carry the faith you instilled in me, the revolutionary spirit of my country, the sensation of complying with the most sacred of duties: to struggle against imperialism wherever it may be. This heals and more than cures any laceration. I say once again that I free Cuba of any responsibility save what stems from her example: that if the final hour comes to me under other skies, my last thought will be of this country, particularly of you.

I thank you for your teachings and your example and I will try to be loyal to you to the last consequences of my acts. I have always been identified with the foreign policy of our revolution and I still am. Wherever I am, I will feel the responsibility of being a Cuban revolutionary and I will act as such. I do not leave my children nor my wife anything material, and I am not ashamed. I am glad it is thus. I do not require anything for them for the state will give them enough with which to live and be educated.

I would have many things to tell you and our people, but I feel that they are unnecessary. Words cannot express what I would like to say, and it is not worthwhile to fill pages. To victory always, fatherland or death, I embrace you with all revolutionary fervor, Che.

54 (b). 1965: FBIS version of Che Guevara's farewell letter to Fidel Castro.

<u>C U B A N   L E A D E R·S H I P</u>

GUEVARA   <u>Castro</u> publicly revealed Che Guevara's departure from the
Cuban scene on 3 October, at a meeting at which the central
committee and secretariat of the reconstituted, renamed "Communist
Party of Cuba" was announced. Applauding Guevara's "merits and virtues,"
he read a letter in which Guevara renounced all "legal ties" to Cuba
in order to serve "other.lands of the world." Guevara "freed Cuba of
any responsibility" for his future actions "save what stems from [the
Cuban] example."

Castro said the letter was "delivered on 1 April"--shortly after Guevara's
return from an African-Asian tour during which he made a number of
statements which must have embarrassed Cuba in its relations with other
communist countries. He attacked Yugoslav economic policies in an interview published in a Cairo magazine which drew an angry complaint from
BORBA. In both Cairo and Algiers he railed against "socialist countries"
which emulate and tacitly collude with capitalist states by engaging in
unequal trade relations with the underdeveloped world. And he called on
"socialist countries" to provide weapons free of charge to peoples
fighting for "liberation."

Havana radio/TV comment has followed up the announcement of Guevara's
departure with praise for his stature as a "revolutionary."

55. 1965: FBIS comments on Che Guevara's farewell letter, attributing Che's absence to
his remarks in Algeria about socialist countries and again demonstrating the need for U.S.
agencies to fabricate discord between Fidel and Che despite all evidence to the contrary.

7 October 1965

CHE GUEVARA LETTER BELIEVED FICTITIOUS

Lima AFP in Spanish 1124 GMT 6 October 1965--P ~~[FOR OFFICIAL USE ONLY]~~

(Excerpts) Buenos Aires--A reporter of the Argentine newspaper EL MUNDO suggests today that the Che Guevara letter read recently by Fidel Castro in Havana is fictitious.

The letter, says the reporter, is dated last 1 April, that is, several days before the Santo Domingo uprising. The letter was publicized, according to Castro, at the opportune moment; it is a typewritten document with no other signature than the word "Che." This would be insufficient proof of authenticity even after an examination by the best graphologist extant.

The letter was read in the presence of Che Guevara's wife who was dressed in strict mourning. Nothing was said of the place where Guevara is at present, nor was mention made of what he had done during these last six months. The relinquishing of Cuban nationality, and the resignation from all the posts he had in Havana absolves the Cuban Government of all responsibility of the future activity of this great revolutionary.

Guevara, the Premier said, had left other letters for his wife, children, and father--who is in Argentina but has not made any statement. Does this all not lead one to believe that Che has died and not precisely in his bed, as most generals are said to die?

Could one not suppose that he had died in the struggle as a true and complete revolutionary?

Is it not logical to believe that the letter, with its political testament nature, has been fabricated after lengthy meditation in order to get out of an embarrassing situation created by the fatality to which combatants are always exposed?

After asking himself if Che Guevara might not have died in Santo Domingo as General Imbert himself says, the article's author writes:

Has Guevara died? Might the letter not be only a ruse to give him more freedom of action? Is his wife's mourning due to the recent death of Celia de la Serna, the revolutionary's mother? The deceased once said: "I am not a Spartan, but I am proud of having given a son to the revolution." The article writer says it must be recognized that, in accord or not with the chosen cause, few times might that bequest have been so complete.

(Editor's note: Montevideo REUTERS in English 0150 GMT 7 October quotes a ranking police official as saying in Buenos Aires on 6 October that nothing would impede former Cuban Industries Minister Ernesto Guevara from returning to his native Argentina if he wished to do so.)

56. 1965: Typical example of the many rumors fabricated by those who disbelieve Fidel Castro about what has happened to Che Guevara. This one claims that the letter is a fake, that Che's wife was dressed in mourning when it was read and concludes that Che is dead.

Havana Domestic Radio & Television Services in Spanish 0412 GMT 3 Dec 65

However, he did not say it for that reason, as he perhaps thought some of us believed. He did not say it for that reason. He said it after he had attended this evening's ceremony. He said it after he had seen the performance of our peasant girls, the same peasant girls (applause) whom we met in the mountains, unshod and poorly dressed, these same daughters of those exploited peasants who opened their arms to us during the difficult days which followed the landing of the Granma; those same peasants of those rugged mountains where there were no hospitals or schools, doctors or teachers, but rather large landholders, foremen, rural guards, exploitation, abuses, mass assassinations, burned homes, and bombed hamlets.

He was expressing the feeling of all of us, the emotion of all of us upon seeing, particularly with that clarity with which one sees on days such as this, the result of the struggle, the result of the effort, upon seeing, with that clarity with which one sees on days such as this, that the blood of the good men was not shed in vain; that those who died in the Moncada Barracks (applause) or on the Granma (applause), in the Sierra or in the lowlands (applause), in the cities, and in the various revolutionary actions, those who died following the victory defending the nation against imperialism, those who died in Giron or fighting the bandit assassins in the Escambray Mountains, the teachers who sacrificed themselves did not do so in vain; and that, thanks to those sacrifices on a day like today we can remember them with profound respect, with profound veneration, and gratitude, for in the work of the revolution, in the successes of the revolution our heroes live and will live eternally. Those who fell will live eternally, as well as those who are absent performing their duty, such as our Comrade Ernesto Guevara. (applause)

And I say absent, I do not say dead, for our enemies rejoice at the idea that Comrade Ernesto Guevara is dead. Naturally, no revolutionary is eternal. Revolutionaries are always running great risks. However, in order to undeceive our enemies and for the benefit of our fellow nationals who wonder or have wondered if he is dead or alive, we can say with infinite satisfaction that he is alive and in good health. (applause) However, evidently the imperialists have not been able to ascertain this with their U-2's. And we also remembered him very much today, because we are thinking of and remembering all those who fought—the men who had faith in their people, who had faith in their cause—and that was the main thing. The number of men is not important. The idea is important, the conviction, the will, and the firmness. That is the main thing. That is why we believe so firmly that the other nations will free themselves. That is why we believe in the future of this continent and of all continents, for while the difficulties are great, our history proves that they are not great enough to prevent the victory of the people.

If in the beginning there are not many of them, it is enough that a few have this conviction, and this faith which will soon become the faith and the conviction of the many, will at a given moment be that of all the people. The history of Vietnam teaches us this very thing. The hundreds of thousands of Yankee soldiers, their armies, their swarms of planes, and their criminal weapons have been dashed to pieces against its heroic resistance. The greater their defeat, the more they threaten to send more and more soldiers, obviously worried in the face of the fact that an unexpected growing resistance to this criminal war has arisen among the American people.

(Live speech by Premier Minister Fidel Castro at ceremonies marking the graduation of the first group of Makarenko primary school teachers, held in Marianao's Pedro Marrero Stadium)

57. 1965: December 3 speech by Fidel Castro in which he remembers the many who died to win the revolution. He also recalls Che Guevara who he says is "absent" and not "dead, for our enemies rejoice at the idea that Comrade Ernesto Guevara is dead." "Naturally, no revolutionary is eternal. Revolutionaries are always running great risks...." He states: "We can say with infinite satisfaction that he [Che] is alive and in good health."

7

1965–1966

Rumors of Che's Activities and Death

★ ★ ★

Che Guevara arrived in Bolivia on November 4, 1966, under an assumed name. However, following his departure from Cuba, there was increasing speculation on Che's whereabouts. The documents that follow cover the period leading up to his arrival in Bolivia. Some are from secondary news sources, while others have obviously been generated by CIA informants in Cuba and possibly exiles in the United States. According to various reports Che was killed trying to invade the Dominican Republic, he was killed by Soviet secret agents and he was killed in a violent argument with Fidel. Elsewhere it is reported that Che is under arrest, that he has lost influence because he is close to the Chinese, that he has cancer, that he is training Cubans to fight in the Congo and many other quite bizarre speculations.

Governments in Latin America had an interest in spreading the rumor that Che Guevara was dead. As one Foreign Minister said: "I do not believe that Guevara is alive; international communism is using the figure of 'Che' Guevara to spread rumors and thus create uneasiness, especially in Latin American countries."

The documents in this chapter reveal a frenzied search for Che. He was supposedly seen in a number of places in South America including Chile, Bolivia, Peru, the Andes, Argentina, Brazil and Paraguay. He was also spotted in the Dominican Republic (in a "yellow-painted pocket submarine") and Zambia. Latin American governments were particularly nervous about Che, fearing that he might lead a revolutionary force capable of overthrowing them.

One source in a document gets close to the truth: On April 23, 1966, a CIA source (Document 83) is quoted as saying that Che was "bound for Bolivia" heading a guerrilla force. The first entry in Che's diary is November 7, 1966, the day Che arrived at the guerrilla base on the Ñacahuazú River in Bolivia.

Why did Che leave Cuba? In an interview with Gianni Minà in 1987, Fidel Castro reflected on Che's decision to lead the Bolivian mission: "Che very much wanted to go to South America. This was an old idea of his, because when he joined us in Mexico — although it is not that he made it a condition — he did ask one thing: 'The only thing I want after the victory of the revolution is to go and fight in Argentina' — his country — 'that you don't keep me from doing so, that no reasons of state will stand in the way.' And I promised him that." [1]

★ ★ ★

---

[1] Published in *Che: A memoir by Fidel Castro* (Ocean Press, 1994).

CENTRAL INTELLIGENCE AGENCY

This material contains information affecting the National Defense of the United States within the meaning of the Espionage Laws, Title 18, U.S.C. Secs. 793 and 794, the transmission or revelation of which in any manner to an unauthorized person is prohibited by law.

INTRY Cuba	**REPORT NO.** QO— K-323/00266-66
JECT "Che" Guevara and Other Latin Americans Leaving Cuba for the Dominican Republic	**DATE DISTR.** 13 Jan 66
	NO. PAGES 1
	REFERENCES DCS
OF Apr 65	

THIS IS UNEVALUATED INFORMATION

1. Early in the spring of 1965 there were 482 Dominicans and Nicaraguans at the Hotel Duvill in Havana. This entire group left for Santo Domingo, D.R., along with "Che" Guevara and 26 Cuban Army officers, the same day in April 1965 that Guevara returned from his trip abroad.

2. These Latin Americans had been attending school and receiving subversive training in Cuba.

—end—

58. 1965: CIA report speculating whether Che Guevara had left for the Dominican Republic.

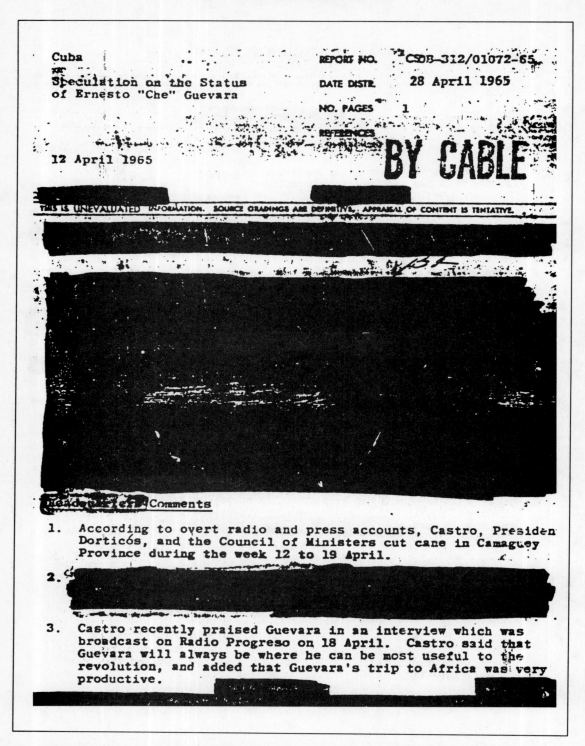

Cuba

Speculation on the Status
of Ernesto "Che" Guevara

REPORT NO. CSDB-312/01072-65

DATE DISTR. 28 April 1965

NO. PAGES 1

REFERENCES

12 April 1965

BY CABLE

THIS IS UNEVALUATED INFORMATION. SOURCE GRADINGS ARE DEFINITIVE. APPRAISAL OF CONTENT IS TENTATIVE.

Headquarters Comments

1. According to overt radio and press accounts, Castro, President Dorticós, and the Council of Ministers cut cane in Camaguey Province during the week 12 to 19 April.

2.

3. Castro recently praised Guevara in an interview which was broadcast on Radio Progreso on 18 April. Castro said that Guevara will always be where he can be most useful to the revolution, and added that Guevara's trip to Africa was very productive.

59. 1965: CIA report on Che Guevara's "status" in April 1965. Fidel Castro is quoted has saying Che "will always be where he can be most useful to the revolution."

COUNTRY Cuba

SUBJECT Rumors Concerning Arrest of Che Guevarra
and Fidel Castro's Attitude Toward Guevarra

REPORT NO. 00-K-323/08C

DATE DISTR. 6 May 65

NO. PAGES 1

REFERENCES

DATE OF
INFO. Apr 65 and earlier

PLACE &
DATE ACQ.

THIS IS UNEVALUATED INFORMATION

1. As of late April 1965, several rumors were circulating among Havana residents concerning "Che" Guevarra. According to one of the rumors, Guevarra had been placed under house arrest by Fidel Castro and subsequently taken to Algiers by the Soviets. According to several persons ▓▓▓▓▓ Guevarra had taken his family and much luggage with him. According to another rumor, he had been imprisoned at La Cabaña Prison. According to still another rumor ▓▓▓▓▓ members of Guevarra's personal escort had attempted to seek asylum in the Mexican Embassy in Havana and after some shooting, some had managed to enter the Embassy and obtain asylum.

2. In my opinion these rumors were prompted by the cool reception Guevarra had received upon his arrival in Cuba from his trip abroad. He also appeared depressed in the photographs of his arrival and ▓▓▓▓▓ he had not been seen or heard from since his arrival. The rumors were given further impetus by Fidel Castro's remarks during a TV interview conducted while he was cutting cane. ▓▓▓▓▓ saw this interview on TV. When asked to comment on the rumors that "Che" was to be assigned as head of the Ministry of Foreign Relations, Castro replied that Guevarra's position would be determined by the needs of the Revolution. When asked to comment on rumors that relations between him and Guevarra were strained, he replied they were "unimprovable".

60. 1965: CIA report on Che Guevara's supposed "arrest" in April 1965. Fidel Castro comments that his relations with Che are "unimprovable."

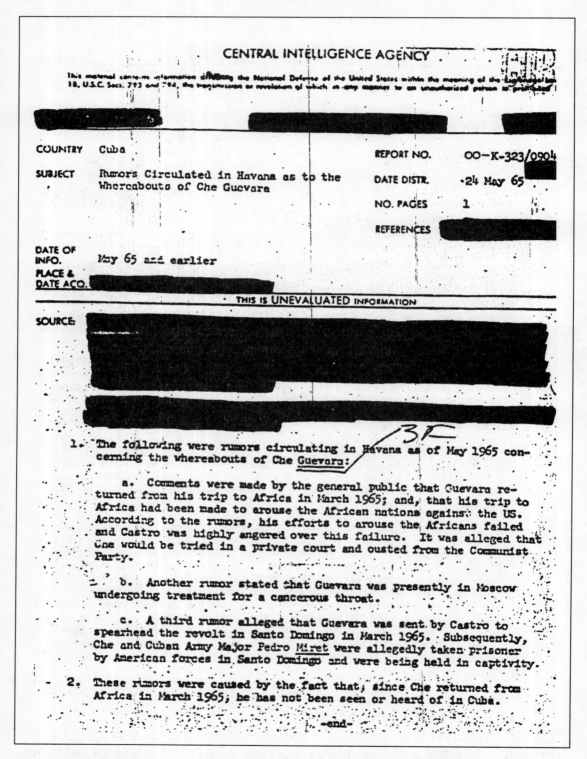

CENTRAL INTELLIGENCE AGENCY

This material contains information affecting the National Defense of the United States within the meaning of the Espionage Laws, 18, U.S.C. Secs. 793 and 794, the transmission or revelation of which in any manner to an unauthorized person is prohibited.

COUNTRY	Cuba	REPORT NO.	OO-K-323/0904
SUBJECT	Rumors Circulated in Havana as to the Whereabouts of Che Guevara	DATE DISTR.	24 May 65
		NO. PAGES	1
		REFERENCES	

DATE OF INFO. May 65 and earlier

PLACE & DATE ACQ.

THIS IS UNEVALUATED INFORMATION

SOURCE

1. The following were rumors circulating in Havana as of May 1965 concerning the whereabouts of Che Guevara:

    a. Comments were made by the general public that Guevara returned from his trip to Africa in March 1965; and, that his trip to Africa had been made to arouse the African nations against the US. According to the rumors, his efforts to arouse the Africans failed and Castro was highly angered over this failure. It was alleged that Che would be tried in a private court and ousted from the Communist Party.

    b. Another rumor stated that Guevara was presently in Moscow undergoing treatment for a cancerous throat.

    c. A third rumor alleged that Guevara was sent by Castro to spearhead the revolt in Santo Domingo in March 1965. Subsequently, Che and Cuban Army Major Pedro Miret were allegedly taken prisoner by American forces in Santo Domingo and were being held in captivity.

2. These rumors were caused by the fact that, since Che returned from Africa in March 1965, he has not been seen or heard of in Cuba.

-end-

61. 1965: CIA report on rumors in Havana on Che Guevara's "whereabouts."

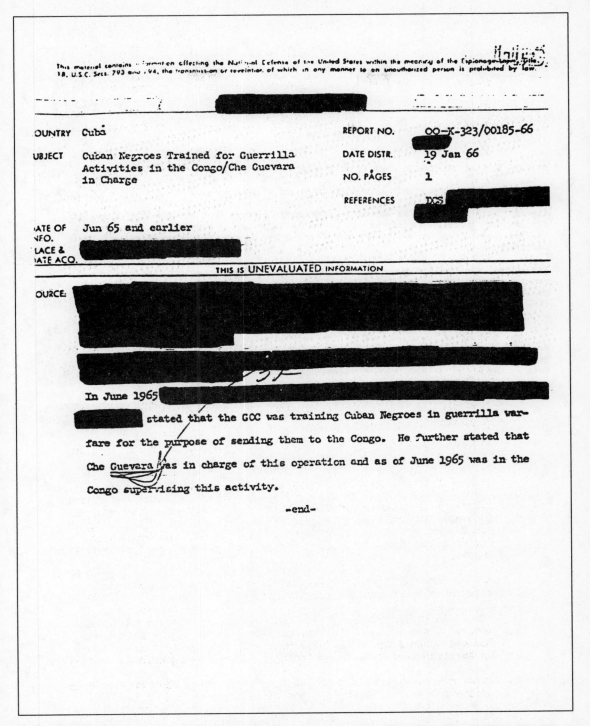

This material contains information affecting the National Defense of the United States within the meaning of the Espionage Laws, Title 18, U.S.C. Secs. 793 and 794, the transmission or revelation of which in any manner to an unauthorized person is prohibited by law.

COUNTRY   Cuba

SUBJECT   Cuban Negroes Trained for Guerrilla
Activities in the Congo/Che Guevara
in Charge

DATE OF
INFO.   Jun 65 and earlier

PLACE &
DATE ACQ.

REPORT NO.   OO-K-323/00185-66

DATE DISTR.   19 Jan 66

NO. PAGES   1

REFERENCES   DCS

THIS IS UNEVALUATED INFORMATION

SOURCE:

In June 1965 _____ stated that the GOC was training Cuban Negroes in guerrilla warfare for the purpose of sending them to the Congo. He further stated that Che Guevara was in charge of this operation and as of June 1965 was in the Congo supervising this activity.

-end-

62. 1965: CIA report stating that the GOC (Government of Cuba) has given Che Guevara responsibility for "training Cuban Negroes in guerrilla warfare for the purpose of sending them to the Congo."

GUEVARA, ERNESTO

CUBA

nnnn 1

G U A T E M A L A

28 June 1965

GUEVARA RUMORED TO PREPARE COUP IN GUATEMALA

Bogota Radio Cadena Nacional in Spanish 1225 GMT 25 June 1965--P

Cabg...

(Text) There are rumors in Guatemalan diplomatic circles that Ernesto "Che" Guevara, former Cuban industries minister, is in Guatemala preparing a communist coup against the government. The rumors do not say when and how Guevara entered Guatemalan territory.

The rumors coincide with anonymous publications, seemingly communist, threatening ranking military leaders deputies to the Congress and other prominent Guatemalan politicians with death. It was reported unofficially that an unidentified plane flew over the eastern sector dropping leaflets againstthe government.

(Editor's Note--E: London REUTERS in English 2118 GMT 27 June reports from Guatemala City that the Guatemalan Government on 27 June refused to comment on rumors that "Che" Guevara is in the country organizing pro-Castro communist elements to overthrow the government. A government spokesman was quoted as saying there was nothing to be said on the matter.)

63. 1965: FBIS document reporting that Che Guevara is "organizing pro-Castro communist elements to overthrow the government" in Guatemala.

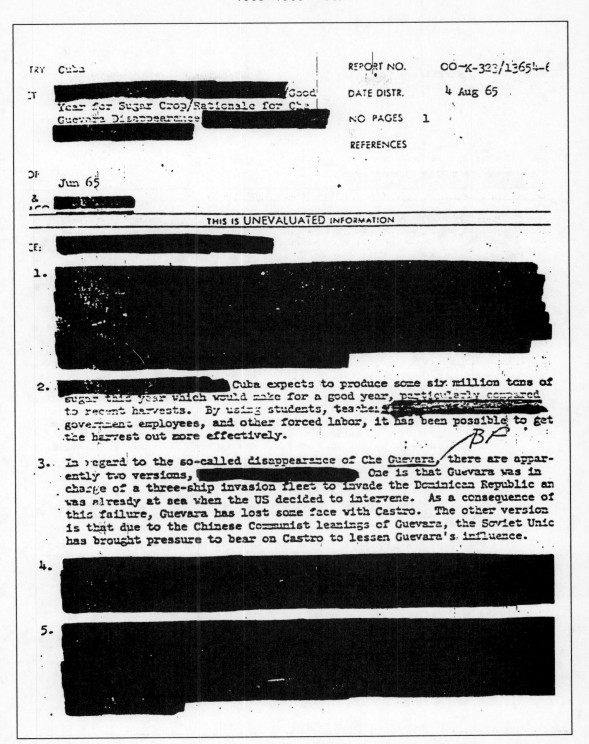

TRY Cuba

IT ▓▓▓▓▓▓▓▓▓▓▓▓▓▓▓▓ Good
Year for Sugar Crop/Rationale for Che
Guevara Disappearance ▓▓▓▓▓▓▓▓

OF Jun 65

&
▓▓▓▓▓▓▓▓▓▓

REPORT NO. OO-K-323/13654-6

DATE DISTR. 4 Aug 65

NO PAGES 1

REFERENCES

THIS IS UNEVALUATED INFORMATION

CE: ▓▓▓▓▓▓▓▓▓▓▓▓▓

1. ▓▓▓▓▓▓▓▓▓▓▓▓▓▓▓▓▓▓▓▓▓▓▓▓▓▓▓▓▓▓▓

2. ▓▓▓▓▓▓▓▓▓▓▓ Cuba expects to produce some six million tons of sugar this year which would make for a good year, particularly compared to recent harvests. By using students, teachers ▓▓▓▓▓▓▓ government employees, and other forced labor, it has been possible to get the harvest out more effectively.

3. In regard to the so-called disappearance of Che Guevara, there are apparently two versions, ▓▓▓▓▓▓▓▓▓▓▓ One is that Guevara was in charge of a three-ship invasion fleet to invade the Dominican Republic and was already at sea when the US decided to intervene. As a consequence of this failure, Guevara has lost some face with Castro. The other version is that due to the Chinese Communist leanings of Guevara, the Soviet Union has brought pressure to bear on Castro to lessen Guevara's influence.

4. ▓▓▓▓▓▓▓▓▓▓▓▓▓▓▓▓▓▓▓▓▓▓▓▓▓▓▓▓

5. ▓▓▓▓▓▓▓▓▓▓▓▓▓▓▓▓▓▓▓▓▓▓▓▓▓▓▓▓

64. 1965: CIA report with two different explanations of Che Guevara's "so-called disappearance."

ꓽTRY Cuba/C̶̶̶̶	REPORT NQ. CO-K-323/22666-65
ꓽ: Decline in Chinese Communist Propaganda/Use of Mailꓽꓽꓽ	DATE DISTR. 27 Dec 65
	NO. PAGES 1
	REFERENCES

ꓽF

Jun 65 and later

&
ꓽCO.   ████████████████████

THIS IS UNEVALUATED INFORMATION

ꓽꓽ   ██
██
██

BF

1. Since July 1965 Spanish editions of Communist Chinese magazines, books and newspapers have disappeared from stores and newstands. Movies depicting life and industrial activities are no longer shown in Cuba. Up to July 1965 much Communist Chinese propaganda was in evidence. This ████████████ is due to Che Guevara's absence. He is a Mao Tze Tung admirer and tried very hard to wean Fidel Castro from the Kremlin. Che wanted Castro to accept Communist China's type of Communism and to put more dependancy on that country rather than on the USSR. However, Castro would never do it. For a time he tried to "keep in" with both countries, but it now appears that he has accepted the USSR as his "big brother". He feels that Communist China will not be able to provide Cuba with economic aid, petroleum and military supplies in the quantities supplied by the USSR so far. Castro realizes that if he should continue to lean towards Mao Tze Tung, even slightly, the USSR will reduce or might even cut off its present aid.

2. Since June 1965 the number of Chinese Embassy personnel has been reduced a great deal. ██████████████████████████
████████

3. The personnel assigned to the Communist China Embassy have always been very cultured, well dressed and appeared friendly towards the Cubans. My observation has led me to believe that they try to win people to Mao Tze Tung theories and ideals through cultural channels rather than through military activities.

4. Since publications from Communist China are no longer available in stores or newstands, the Embassy has been compiling a mailing list of Cubans, to whom they are sending, free of charge, literature of all types. ████████████

-end-

65. 1965: CIA report describing Che Guevara as a "Mao Tse Tung admirer" and that he "tried very hard to wean Fidel Castro from the Kremlin."

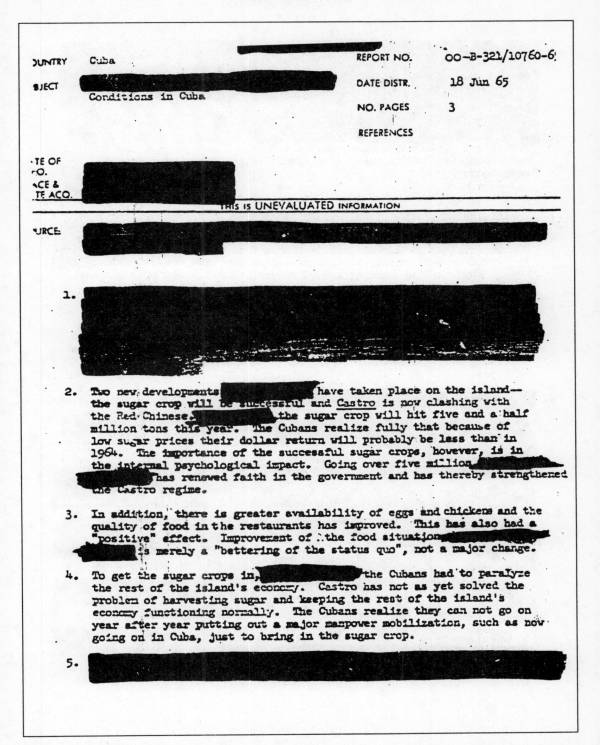

COUNTRY   Cuba   REPORT NO.   00-B-321/10760-6

SUBJECT   Conditions in Cuba   DATE DISTR.   18 Jun 65

NO. PAGES   3

REFERENCES

DATE OF INFO.

PLACE & DATE ACQ.

SOURCE

1.

2. Two new developments [blacked out] have taken place on the island—the sugar crop will be successful and Castro is now clashing with the Red Chinese. [blacked out] the sugar crop will hit five and a half million tons this year. The Cubans realize fully that because of low sugar prices their dollar return will probably be less than in 1964. The importance of the successful sugar crops, however, is in the internal psychological impact. Going over five million [blacked out] has renewed faith in the government and has thereby strengthened the Castro regime.

3. In addition, there is greater availability of eggs and chickens and the quality of food in the restaurants has improved. This has also had a "positive" effect. Improvement of the food situation [blacked out] is merely a "bettering of the status quo", not a major change.

4. To get the sugar crops in, [blacked out] the Cubans had to paralyze the rest of the island's economy. Castro has not as yet solved the problem of harvesting sugar and keeping the rest of the island's economy functioning normally. The Cubans realize they can not go on year after year putting out a major manpower mobilization, such as now going on in Cuba, just to bring in the sugar crop.

5.

66 (a). 1965: CIA report on the problems of the Cuban economy and assessing Che Guevara's trip to Africa.

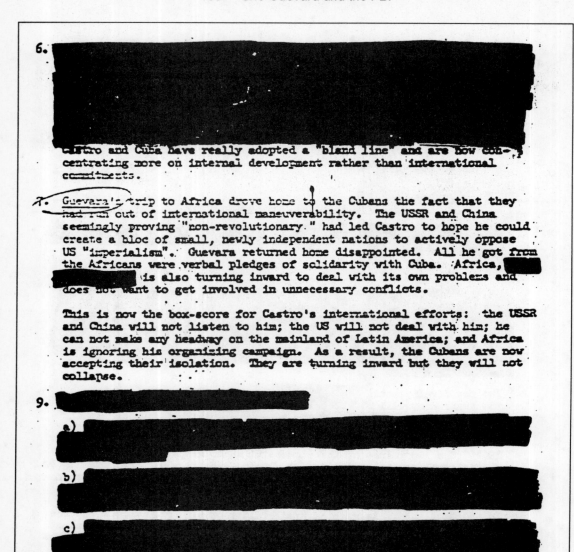

6.

Castro and Cuba have really adopted a "bland line" and are now concentrating more on internal development rather than international commitments.

7.   Guevara's trip to Africa drove home to the Cubans the fact that they had run out of international maneuverability. The USSR and China seemingly proving "non-revolutionary," had led Castro to hope he could create a bloc of small, newly independent nations to actively oppose US "imperialism". Guevara returned home disappointed. All he got from the Africans were verbal pledges of solidarity with Cuba. Africa, ▓▓▓▓▓ ▓▓▓▓▓▓▓▓ is also turning inward to deal with its own problems and does not want to get involved in unnecessary conflicts.

This is now the box-score for Castro's international efforts: the USSR and China will not listen to him; the US will not deal with him; he can not make any headway on the mainland of Latin America; and Africa is ignoring his organizing campaign. As a result, the Cubans are now accepting their isolation. They are turning inward but they will not collapse.

9.

a)

b)

c)

d)

e)

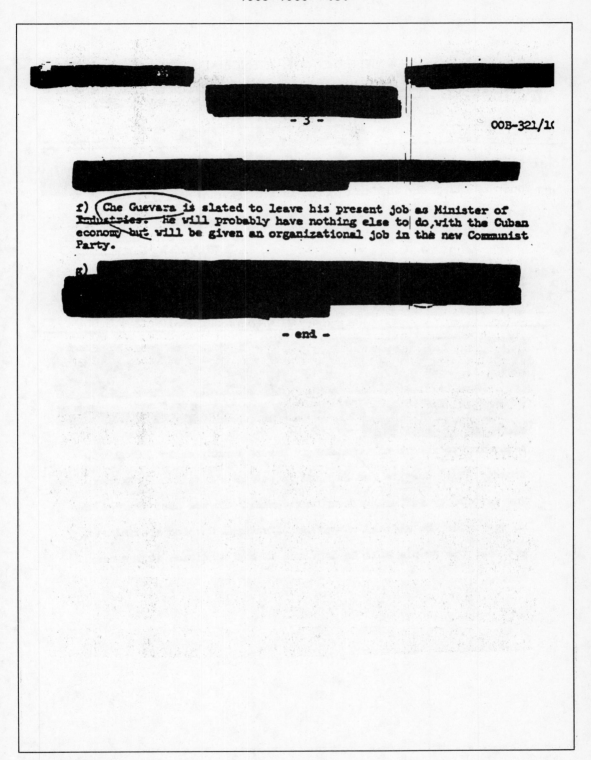

- 3 -

OOB-321/1(

f) Che Guevara is slated to leave his present job as Minister of Industries. He will probably have nothing else to do, with the Cuban economy but will be given an organizational job in the new Communist Party.

g)

- end -

CENTRAL INTELLIGENCE AGENCY

This material contains information affecting the National Defense of the United States within the meaning of the Espionage Laws, Title 18, U.S.C. Secs. 793 and 794, the transmission or revelation of which in any manner to an unauthorized person is prohibited by law.

COUNTRY Cuba	REPORT NO. OO— K-323/13
SUBJECT Guevara Allegedly Suffering from Lung Cancer	DATE DISTR. 27 Jul 65
	NO. PAGES 1
	REFERENCES
DATE OF INFO. 5 Jul 65 and earlier	
PLACE & DATE ACQ.	

THIS IS UNEVALUATED INFORMATION

SOURCE:

3F

According to rumors circulating in Havana during early July 1965, Ernesto "Che" Guevara was ill and in bed at a hospital in Havana. He was reportedly suffering from lung cancer. It was also rumored that he was under the medical attention of several Sovbloc specialists, and that the people will be informed of his condition in the near future.

-end-

67. 1965: CIA document speculating that Che Guevara is suffering from lung cancer.

CENTRAL INTELLIGENCE AGENCY

This material contains information affecting the National Defense of the United States within the meaning of the Espionage 78, U.S.C. Secs. 793 and 794, the transmission or revelation of which in any manner to an unauthorized person is prohibited

COUNTRY	Cuba	REPORT NO. OO—K-323/12
SUBJECT	Alleged Currency Change to Take Place on 26 Jul 65	DATE DISTR. 19 July 65
		NO. PAGES 1
		REFERENCES

DATE OF
INFO.

PLACE &
DATE ACQ

THIS IS UNEVALUATED INFORMATION

During June 1965, it was rumored in Havana, that on 26 Jul 65 the GOC would have a complete currency change. The reason was to remove from circulation all bills with "Che" Guevara's signature and render worthless currency being hoarded.

-end-

68. 1965: CIA speculation on the significance of the removal of all Cuban currency with Che Guevara's signature.

CENTRAL INTELLIGENCE AGENCY

This material contains information affecting the National Defense of the United States within the meaning of the Espionage Laws, Title 15, U.S.C. Secs. 793 and 794, the transmission or revelation of which in any manner to an unauthorized person is prohibited by law.

COUNTRY	Cuba	REPORT NO.	OO—K-323/18986-65
SUBJECT	Ernesto Guevara's Name Included with Other GOC "Martyrs"	DATE DISTR.	29 Oct 65
		NO. PAGES	1
		REFERENCES	

DATE OF INFO.   24-26 Jul 65

PLACE & DATE ACQ.

THIS IS UNEVALUATED INFORMATION

SOURCE:

1. On 24 Jul 65, on several store windows in Sagua La Grande, Las Villas, the GOC displayed two five feet square posters in celebration of the anniversary of the 26th of July Movement. One poster illustrated Cuban soldiers fighting against "Yankee Imperialism". Overlooking the battle-ground was a portrait of the face of the late Camilo Cienfuegos. The other poster had a similar scene but the portrait face was that of Ernesto (Che) Guevara.

2. _____ 26th of July celebrations _____ held in Santa Clara, Las Villas. The celebrations lasted until the early hours of 27 Jul 65. One of the principal speakers, who was from Havana and unknown to _____, spoke for over three hours. His closing statement was quoted as follows, "Let us acknowledge here tonight the sacrifice of the glory of the fallen ones, and that their sacrifice will not be wasted. Among these martyrs I must include Major E. Guevara."

-end-

69. 1965: CIA information report on a reference to Che Guevara as a "martyr."

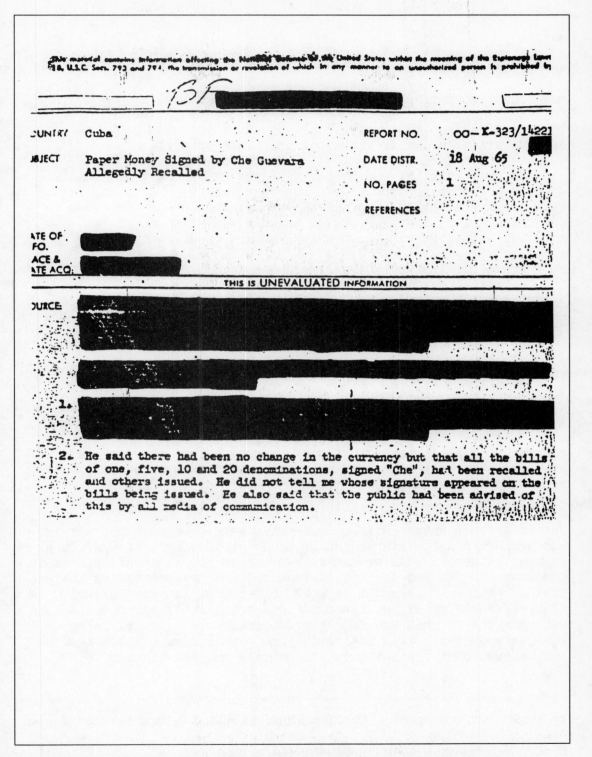

BF

COUNTRY	Cuba
SUBJECT	Paper Money Signed by Che Guevara Allegedly Recalled

REPORT NO.	00-K-323/14221
DATE DISTR.	18 Aug 65
NO. PAGES	1
REFERENCES	

DATE OF INFO.

PLACE & DATE ACQ.

THIS IS UNEVALUATED INFORMATION

SOURCE

1.

2. He said there had been no change in the currency but that all the bills of one, five, 10 and 20 denominations, signed "Che", had been recalled and others issued. He did not tell me whose signature appeared on the bills being issued. He also said that the public had been advised of this by all media of communication.

70. 1965: CIA document: "Paper Money Signed by Che Guevara Allegedly Recalled."

```
FBIS

REPORT ON GUEVARA DEATH

FOR YOUR INFORMATION

THE SANTO DOMINGO NATIONAL RECONSTRUCTION GOVERNMENT RADIO IN
SPANISH AT 03.10 GMT 21 AUGUST CARRIED THIS BULLETIN:

'IT HAS JUST BEEN LEARNED BY OUR REPORTER AT THE NATIONAL PALACE,
WHERE THE RECONSTRUCTION GOVERNMENT TEMPORARILY IS LOCATED, THAT
CUBAN COMMUNIST LEADER CHE GUEVARA WAS KILLED IN SANTO DOMINGO
DURING THE FIRST ARMED ENCOUNTER BETWEEN FORCES LOYAL TO THE
NATIONAL RECONSTRUCTION GOVERNMENT AND THE REBEL FORCES.'

NO FURTHER DETAILS WERE GIVEN IN THE BROADCAST.

21 AUG

                              * * *

FBIS

COMMENT ON GUEVARA

MONTEVIDEO CORRESPONDENT'S DISPATCH IN SPANISH TO PRENSA LATINA
2 SEP 65

MONTEVIDEO - AFTER SEVERAL DAYS OF SILENCE ON THE SUBJECT, THE
RIGHTIST NEWSPAPER EL DIA IS AGAIN WONDERING 'WHERE CHE GUEVARA IS'
AND TRIES TO INDICATE AGAIN THE WHEREABOUTS OF THE CUBAN
REVOLUTIONARY.

THE PAPER THEN SAYS: 'HIS SUCCESSOR HAS BEEN APPOINTED BUT NOTHING
HAS BEEN SAID ABOUT HIS RESIGNATION, IF HE RESIGNED, OR WHETHER HE
IS DEAD OR ALIVE… WHAT WE ARE INTERESTED IN AS FAR AS HIS PERSON IS
CONCERNED IS THE POSSIBILITY THAT HE IS STILL TRANSGRESSING AGAINST
FREEDOM. AND WHAT IS STILL OF MORE CONSEQUENCE IS THAT THE WORLD'S
(INDIFFERENCE) TO HIS WHEREABOUTS IS A MUTE AND (IRREVOCABLE)
CONDEMNATION OF THE FRIGHTFUL SYSTEM PREVAILING IN CUBA… IN NO
DEMOCRACY DO THE RULERS DISAPPEAR FROM PUBLIC LIFE WITHOUT LEAVING
ANY TRACES… ONLY TYRANNY GETS RID OF THEM IN THAT FASHION.'
```

71. 1965: Two FBIS reports: (i) Che Guevara has been killed in Santo Domingo (August 21).
(ii) Che's whereabouts still unknown (September 2)
These documents have been retyped from the originals.

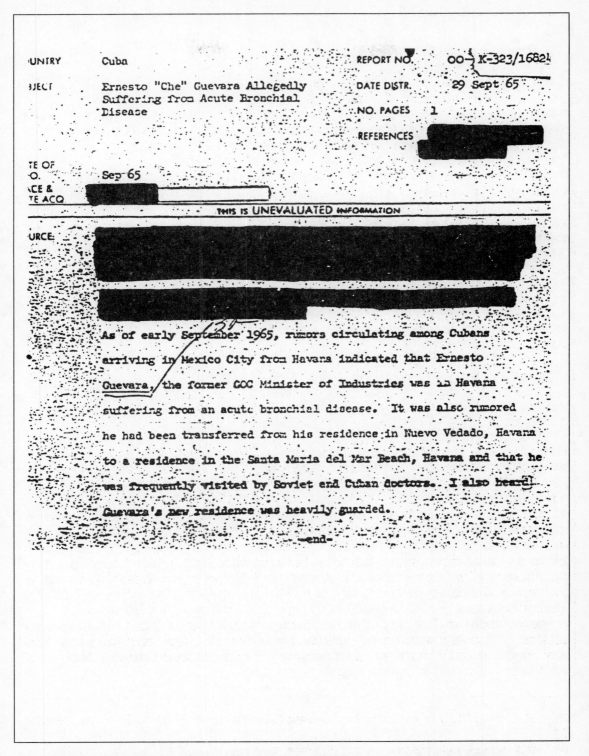

COUNTRY   Cuba   REPORT NO.   00-X-323/16824

SUBJECT   Ernesto "Che" Guevara Allegedly   DATE DISTR.   29 Sept 65
            Suffering from Acute Bronchial
            Disease   NO. PAGES   1

                                                    REFERENCES   ████████

DATE OF
INFO.   Sep 65

PLACE &
DATE ACQ   ████████

THIS IS UNEVALUATED INFORMATION

SOURCE: ██
           ██
           ██

As of early September 1965, rumors circulating among Cubans
arriving in Mexico City from Havana indicated that Ernesto
Guevara, the former GOC Minister of Industries was in Havana
suffering from an acute bronchial disease. It was also rumored
he had been transferred from his residence in Nuevo Vedado, Havana
to a residence in the Santa Maria del Mar Beach, Havana and that he
was frequently visited by Soviet and Cuban doctors. I also heard
Guevara's new residence was heavily guarded.

—end—

72. 1965: CIA report on Guevara "Allegedly Suffering from Acute Bronchial Disease."

```
FBIS
REPORTS OF GUEVARA CAPTURE

LIMA AFP IN SPANISH 9 OCT 65

LIMA - TWO NEWSPAPERS TODAY REPORTED THAT 'CHE' GUEVARA HAS BEEN
CAPTURED IN THE QUILLABAMBA GUERRILLA ZONE, IN THE SOUTHEASTERN
PORTION OF THE COUNTRY. THE PAPERS REPORT THAT THIS IS A RUMOR AND
EMPHASIZE THAT THEY DO NOT HAVE OFFICIAL CONFIRMATION....

                              *  *  *


FBIS
REPORTED CAPTURE OF GUEVARA

LONDON REUTERS IN ENGLISH 9 OCT 65

LIMA, PERU, 9 OCTOBER - REPORTS REACHING HERE FROM CUZCO SAY FORMER
CUBAN INDUSTRIES MINISTER ERNESTO 'CHE' GUEVARA HAS BEEN CAPTURED,
IT WAS LEARNED TODAY....

                              *  *  *


FBIS
GUEVARA WHERE ABOUTS

MONTEVIDEO REUTERS IN SPANISH 9 OCT 65

LIMA - IT WAS REPORTED TODAY THAT A POLICE PATROL WAS SENT ... TO THE
REMOTE AMAZON JUNGLE REGION OF TIRUSTAN, DUE TO RUMORS THAT ERNESTO
'CHE' GUEVARA WAS TRAINING GUERRILLAS IN THAT AREA. ...

... IT IS INDICATED THAT DETECTIVES AND SECURITY AGENTS ARE KEEPING
CLOSE WATCH ON THE HOMES OF KNOWN COMMUNISTS WHO COULD SERVE AS A
REFUGE FOR THE REVOLUTIONARY ...

... GOVERNMENT MINISTER, DEPUTY [NAME ILLEGIBLE] SAID IN HUANCAYO
DURING THE WEEK THAT THE FORMER CUBAN LEADER WAS NOT IN PERU AND
EXPRESSED DOUBTS THAT THE LETTER ATTRIBUTED TO CHE GUEVARA AND READ
BY CASTRO HAD BEEN REALLY WRITTEN BY HIM.
```

73. 1965: Examples of the many FBIS reports that Che Guevara is training guerrillas in Peru. The documents have been retyped from the originals.

CENTRAL INTELLIGENCE AGENCY

This material contains information affecting the National Defense of the United States within the meaning of the Espionage Laws, Title 18, U.S.C. Secs 793 and 794, the transmission or revelation of which in any manner to an unauthorized person is prohibited by law.

NTRY   ~~Lxxcaxshxa~~/Cuba

REPORT NO: OO— B-321/0C830-66

CT.   Claim that "Che" Guevara is Still Living

DATE DISTR.   22 Apr 66

NO. PAGES   1

REFERENCES

OF   Nov 65 and earlier

E &
ACO

THIS IS UNEVALUATED INFORMATION

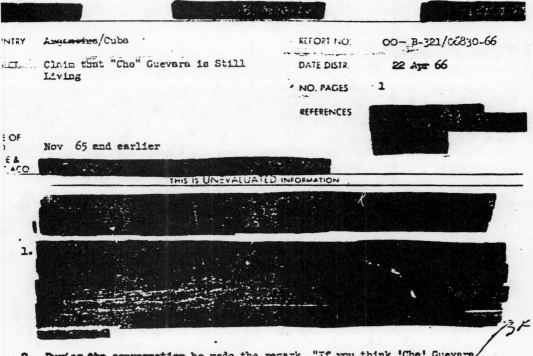

1.

2. During the conversation he made the remark, "If you think 'Che' Guevara is dead, you are badly mistaken. We will hear much more from him. He went into no further details.

                    -end-

74. 1965: CIA reports an unidentified person remarking: "If you think 'Che' Guevara is dead, you are badly mistaken. We will hear much more from him."

GCC Subversive Activities/Claims that
Che Guevara Is Alive
████████████

DATE DISTR.   29 Nov 65

NO. PAGES·   1

REFERENCES   This report was pre
                  disseminated as TD-
                  20619-65

Early Nov 65
████████████

THIS IS UNEVALUATED INFORMATION

████████████████████████████████
████████████████████████████████

1. ████████████████████████████████
████████████████████████████████
████████████████████████████████

2. ████████████████████████████████

3. "Cuba is the recognized leader in training and supplying dissident
groups throughout Latin America who want to liberate their countries.
As a result of a scheduled December 1965 "Tri-Continent Conference"
(Asia, Africa and South America) to be held in Havana, Cuba hopes to
become the leader of such activities in Africa and Asia too. Africa
has priority and some Cuban agents are already at work there. So,
also, Cuba presently has agents operating in South Viet Nam.

4. "Several months ago the Cuban government ordered the surrender of
all personal weapons to the authorities. One of the main objects of
this was to acquire weapons of US manufacture for export to subversive
elements. Not only will these guns help satisfy the increased demand
for weapons, as a result of stepped up activities, but also they can
be used for propaganda purposes in the event of capture.

5. "Regarding Che Guevara, he is definitely alive and probably in
Latin America. ████ ████ Colombia or Peru are the most likely places.

6. ████████████████████████████

75. **1965:** CIA report on Cuba's "Subversive Activities" and claims that Che Guevara is
"definitely alive and probably in Latin America."

CENTRAL INTELLIGENCE AGENCY

This material contains information affecting the National Defense of the United States within the meaning of the Espionage Laws, Title 18, U.S.C. Secs. 793 and 794, the transmission or revelation of which in any manner to an unauthorized person is prohibited by law.

ITRY ▮▮▮▮/Cuba

CT Ernesto "Che" Guevara Allegedly
Working Among Quechua Indians

OF ▮▮▮▮

&
ACO.

REPORT NO. 00- K-323/02647-66

DATE DISTR. 21 Feb 66

NO. PAGES 1

REFERENCES

THIS IS UNEVALUATED INFORMATION

He was told that the Peruvian military
were conducting an extensive search among the Quechua Indians for Ernesto
"Che" Guevara, who was said to be working among these Indians. He is reported
to have cut off his beard. ▮▮▮▮▮▮ that Guevara learned to speak the
Quechuan language in Cuba.

-end-

76. 1965: CIA report that Che Guevara is "allegedly working among Quechua Indians." The informant mentions that Guevara is "reported to have cut off his beard."

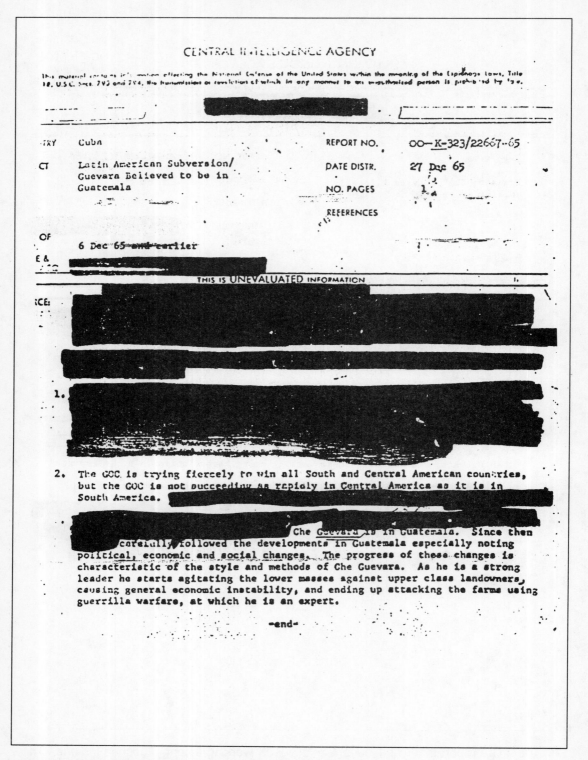

CENTRAL INTELLIGENCE AGENCY

This material contains information affecting the National Defense of the United States within the meaning of the Espionage Laws, Title 18, U.S.C. Secs. 793 and 794, the transmission or revelation of which in any manner to an unauthorized person is prohibited by law.

TRY   Cuba

CT   Latin American Subversion/
Guevara Believed to be in
Guatemala

REPORT NO.   OO-K-323/22667-65

DATE DISTR.   27 Dec 65

NO. PAGES   1

REFERENCES

OF

E &

6 Dec 65 and earlier

THIS IS UNEVALUATED INFORMATION

CE:

1.

2.   The GOC is trying fiercely to win all South and Central American countries,
but the GOC is not succeeding as rapidly in Central America as it is in
South America.

Che Guevara is in Guatemala. Since then
carefully followed the developments in Guatemala especially noting
political, economic and social changes. The progress of these changes is
characteristic of the style and methods of Che Guevara. As he is a strong
leader he starts agitating the lower masses against upper class landowners,
causing general economic instability, and ending up attacking the farms using
guerrilla warfare, at which he is an expert.

-end-

77. 1965: CIA report that Che Guevara is in Guatemala.

CENTRAL INTELLIGENCE AGENCY

This material contains information affecting the National Defense of the United States within the meaning of the Espionage Laws, Title 18, U.S.C. Secs. 793 and 794, the transmission or revelation of which in any manner to an unauthorized person is prohibited by law.

COUNTRY Cuba

SUBJECT Alleged_Expulsion_of_Che Guevara from Cuban Communist Party

REPORT NO. 00- K-323/01512-66

DATE DISTR. 28 Jan 66

NO. PAGES 1

REFERENCES DCS

DATE OF INFO. 10 Jan 66 and earlier

PLACE & DATE ACQ

THIS IS UNEVALUATED INFORMATION

SOURCE:

According to rumors in Havana, "Che" Guevara was expelled from the Cuban Communist Party at the insistence of the USSR. ████████ that economic sanctions were to be imposed against Cuba if Fidel Castro did not comply with the Soviet request.

—end—

78. 1965: CIA report: "Alleged Expulsion of Che Guevara from Cuban Communist Party."

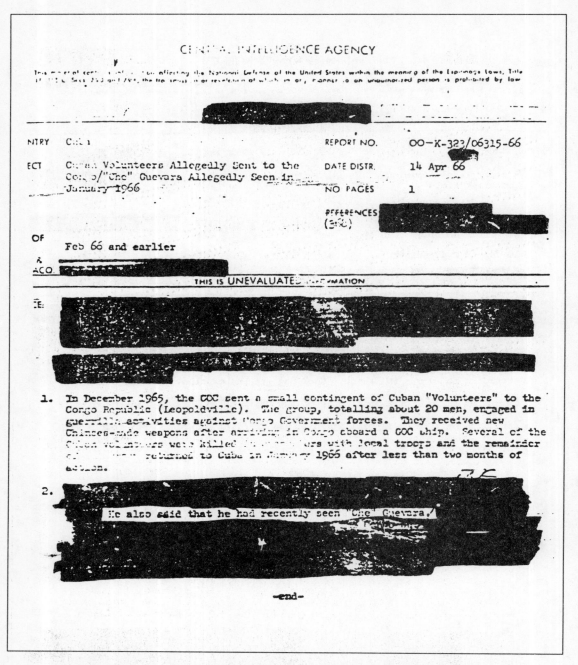

CENTRAL INTELLIGENCE AGENCY

This material contains information affecting the National Defense of the United States within the meaning of the Espionage Laws, Title 18, U.S.C., Secs. 793 and 794, the transmission or revelation of which in any manner to an unauthorized person is prohibited by law.

NTRY   Cuba   REPORT NO.   OO-K-323/06315-66

ECT   Cuban Volunteers Allegedly Sent to the   DATE DISTR.   14 Apr 66
        Congo/"Che" Guevara Allegedly Seen in
        January 1966   NO PAGES   1

                                          REFERENCES
                                          (RID)

OF   Feb 66 and earlier

ACQ.

THIS IS UNEVALUATED INFORMATION

1. In December 1965, the GOC sent a small contingent of Cuban "Volunteers" to the
    Congo Republic (Leopoldville). The group, totalling about 20 men, engaged in
    guerrilla activities against Congo Government forces. They received new
    Chinese-made weapons after arriving in Congo aboard a GOC ship. Several of the
    Cuban volunteers were killed in encounters with local troops and the remainder
    of them returned to Cuba in January 1966 after less than two months of
    action.

2. He also said that he had recently seen "Che" Guevara.

-end-

79. 1966: CIA report that the GOC (Government of Cuba) has sent "Volunteers" to the Congo. "The group, totalling about 20 men, engaged in guerrilla activities against Congo Government forces. They received new Chinese-made weapons after arriving in Congo aboard a GOC ship. Several of the Cuban volunteers were killed in encounters with local troops and the remainder [illegible] returned to Cuba in January 1966 after less than two months of action." Significant details of this report remain deleted. Report also mentions recent sighting of Che Guevara.

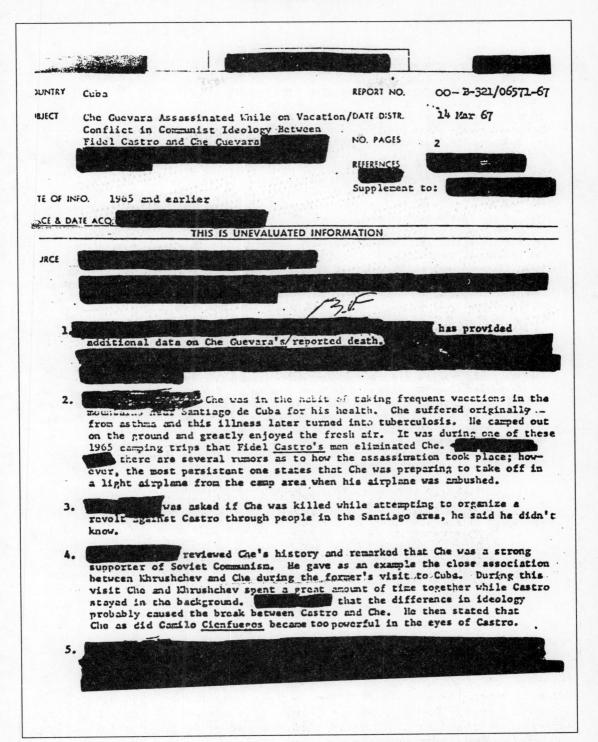

COUNTRY   Cuba

REPORT NO.   OO— B-321/06571-67

SUBJECT   Che Guevara Assassinated While on Vacation/
Conflict in Communist Ideology Between
Fidel Castro and Che Guevara

DATE DISTR.   14 Mar 67

NO. PAGES   2

REFERENCES

Supplement to:

DATE OF INFO.   1965 and earlier

SOURCE & DATE ACQ

THIS IS UNEVALUATED INFORMATION

SOURCE

1. ████████ has provided additional data on Che Guevara's/reported death.

2. ████████ Che was in the habit of taking frequent vacations in the mountains near Santiago de Cuba for his health. Che suffered originally from asthma and this illness later turned into tuberculosis. He camped out on the ground and greatly enjoyed the fresh air. It was during one of these 1965 camping trips that Fidel Castro's men eliminated Che. ████████ there are several rumors as to how the assassination took place; however, the most persistent one states that Che was preparing to take off in a light airplane from the camp area when his airplane was ambushed.

3. ████████ was asked if Che was killed while attempting to organize a revolt against Castro through people in the Santiago area, he said he didn't know.

4. ████████ reviewed Che's history and remarked that Che was a strong supporter of Soviet Communism. He gave as an example the close association between Khrushchev and Che during the former's visit to Cuba. During this visit Che and Khrushchev spent a great amount of time together while Castro stayed in the background. ████████ that the difference in ideology probably caused the break between Castro and Che. He then stated that Che as did Camilo Cienfuegos became too powerful in the eyes of Castro.

5. ████████████████

80. 1965: CIA report on "Che's assassination" and "Conflict in Communist ideology." All information on the second page (not reproduced here) has been deleted.

GUEVARA DIED IN ACTION OFF BARAHONA PORT

Santo Domingo Radio Mil in Spanish 1145 GMT 11 February 1966--C

(Text) Caracas--Ernesto "Che" Guevara died in action off Barahona port on the Dominican coast. This declaration was made yesterday in Caracas by Dr. Buenaventura Sanchez Feliz, former education minister during Bosch's administration.

Dr. Sanchez Feliz affirmed that Guevara was killed off the Barahona coast when a vessel loaded with men was sunk by warships. He added that the second "strong man" of Cuba had tried to land on the Dominican Republic during the most hectic days of the past Dominican revolt.

Dr. Sanchez Feliz' declarations were made during an interview with reporters of the Caracas daily ULTIMAS NOTICIAS. He based his version on the fact that a Neiba fisherman had affirmed he was witness to the naval action and the sinking of the vessel commanded by "Che" Guevara. He concluded his declarations affirming that the sinking of a vessel on that date and place was confirmed by diplomatic circles linked with Washington, and that it has been practically assured that such a vessel was captained by Guevara.

GUEVARA WHEREABOUTS--Foreign Minister Juracy Magalhaes told newsmen in Rio de Janeiro that he knows nothing about reports disseminated by some news agencies to the effect that "Che" Guevara is somewhere in the border area between Brazil and (?Peru). According to a CORREIO DO POVO report published on 6 March, Magalhaes said that "I do not believe that Guevara is alive" and added that "international communism is using the figure of 'Che' Guevara to spread rumors and thus create uneasiness, especially in Latin American countries." (Text) (Montevideo Correspondent's Dispatch Spanish PRENSA LATINA Havana 2140 GMT 8 March 1966--E) (FOR OFFICIAL USE ONLY)

81. **1966:** Two FBIS press reports that
(i) Che Guevara died trying to invade Dominican Republic (February 11).
(ii) Argentine foreign minister says that Che is dead (March 8).

GUEVARA REPORTED AT MEETING IN CONCEPCION
Lima XPP in Spanish 1439 GMT 4 March 1966--P (FOR OFFICIAL USE ONLY)

(Text) Lima--A communist meeting chaired by Che Guevara took place in Concepcion,
Chile, according to information from Tacna published today by LA PRENSA.

The report was signed by LA PRENSA's correspondent, who stated that the disclosure
had been made by a ranking leftist leader several days ago.

According to the report, the communist meeting was attended by extreme leftist
Peruvians in May, 1965 and among those present were Guillermo Lobaton and Luis
de la Puente Uceda. Both guerrilla leaders were killed recently by the armed forces.
And, according to the LA PRENSA correspondent, they had stolen into Chile by landing
at some spot along the coast.

Guevara was said to have been without whiskers and wearing makeup. Peruvian guerrilla
warfare, which as yet had not gone into action, was discussed at length at the
meeting. The Red Chilean leader who spoke explained that the weapons earmarked for
subversion in Peru had entered through Chile, where they had been unloaded after
arrival from Czechoslovakia.

The report says that Che Guevara did not personally take part in any of the
Peruvian guerrillas' actions. It also notes that the former number two man of the
Cuban revolution now should be on the Argentine-Brazil border, and that it is therefore
false that he had vanished or fallen from grace under Fidel Castro.

82. 1966: FBIS report from Peru that Che Guevara was seen at a "communist meeting" in
Chile in May 1965 "without whiskers and wearing makeup."

CENTRAL INTELLIGENCE AGENCY

This material contains information affecting the National Defense of the United States within the meaning of the Espionage Laws, T. 18, U.S.C Secs. 793 and 794, the transmission or revelation of which in any manner to an unauthorized person is prohibited by la

COUNTRY Cuba/~~Bolivia~~	REPORT NO. 00-K-323/06978-6
SUBJECT Revolutionary Group Allegedly Bound For Bolivia	DATE DISTR. 23 Apr 66
	NO. PAGES 1
	REFERENCES

THIS IS UNEVALUATED INFORMATION

In the very near future 90 Cuban-trained revolutionaries will depart for Bolivia. They have undergone extensive training in guerrilla warfare and regional Bolivian cultural customs. The majority of the group are Cuban, but it includes several undersigned foreigners. This is the first group of five thousand guerrillas who are reported to be sent to various Latin American countries during 1966.

[Collectors Comment: Another source quoted as saying that "Che" Guevara allegedly was in Bolivia heading a force of guerrillas in the Andes Mountains.]

- end -

83. 1966: CIA document of April 23, 1966, titled "Revolutionary Group Allegedly Bound For Bolivia" states that "Cuban-trained revolutionaries" are going to Bolivia and that Che Guevara is leading a force of guerrillas in the Andes.

BRAZILIAN SAYS GUEVARA DEAD -- Belo Horizonte, Diario de Minas, 1 May 66

3F

    Columnist Ibrahim Sued reported in his column that the mysterious disappearance of Che Guevara is beginning to become clear. He reports   that he has just found out through a person he knows who is linked to the secret service of an American nation, that a high hemispheric source has obtained the following information: Guevara was assassinated or kidnaped in Cuba by Soviet secret agents because of the divergencies between the Communist lines of Moscow and Peking. He wanted Fidel Castro to follow the Peking line, abandoning the Kremlin. Fidel, who was resisting the wishes of Guevara, was consequently threatened by a plot which Guevara was developing to remove him from power. In the face of this danger Soviet secret agents eliminated Guevara on orders from Moscow. To prevent an international scandal, and to justify himself to the Cuban people, Fidel Castro, preferred to adopt the version of the story that Guevara was with guerrillas at some location in Latin America.

PORTUGUESE MINISTER DENIES GUEVARA IN ZAMBIA

Paris AFP in English 1402 GMT 3 May 1966--E (FOR OFFICIAL USE ONLY)

3,

(Text) Lisbon, 3 May--Portuguese Foreign Minister Franco Nogueira today denied any knowledge that the missing Cuban revolutionary Ernesto Che Guevara is in Zambia training African terrorists. Newspaper reports here had said the terrorists would be sent to Mozambique. Nogueira admitted at a press conference it was possible some Mozambique nationalists were being trained in People's China. That would fit in with that country's policy towards Africa, he said. But their target would not only be Portugal.

84. 1966: Two contradictory news reports monitored by FBIS:
(i) A "high hemispheric source" reports that Che Guevara was "assassinated or kidnapped in Cuba by Soviet secret agents because of the divergences between the Communist lines of Moscow and Peking."
(ii) The foreign minister of Portugal denies that Che has been in Zambia "training African terrorists."

FBIS 73 ~~FOR OFFICIAL USE ONLY~~ (SEE 06 OF 4 MAY)

TALK WITH CHE

MONTEVIDEO CORRESPONDENT'S DISPATCH IN SPANISH TO PRENSA LATINA
HAVANA 1425Z 4 MAY 66 E

(TEXT) MONTEVIDEO, 4 MAY--I TALKED TO CHE IN THE ANDES, SAYS
AN ITALIAN JOURNALIST. "HE MIGHT HAVE BEEN IN PERU," SAYS THE BUENOS
AIRES MORNING PAPER EL MUNDO IN ITS HEADLINES. IN ITS INSIDE PAGES,
THE PAPER CARRIES A FIVE-COLUMN ARTICLE: "I TALKED TO 'CHE'
GUEVARA, SAYS A JOURNALIST."

ANOTHER MORNING PAPER WHICH CARRIES THE CABLED REPORT IS CLARIN.
IN ITS INSIDE PAGES IT CARRIES A SHORT ARTICLE UNDER THE
HEADLINE: "REPORTAGE ON 'CHE' GUEVARA."

THE TWO OTHER ARGENTINE DAILES RECEIVED HERE, LA NACION AND LA
PRENSA, CARRY THE REPORT COMING FROM ITALY. LA PRENSA PUBLISHES
IN BRIEF ONE OF ITS REGULAR COLUMNS FROM ITS CORRESPONDENT
GUILLERMO MARTINEZ MARQUEZ. FROM NEW YORK, HE SENDS AN ARTICLE
ENTITLED: "OTHER VERSIONS ON THE GUEVARA CASE"--BASED ON MATERIAL
PUBLISHED (IN THE NEW YORK--ED.) EL TIEMPO BY CUBAN JOURNALIST
ENRIQUE PIZZI DE PORRAS.

CHE GUEVARA PHOTO

~~MONTEVIDEO CORRESPONDENT'S DISPATCH IN SPANISH TO PRENSA LATINA~~
HAVANA 2140Z 13 MAY 66 E

(TEXT) THE CARACAS DAILY ULTIMAS NOTICIAS ON THE FRONT PAGE
OF ITS WEDNESDAY EDITION PUBLISHES A PHOTGRAPH AND SAYS THAT THIS
IS "THE FIRST PHOTOGRAPH OFCHE GUEVARA IN HIS HIDEOUT IN THE
ANDES." THE PHOTOGRAPH, WHICH OCCUPIES SEVEN 20-CENTIMETER
COLUMNS ON THE TABLOID'S FRONT PAGE, CARRIES THIS CAPTION:
"CHE GUEVARA, WHO HAS BEEN REPORTED DEAD SO MANY TIMES, IS ON
THE TOP OF THE ANDES MOUNTAINS. ULTIMAS NOTICIAS PUBLISHED
A LONG INTERVIEW ABOUT HIS PLANS ON 10 MAY. TODAY, WE PUBLISH
THE FIRST PHOTOGRAPH OF THE MAN WHO IS CONSIDERED FIDEL CASTRO'S
'SECOND.' IT WAS TAKEN IN THE HEART OF THE ANDES, WHERE HE IS
ORGANIZING THE GUERRILLAS IN LATIN AMERICAN AND WHERE HE STATED
THAT WITHIN FIVE YEARS ALL AMERICA WILL BE CASTROITE."

INAS MUCH AS WE DO NOT HAVE THE TUESDAY EDITION
MENTIONED BY THE NEWSPAPER, IT IS NOT KNOWN HERE IF THE MENTIONED
INTERVIEW IS THE SAME AS THAT PUBLISHED RECENTLY BY AN ITALIAN
MAGAZINE.

85. 1966: Two FBIS press reports that Che Guevara is in the Andes.

CHE GUEVARA DEATH ALLEGED BY HUERTAS

Paris AFP in French 1624 GMT 14 May 1966--E (FOR OFFICIAL USE ONLY)

(Text) Buenos Aires, 14 May--According to Dr. Enrique Huertas, president of the Cuban Free Medical College and an active anti-Castorite, Maj. Ernesto Che Guevara, former Cuban minister of industry, was killed on 24 April 1964, while attempting to land in Santo Domingo. Dr. Huertas made this statement in the course of a press conference.

According to Dr. Huertas, the event took place after Che Guevara had taken his place in a yellow-painted pocket submarine, launched from a ship carrying arms and munitions. When the little submarine reached the coast, it was caught under artillery fire and exploded. Guevara was mortally wounded, but a man accompanying him survived and later told of the end of the former Cuban minister.

(Editor's note: Montevideo Correspondent's Dispatch in Spanish to PRENSA LATINA 1410 GMT 15 May Quotes Huertas as saying: "The second version is that Guevara, together with Major Piñeiro, known as 'Red Beard,' is on the Colombian-Venezuelan border, organizing the guerrilla fighters of those countries and also in Peru and Ecuador. This plan, originally called 'Bolivar,' is now known as the 'Fidelot' plan." According to Huertas, the "Fidelot" plan is based on an old Castro theory about the possibility of converting the Andes into a second Sierra Maestra. He was quoted as saying that, according to the reports, Castro would mysteriously disappear from Cuba at the opportune moment in order to go to that area, from where he would broadcast by radiotelephone.)

86. 1966: FBIS reports a Castro opponent saying Che Guevara was killed while landing on coast of the Dominican Republic in a "yellow-painted pocket submarine." Also, says Che could be on the Colombian-Venezuelan border with Major Piñeiro and that Fidel Castro will secretly leave Cuba to go to the area and make a radio broadcast.

CHE RUMORED TRAINING GUERRILLAS IN PERU -- Lima, La Cronica, 30 May 66

Reports from Cuzco state that heavily armed forces of the Army and the Civil Guard were mobilized on 29 May to the Vilcabamba area for the purpose of putting down a new subversive outbreak which, it is said, has broken out in the village of Espiritu Pampa. Other rumors, still not confirmed, report that Che Guevara was at that place a short time ago. It is said that he was the one who was in charge of the organization and training of this revolutionary group which has set up its redoubt in the Vilcabamba highlands.

The General Directorate of the Civil Guard categorically denies the existence of any new subversive outbreak and states the Civil Guard forces have not been mobilized for this reason at the present time. It has been announced   that four helicopters of the Peruvian Air Force will fly over the area in the coming days to reconnoiter   the characteristics of the area and verify the existence of the guerrillas.

GUEVARA REPORTED IN MISIONES PROVINCE

Paris AFP in French 0032 GMT 4 July 1966--E (FOR OFFICIAL USE ONLY)

(Text) Buenos Aires, 4 July--Ernesto Che Guevara has reportedly been seen in Misiones Province, the remote northeasterly strip of Argentina that extends between Paraguay and Brazil. The correspondent of the big evening paper LA RAZON who reports this news says Guevara is supposed to have (?shaved) his beard and cut his hair very short, and has a broken arm from a recent auto accident. He is reported to be hiding in the Obera area, not far from the Brazilian border. Presumably, he entered Argentina through Brazil. The entire region is covered with dense growth, and crossing from one country to the other is greatly facilitated by the many smugglers, who are familiar with all the paths.

Misiones Province is Guevara's native country. In its capital, Posadas, the territory's security services remain silent on these reports, which they have not denied. Troops and national gendarmes (?have) gone to the Obera area to prevent the possible infiltration of communist activists from Brazil, but Posadas residents believe this troop movement is chiefly intended to ferret out Guevara's hiding place.

87. 1966: Two FBIS press reports
(i) Che Guevara is training guerrillas in Peru (May 30).
(ii) Che Guevara is in Argentina, that he has broken his arm, cut his hair and shaved off his beard (July 4).

CENTRAL INTELLIGENCE AGENCY

This material contains information affecting the National Defense of the United States within the meaning of the Espionage Laws, Title 18, U.S.C. Secs. 793 and 794, the transmission or revelation of which in any manner to an unauthorized person is prohibited by law.

COUNTRY	Cuba	REPORT NO. OO—X-323/12254-66
SUBJECT	Che Guevara's Picture Given Prominence	DATE DISTR. **3 Aug 66**
		NO. PAGES 1
		REFERENCES

DATE OF
INFO.   18 Jul 66 and earlier

PLACE &
DATE ACQ.

THIS IS UNEVALUATED INFORMATION

SOURCE:

1. The latter part of May 1966   in the America building   Fidel Castro's picture had been replaced by a colored picture of Che Guevara about 2X3 meters in size. Castro's picture had hung there for several years.

2. In April 1966 a very large picture of Che Guevara was painted in colors on the wall of the bus terminal for routes 60 and 65 in El Cerro, Havana.

3. Early June 1966, a picture of Che Guevara and one of Camilo Cienfuegos were hung side by side on one of the walls of the Telephone Company at Aguila and Dragones Streets.

4. At El Laguito in Havana, where all airlift passengers report, a picture of Che Guevara is hung on the wall. It is about 2 X 1 and 1/2 meters in size.

   [Collector's note: Several sources have commented about Guevara's picture at El Laguito, as well as at the Reforma Urbana Building on 25 and 0 Streets in Vedado, Havana.]

   —end—

88. 1966: FBIS reports from informant[s] of various places in Cuba displaying Che Guevara's picture.

Che Guevara

BRAZILIANS REPORT GUEVARA IN SOUTH AMERICA -- Buenos Aires, Ultima Hora, 19 July 66

/3F

Porto Alegre -- the Secretary of Public Security of Rio Grande do Sul, Brazil, affirmed that he had knowledge of the presence of leftist leader Ernesto Che Guevara in Southern   South America.

CUBAN EXILES ANNOUNCE DEATH OF GUEVARA -- Belo Horizonte, Diario de Minas, 28 July 66

Angel Gonzalez Fernandez, delegate in Mexico of the Cuban Revolutionary Student Directorate, an anti-Castro exile organization, has reported that Che Guevara probably died in a violent political argument which he had with Fidel Castro and his advisors. He bases his idea on letters from two Cubans who sought freedom about two weeks ago and are presently in Jamaica: pilot Ignacio del Valle and mechanic Luis Miguel Paredes. These letters, which he has just

published, were sent from Kingston by these two exiles.

According to del Valle, who was the personal pilot for Che, the latter had various arguments with Fidel and his advisors about economic planning, China, and the activities of the Communist old guard. Del Valle said that Guevara disappeared on returning from a long trip through Asia and Africa and that Che's new pilot, Eliseo de Campa, told him that Che had an argument with Fidel. Another associate of Guevara told him that during this argument he heard shots, that some people were wounded, and that Guevara probably died during it.

89. 1966: Contradictory news items carried in the same FBIS report: A government official says Che Guevara is in southern South America. Report from anti-Castro leader that Che died in "violent political argument" with Fidel regarding "economic planning, China, and the activities of the Communist old guard."

Che Guevara

EXILED CUBANS AFIRM GUEVARA AND CIENFUEGOS DEAD -- Mexico. City,
Excelsior, 27 July 66

An airplane pilot and a mechanic, who fled recently from Cuba
with their families and are now in Jamaica, have stated that it is
almost certain that Che Guevara is dead, and that Camilo Cienfuegos
died   by order of Raul Castro.

The Cuban Revolutionary Student Directorate, headed by Angel
Gonzalez Fernandez, made public last night parts of a letter
stating. the above which allegedly was received from Kingston,
Jamaica, from Ignacio del Valle, a pilot of the Cuban Air Force,
and Luis Paredes, an aviation mechanic.

In regard to the "almost certain death of Ernesto Guevara,".
Ignacio del Valle states that he was pilot for Che and was present
during disputes between Che and aides of Fidel Castro and with
Castro, himself. Del Valle says:

(The letter is addressed to Angel Gonzalez Fernandez) "Thus I
can tell you that one day, after Che returned from a long trip
through the Afro-Asian countries, he disappeared with his three
aides. The general comment was that he had gone to the Dominican Republic to reach agreements with the leaders of the revolution taking place there. We knew nothing more about him until his aides and
his then personal pilot Eliseo de la Campa returned and told us
that Che, then Minister of Industries, would not return to his post
because he had failed in his mission and had had a great altercation   with Fidel Castro. To this we connected other information
from one of the aides which slipped out in our presence, as Paredes
told you, 'that we were more Communist then Lenin, that during the
altercation there were shots and even persons wounded, and that Che
probably did not survive.'

Mechanic Luis Paredes, concerning the death of Camilo
Cienfuegos, who at one time was considered the right hand of Fidel
Castro, stated in his letter to Gonzalez Fernandez:

"On 28 October 1959 I was working as an aviation mechanic at
the Camaguey military airport. I was present when a Cessna airplane took off en route to Havana about 1830 hours carrying Major Cienfuegos. A few minutes later I saw a Seafury airplane, number 530, take off in the same direction.

"The unusual aerial movement at that hour surprised us and,
taking advantage of the fact that I was repairing a Seafury, number
510, I turned on the radio and heard the control tower order
Seafury number 530 to follow and shoot down a small Cessna airplane
that was 'burning cane fields. 'The order was described as being
given directly by Raul Castro.

90. 1966: FBIS quotes a recent Cuban exile saying it is "almost certain Che Guevara is
dead, and that Camilo Cienfuegos died by order of Raúl Castro." Also, interesting fictitious
report on Camilo's death by same source.

Buenos Aires, La Razon, 3 July 1966

[Following is the complete text of the report referred to in the above article. This report appeared under the headline "Che Guevara Disguised and With a Broken Arm Reported Hidden in Misiones."]

Since the end of June a rumor has been circulating in Misiones that Dr Ernesto "Che" Guevara (the former right-hand man of Fidel Castro in Cuba who mysteriously disappeared) was hidden "somewhere" in Misiones Province Later, the area of Obera was pinpointed. It was even said that Guevara was traveling in disguise: the beard that distinguishes the Castro Communists had been shaved, his hair was cut short, and he had a broken arm as a result of an automobile accident. This rumor came into especially sharp focus in the provincial capital of Posadas. Although this possibility was rejected in certain circles, in many the news was believed, considering that the presumed death of Che in Santo Domingo had been no more than a scheme to facilitate his move to other countries of the continent to work in the organization of groups of guerrillas, or "national liberation forces," as they are called.

Those who believe that Guevara is in Argentina or in a bordering country base this on the coincidence of the stories of the Mexican journalists who, after returning home from a visit from Cuba, declared that the Castro regime was trying by all means to bring about popular uprisings in some South American countries (such as Colombia, Peru, and Brazil, whereas is known armed civilian brigades have been active for some time in the mountains). It should be remembered that although Guevara was said to have been killed during a skirmish between the two opposing bands during the Dominican revolution, later that information was denied. Furthermore, later news reports placed him in Peru cooperating with the Peruvian guerrillas. Thus, there are doubts about his fate.

As for the supposed presence of Che Guevara in Misiones, on seeking information from the security services, they maintained strict and logical silence, neither confirming nor denying the rumors. However, despite their silence, it was possible to learn that Army troops and the Misiones police had then detached to the area of Obera and that the National Gendarmerie is redoubling its vigi-

lance along the Brazilian border in view of the presumption that Castro-Communist-type uprisings could break out.

On being alive and hidden in Misiones, such as is said, it is considered that Guevara would have entered from Brazil -- one of those countries reported by Cuban Communist Party Organization Secretary Armando Hart where Cuba would be supporting guerrilla movements, just as occurs in Venezuela, Nicaragua, and Colombia.

91. 1966: FBIS report on Che Guevara's presence in Misiones, Argentina.

DOMINICAN COLONEL REPORTS HE SAW GUEVARA IN DOMINICAN REPUBLIC --
Buenos Aires, La Razon, 7 July 1966

ANSA, New York -- Ernesto "Che" Guevara, the Argentine Communist
who disappeared 16 March 1965, was seen in the Presidential Palace
in Santo Domingo by the then president of the military junta
Col Pedro Bartolome Benoit, according to what the colonel told the
director of the New York daily El Tiempo. Colonel Benoit, the man
who asked US Marines to land to save the Dominican situation, added
that he was not completely sure if Guevara was the Cuban he saw with
a group of 10 foreigners in the palace on that 26 April 1965. But,
he said that he believes he recognized the then Cuban Minister of
Economy dressed in the Castroite uniform, with brassard and beret.
Guevara, or whoever it was that looked like him, was part of a
group of 10 similarly dressed men who seemed to be in command in
the palace during the period when the followers of Francisco
Caamano and Juan Bosch had taken possession of the building. "Afterwards, I did not again see or hear news of those foreigners,"
said the colonel. "I heard many rumors of the presence of
Guevara, and I am aware of the rumor that he has been assassinated or was killed in the war," he added. "However, I have
absolutely no confirmation of any of those rumors. What I do
know, because I saw it, is that a man was there that I thought I
recognized as Che Guevara, from his photos. He was in the palace
with 10 other foreigners when I went there twice to confer with
the rebels in the name of the Air Force." Colonel Benoit said it
was possible that Guevara, on seeing that the revolution was not going to triumph immediately and that the US troops were already on
the way to Santo Domingo, left the country or that he really was li-
quidated by orders of Fidel Castro in the Dominican Republic and
his body secretly buried. Colonel Benoit added that one of the
reasons he asked for US troops -- on assuming power as chief of the
military junta -- was that he saw "that the revolution apparently headed by Francisco Caamano was in reality directed by foreigners and was the fruit of more than a year of preparation."

92. 1966: FBIS report that Che Guevara was seen in the Dominican Republic in April 1965.

Che Guevara   FPIR 0285/66
                                22 Jul 1966

GUEVARA REPORTED in ARGENTINA'S MISIONES PROVINCE -- Buenos Aires,
La Razon, 6 July 1966

            [The following article, datelined Posadas, Argentina, appeared
under the front-page headline "Che Guevara in Argentina?"]

      Ernesto "Che" Guevara, the noted guerrilla and Communist lead-
er who disappeared mysteriously from Cuba, must have been in
Misiones Province. Thus it would appear from a series of indications collected by the provincial police after a widespread operation against the extremist group whose local offices were closed,
an operation which culminated in the detention of 70 members who
were later released. La Razon advanced this idea in its 3 July issue based on the testimony of several persons from Obera and Campo
Grande (the center of Misiones). This testimony allows one to af-
firm that a person with Guevara's characteristics was hidden on
small farms in the area and there held meetings with persons from
outside the area, who perhaps came from Brazil and Paraguay.
This news, which has made such an impact on public opinion, came
from Misiones Deputy Police Chief Capt Mario Oscar Davico, who referred in a press meeting to the operation undertaken and admitted
that through various confidential reports it had been possible to i-
dentify the Communist leader in various localities.

      It is known that, simultaneously, various commissions have
gone out, employing native guides of the area to establish where
Che was going after his mysterious talks. It is conjectured
that he may have a hiding place in the jungle in the Alto Parana,
terrain particularly favorable for evading pursuers. Guevara,
lived in Puerto Avellaneda in his childhood; there his father was
administrator of the port. The topography of the region is familiar to him, with its small farms, plantations of yerba mate, tobacco, tung, and great pine groves. The tortuous terrain crossed by
brooks and covered by underbrush is taken advantage of by smugglers and by those who cross clandestinely from one bank to the other. This traffic from San Ignacio to Puerto Iguazu cannot be controlled by the authorities since it is easy to cross the river in
canoes during the night. The same is true of the coast of the
Uruguay River, to go into Brazil.

      In well-informed circles, it is said that Guevara's presence
could not be accidental but was the result of a well thought out
plan which places Misiones as an enclave strategically located between the two neighbor countries and with an ideal geography for

furtive movement, with narrow paths known at times only to the native guides. Captain Davico reported to newsmen that 21 Argentine
Communist Party locals have been closed and that guns and a variety
of propaganda have been seized.

93. 1966: FBIS report that Che Guevara was in Misiones, Argentina.

CHE GUEVARA REPORTED SEEN IN BARRACAO

Lima AFP in Spanish 2055 GMT 3 August 1966--P (FOR OFFICIAL USE ONLY)

(Excerpts) Rio de Janeiro--Ernesto Che Guevara has been seen in Barracao, affirmed
the mayor of that community today. He said he was convinced of the veracity of some
citizens' reports in this respect. The former Cuban revolutionary leader, according to
rumors accepted by the mayor and reported from Curitiba today, was seen in a local
restaurant.

According to the version offered by Mayor Alfonso Sandino, the stranger, tall and cordial,
arrived one morning at the frontier village in a taxi bearing a Corrientes Province
license plate from Argentina. He was accompanied by another person who spoke Portuguese
and acted as interpreter. The stranger had lunch in a local dining place, left a 10,000-
cruzeiro tip, and disappeared. The mayor said the strangers spent some 24 hours in
Barracao, although they lost sight of them after the meal.

Some observers have recalled that the Brazilian authorities seemed to agree, in principle,
in giving credit to all rumors which up to now have pointed to the presence of Guevara
within the Argentina-Brazil-Paraguay frontier triangle.

GUEVARA WHEREABOUTS

BUENOS AIRES CORRESPONDENT'S DISPATCH IN ENGLISH TO REUTERS
LONDON 2110Z 10 AUG 66 E

(TEXT) CURITIBA, BRAZIL--THE LOCAL DELEGATE OF THE BRAZILIAN
POLITICAL SECURITY POLICE, OSIAS ALGAUER, CONFIRMED
TO REPORTERS THAT THE FORMER CUBAN MINISTER OF INDUSTRY,
ARGENTINE-BORN ERNESTO "CHE" GUEVARA, HAD RECENTLY BEEN IN THE
NEIGHBOORHOOD OF CURTIBA, BRAZIL. HE SAID HE WAS NOT "ABSOLUTELY
SURE" BUT THAT "ALL THE INVESTIGATIONS CARRIED OUT BY THE POLITICAL
SECURITY POLICE HAVE CONFIRMED THE PRESENCE OF GUEVARA OU SOMEONE
WHO LOOKS EXACTLY LIKE HIM," IN SOUTHWEST
PARANA. RECENTLY, MAYOR AFONSO SANVIDO, OF BARRACO, PARANA,
REPORTED THAT GUEVARA HAD SPENT THE NIGHT IN HIS (WORD
INDISTINCT).

MEANWHILE, IN THE TOWN OF MARINGA, JOSE ROCHA, OWNER OF THE
HOTEL CANADA, SAID HE WAS SURE HE HAD SEEN "CHE" IN MARINGA.
"IT WAS EARLY IN THE MORNING," HE SAID, "AND CHE GUEVARA WAS SITTING
IN A PARKED CAR." HE WAS SURE OF THE IDENTITY, HE SAID, BECAUSE
HE HAD MET GUEVARA WHEN HE WAS IN BRAZIL AS A GUEST OF FORMER
PRESIDENT JANIO QUADROS.

POLICE DELEGATE ALAGUER SAID THE POLICE BELIEVE GUEVARA IS
LOOKING OVER THE GROUND AND SOUNDING OUT POSSIBILITIES OF
GUERRILLA ACTIVITIES WITH THE SUPPORT OF LOCAL INHABITANTS.
"WE BELIEVE THIS (SOUTHWESTERN REGION) WAS CHOSEN NOT
ONLY BECAUSE OF ITS PROXIMITY TO THE ARGENTINE AND PARAGUAYAN
BORDERS, BUT ALSO BECAUSE THE LACK OF COMMUNICATIONS FOUND THERE
IS PROPITIOUS FOR ACTIVITIES OF THAT TYPE," HE SAID.

94. 1966: Two FBIS press reports that Che Guevara has been seen in Brazil.

DIPLOMAT REPORTS GUEVARA KILLED ON SOVIET ORDERS -- Lima, La Prensa, 6 Oct 66

Fidel Castro, pressured by the USSR, has eliminated Ernesto "Che" Guevara, according to a foreign diplomat who was recently in Cuba. The diplomat, who asked that his name not be revealed, reported that the Soviet order was given in view of the open sympathy of Guevara toward the Chinese Communist regime. He said that Guevara favored the introduction of Castroism in Latin America, employing violence as proposed by Peiping rather than the Soviet method of introducing its doctrine by peaceful means.

"The fate of Guevara is the same as that of Camilo Cienfuegos," asserted the diplomat. Calling Castro "inept," the diplomat reported that approximately 75,000 people have been imprisoned in the La Cabana prison. Of these, 25,000 fought with Castro against the dictator Batista. He said that Hubert Matos was imprisoned there by Castro when he expressed a desire to return to teaching, his profession before joining with Castro.

95. 1966: FBIS reports the claim of an unnamed foreign diplomat who visited Cuba that "Fidel Castro, pressured by the USSR, has eliminated Ernesto 'Che' Guevara."

CUBA

CHILEAN DAILY ASSERTS GUEVARA STILL ALIVE -- Santiago, Las Noticias de Ultima Hora, 31 Oct 66

"Che" Guevara has become the most useful myth of the enemies of Cuba. It is known that he is no longer in the Cuba he helped liberate, that he left a letter to Fidel Castro saying that new battles awaited him in other places. There is no doubt that Guevara is not dead, that he is loyal to his fate that previously took him to fight for Guatemala, that it is impossible, for now, to say to the world where he now is since that would mean putting him on the threshhold of death. Enemies of Cuba use the lack of news of his whereabouts to weave the most fantastic stories. One recent report from the US, saying he was assassinated...by Castro. Such legends are not so strange; they belong to the old arsenal of those who dream of the defeat of all conquests of the people. On the eve of the Russian Revolution, it was said that Lenin was a German agent and that the Bolsheviks were demons paid by the Kaiser.

Since Cuba proclaimed socialism, subtitles of horror movies have been spread in slick paper books, on the radio, in the movies, and on television. There are specialists for coloring these stories and providing the psychological means necessary to make good people horrified and think that barbarians are in power in Cuba. Repeatedly, Castro has been given up for dead, reportedly perishing at the hands of his own collaborators; it has been said that he was imprisoned, that he was the object of a terrorist attempt, etc. Guevara has been reported dead in diverse places: a tomb in Santo Domingo. His body has been seen in the Peruvian jungles, in Vietnam. He has been reported crossing the Argentine Pampas, or with a machinegun crossing Paraguay, Brazil, Nicaragua. The great revolutionary is an omnipotent shadow, capable of being everywhere at once. The publicists of these adventures would like for Guevara to be dead, for his actions not to threaten any satrap. Thus, they have given as fact the news of his death. But the truth is that all indications are that at any time, "Che" Guevara will emerge with the good health of the dead that the reactionary imagination has dreamed up.

96. 1966: FBIS report on an article from a Chilean paper saying that Che Guevara is not dead and that "the publicists of these adventures would like for Guevara to be dead, for his actions not to threaten any satrap. Thus, they have given as fact the news of his death."

8

1967–1968

Che in Bolivia:
His Disappearance,
Reappearance and Murder

★ ★ ★

The twelve documents in this chapter cover the period of Che Guevara's mission in Bolivia. They are concerned with speculation over his whereabouts, his capture and death, the fate of his corpse, and finally, with his diary from Bolivia. When Che disappeared from Cuba there was speculation worldwide as to why he vanished and where he went. His observation that the Cuban revolution "may be mistaken, but it never lies" was widely ignored. Cynics, as well as enemies, spread rumors about a split between Che Guevara and Fidel Castro for various reasons. Some had him dead, others murdered. Dead or alive, he was spotted all over the world. In fact, he did travel widely, in disguise, before coming to Bolivia. These documents reflect the rumor mongering that the FBI recorded, ever alert to the various speculations.

On November 7, 1966, Che arrived at the guerrilla base on the Ñacahuazú River in Bolivia. Four months later on March 23, 1967, Che's guerrilla unit, called the Army of National Liberation of Bolivia, began its military operations.

Why did Che choose Bolivia? Bolivia was the most unstable country in Latin America, having gone through 189 changes in government since it became an independent republic in 1825. Like Mexico in the years 1910 to 1920 and Cuba more recently, Bolivia was a Latin American country that had had a revolution based on popular participation in 1952. And it is next to Argentina.

Constantino Apasa, a Bolivian tin miner, summed up the political situation in his country in the year that Che arrived: "When the MNR came to power in 1952, we felt it was a workers' party and things would be different. But then the MNR politicians organized a secret police and filled their pockets. They rebuilt the army which we had destroyed, and when it got big enough, the army threw them out. Now the army has new weapons which we cannot match." Landlocked, Bolivia is Latin America's poorest, most illiterate, most rural and most Indian country. The 1964 military coup ended the MNR's twelve year reign. The military officers who now ran Bolivia were all U.S. trained.

Che went to fight in alliance with Inti Peredo, Bolivian chief of the ELN (National Liberation Army). The mission of Che and the ELN was, in Che's words, to create "two, three, many Vietnams." A rift developed between Che and a section of the leadership of the Bolivian Communist Party a month after his arrival, Che noting in his diary that "the party is now taking up ideological arms against us."

Two men defected from his camp in March 1966. And one, for money, betrayed the guerrilla troop's whereabouts to the CIA even before their struggle commenced. As soon as the information from the defector was received, the United States set up a counterinsurgency camp in La Esperanza and the CIA advised the Bolivian government on the methods needed to defeat the guerrilla movement. U.S. Green

Berets, experienced in Vietnam, proceeded to train Bolivian Rangers in counter-guerrilla warfare. It was this unit that captured and murdered Che.

For Washington, defeating Che was crucial. The U.S. government was terrified that Che would succeed in igniting revolution among the impoverished masses of Latin America. At stake was the future of the region. The Cuban example could not be allowed to take root in the continent. Che had to be stopped. General Barrientos's Bolivian Rangers remained hot on Che's trail. Che did not know that researchers at the University of Michigan had perfected the use of infrared photographic sensors that detected human body heat from long distances. Che's troops were isolated and increasingly depleted. On August 31, 1967, the unit headed by Joaquín, which included Tania (Tamara Bunke), the revolutionary guerrilla, was wiped out.

On October 8, 1967, eleven months after he had begun, Che was wounded, captured and taken to a school room in La Higuera near the Vallegrande military base. A day later an obscure Bolivian soldier fired shots into Che's neck on orders from the CIA. The next day a small airplane flew his body out from Vallegrande. No one has told where Che's remains are located. His hands were cut off. His finger was sent to Langley, Virginia, headquarters of the CIA.

Michèle Ray, a French journalist, was one of the first to investigate the circumstances of Che's death in Bolivia. She was interviewed in the Havana newspaper *El Mundo* on January 4, 1968. Ray had published her account of Che's death in the magazine *Paris Match* and later in the March 1968 issue of *Ramparts*. In her *Ramparts* article, titled "In Cold Blood: How the CIA Executed Che," Ray named the CIA operatives Felix Ramos and Eduardo Gonzales as being present in La Higuera when Che was assassinated.

Following Che's death, a dispute emerged concerning the authenticity of his Bolivian diary. Cuba eventually published the diary with Fidel Castro's "Necessary Introduction." In it, Castro defends Che from his detractors, writing: "They have not hesitated, however, to call Che a mistaken adventurer or, more benignly, an idealist whose death marked the swan song of the revolutionary armed struggle in Latin America."

Fidel Castro continued: "Che considered himself a soldier of this revolution, with absolutely no concern about surviving it. Those who imagine that Che's ideas failed because of the outcome of the struggle in Bolivia might as well use this simplistic argument to say that many of the great revolutionary precursors and thinkers, including the founders of Marxism, were also failures because they were unable to see the culmination of their life's work and died before their noble efforts were crowned with success."[1]

---

[1] Published in *Che: A memoir by Fidel Castro* (Ocean Press, 1994).

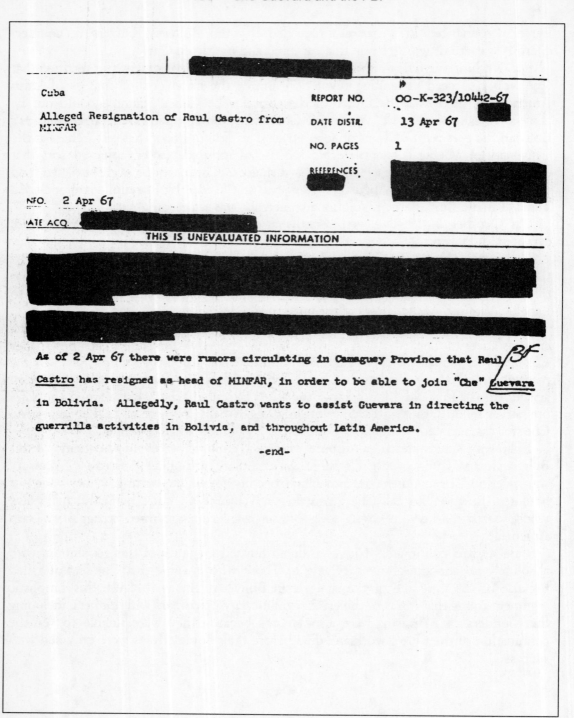

Cuba

Alleged Resignation of Raul Castro from
MINFAR

REPORT NO.   OO-K-323/10442-67

DATE DISTR.   13 Apr 67

NO. PAGES   1

REFERENCES

NFO.   2 Apr 67

ATE ACQ.

THIS IS UNEVALUATED INFORMATION

As of 2 Apr 67 there were rumors circulating in Camaguey Province that Raul
Castro has resigned as head of MINFAR, in order to be able to join "Che" Guevara
in Bolivia. Allegedly, Raul Castro wants to assist Guevara in directing the
guerrilla activities in Bolivia, and throughout Latin America.

-end-

97. 1967: Although Che Guevara's whereabouts are not yet known, this CIA document of
"unevaluated information" states that Che is in Bolivia and reports rumors that Raúl Castro
is about to join him. It is dated April 2, 1967.

CENTRAL INTELLIGENCE AGENCY

This material contains information affecting the National Defense of the United States within the meaning of the Espionage Laws, Title 18, U.S.C. Secs. 793 and 794, the transmission or revelation of which in any manner to an unauthorized person is prohibited.

▓▓▓▓▓▓▓▓▓▓▓▓▓▓▓▓▓▓

COUNTRY   Cuba/~~Argentina~~   REPORT NO   OO- K-323/10910-

SUBJECT   Ernesto "Che" Guevara - His Whereabouts   DATE DISTR   28 Apr 67

                                                   NO PAGES   1

                                                   REFERENCES ▓▓▓▓▓▓

DATE OF INFO   Early Apr 67

PLACE & DATE ACQ ▓▓▓▓▓▓▓▓▓▓▓

THIS IS UNEVALUATED INFORMATION

SOURCE ▓▓▓▓▓▓▓▓▓▓▓▓▓▓▓▓▓▓▓▓▓

▓▓▓▓▓▓▓▓▓▓▓▓▓▓▓▓▓▓▓▓▓▓▓▓▓▓ said that he saw
Ernesto "Che" Guevara early in April 1967 ▓▓▓▓▓▓ Guevara was dressed in priestly
garments and that his hair had been bleached blond. ▓▓▓▓▓▓▓▓ that
if there had been any doubts in his mind that the man he saw was, indeed,
Guevara they were dispelled when a trusted friend confided in him that he,
also had seen Guevara in the same garb and roughly in the same locality at
approximately the same time.

2. ▓▓▓▓▓▓▓▓▓▓▓▓▓▓▓▓▓▓▓▓▓▓▓▓▓▓▓▓▓▓▓▓▓▓▓
▓▓▓▓▓▓▓▓▓▓▓▓▓▓▓ He described Guevara as blond and wearing
face make-up and said he was at that time on his way to Uruguay and thence
to Brazil ▓▓▓▓▓▓▓▓▓▓▓▓▓▓▓▓▓▓

- End -

98. 1967: This CIA document presents further "unevaluated information" from a source reporting Che Guevara is in Uruguay en route to Brazil.

(TEXT) A VERY IMPORTANT POLITICAL DOCUMENT WAS SENT BY MAJ. ERNESTO CHE GUEVARA FROM "SOMEWHERE IN THE WORLD" FOR PUBLICATION IN THE MAGAZINE TRICONTINENTAL, WHOSE FIRST NUMBER --IN ENGLISH, FRENCH, AND SPANISH--WILL COME OUT THIS JUNE. OSMANY CIENFUEGOS, SECRETARY GENERAL OF THE EXECUTIVE SECRETARIAT OF THE AFRO-ASIAN-LATIN AMERICAN PEOPLES SOLIDARITY ORGANIZATION (AALAPSO), SAID AT A PRESS CONFERENCE THIS AFTERNOON THAT "IT HAS BEEN DECIDED TO PUBLISH THIS VITAL MESSAGE TO THE PEOPLES OF THE WORLD FROM THE HEROIC, LEGENDARY FIGHTER WITHOUT WAITING FOR THE FIRST ISSUE OF OUR MAGAZINE."

OSMANY SAID THAT THE MAGAZINE HAD REQUESTED ARTICLES FROM THE WORLD'S MOST OUTSTANDING REVOLUTIONARY LEADER AND THAT "MAJ. ERNESTO CHE GUEVARA WAS AMONG THE FIRST CONTRIBUTORS, WITH AN ARTICLE WHICH HE SENT OUR ORGANIZATION FOR PUBLICATION."

AS HE PREPARED TO READ AN INTRODUCTION TO THE PAMPHLET CONTAINING GUEVARA'S POLITICAL PAPER, OSMANY CIENFUEGOS WENT ON TO SAY THAT "BECAUSE OF ITS CONTENT, BECAUSE OF THE CLARITY WITH WHICH IT DISCUSSES PROBLEMS OF VITAL IMPORTANCE TO THE REVOLUTIONARY MOVEMENT, BECAUSE OF ITS VIGOROUS DENUNCIATION OF YANKEE IMPERIALISM'S POLICY IN SENDING U.S. SOLDIERS TO PUT DOWN REVOLUTIONARY LIBERATION MOVEMENTS ANYWHERE THEY CROP UP--AS IT HAS DONE NOT ONLY IN VIETNAM AND THE DOMINICAN REPUBLIC, BUT ALSO IN GUATEMALA, COLOMBIA, VENEZUELA, AND BOLIVIA, COUNTRIES WHERE MANY GREEN BERETS OF THE SPECIAL FORCES ALREADY EXIST-- AND BECAUSE OF ITS VIGOROUS EXHORTATION TO THE PEOPLES TO GIVE A FITTING REPLY TO THIS CRIMINAL POLICY, THE AALAPSO EXECUTIVE SECRETARIAT HAS DECIDED TO PUBLISH THIS VITALLY IMPORTANT MESSAGE TO THE PEOPLES OF THE WORLD FROM THE HEROIC, LEGENDARY FIGHTER WITHOUT WAITING FOR PUBLICATION OF THE FIRST ISSUED OF OUR MAGAZINI

THE PAMPHLET HANDED OUT TODAY TO THE DOMESTIC AND FOREIGN PRESS CONTAINS SIX PHOTOS OF CHE GUEVARA, FOUR OF THEM IN GUERRILLA FIELD DRESS AND TWO IN CIVILIAN CLOTHES. IN ONE OF THE LATTER PHOTOS CHE GUEVARA IS BEING SHAVED WITH A ELECTRIC RAZOR. IN THE OTHER HE APPEARS ALMOST IN PROFILE, WITH A COLLAR AND CHECKERED TIE, SMOKING A CIGAR.

THE CAPTION FOR THE LAST PHOTO, SHOWING CHE WITHOUT A BEARD OR MUSTACHE AND WITH BIG FIELD GLASSES HANGING FROM HIS NECK, SAYS: "LIKE THE PHOENIX, HE WAS REBORN FROM HIS ASHES, A WAR- HARDENED GUERRILLA."

THE PAMPHLET'S TITLE PAGE IS RED. IT READS: "TRICONTINENTAL, SPECIAL SUPPLEMENT, MAJ. ERNESTO CHE GUEVARA: MESSAGE TO THE TRICONTINENTAL." THIS LETTERING IS IN WHITE ON A PHOTO OF TH HEROIC, LEGENDARY FIGHTER READING A DOCUMENT. AT THE END OF THE 24-PAGE ARTICLE IS JUST THE SIGNATURE BY WHICH MAJ. ERNESTO GUEVARA IS INTERNATIONALLY KNOWN: CHE.

99. 1967: FBIS report of a press conference held by Osmany Cienfuegos, Secretary General of the Executive Secretariat of the Afro-Asian-Latin American People's Solidarity Organization, on April 16, 1967. In the interval between his disappearance in the spring of 1965 and his death in Bolivia in October 1967, Guevara made one public statement which became known as his "Message to the Tricontinental."

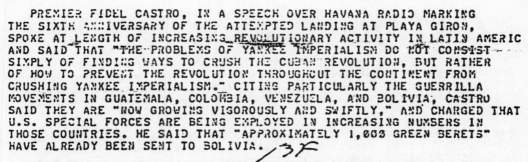

GUEVARA, ERNESTO

FBIS 55 ~~FOR OFFICIAL USE ONLY~~

FBIS BULLETIN FOR 20 APR 1967

CASTRO SPEECH

PREMIER FIDEL CASTRO, IN A SPEECH OVER HAVANA RADIO MARKING THE SIXTH ANNIVERSARY OF THE ATTEMPTED LANDING AT PLAYA GIRON, SPOKE AT LENGTH OF INCREASING REVOLUTIONARY ACTIVITY IN LATIN AMERIC AND SAID THAT "THE PROBLEMS OF YANKEE IMPERIALISM DO NOT CONSIST SIMPLY OF FINDING WAYS TO CRUSH THE CUBAN REVOLUTION, BUT RATHER OF HOW TO PREVENT THE REVOLUTION THROUGHOUT THE CONTINENT FROM CRUSHING YANKEE IMPERIALISM." CITING PARTICULARLY THE GUERRILLA MOVEMENTS IN GUATEMALA, COLOMBIA, VENEZUELA, AND BOLIVIA, CASTRO SAID THEY ARE "NOW GROWING VIGOROUSLY AND SWIFTLY," AND CHARGED THAT U.S. SPECIAL FORCES ARE BEING EMPLOYED IN INCREASING NUMBERS IN THOSE COUNTRIES. HE SAID THAT "APPROXIMATELY 1,000 GREEN BERETS" HAVE ALREADY BEEN SENT TO BOLIVIA.

CASTRO SAID THAT CHE GUEVARA'S "MESSAGE" WILL SERVE TO INSPIRE REVOLUTIONARIES IN ASIA, AFRICA, AND LATIN AMERICA AND THAT HIS "APPEARANCE" MUST HAVE BEEN "TRAUMATIC" FOR THE IMPERIALISTS, WHO WOULD GIVE ANYTHING TO KNOW WHERE HE IS AND WHETHER HE IS "ORGANIZING LIBERATION MOVEMENTS, OR FIGHTING ON ONE OF THE LIBERATION FRONTS." CASTRO EXPRESSED CERTAINTY THAT "FRESH NEWS" WILL BE RECEIVED FROM GUEVARA IN THE "DAYS, WEEKS, MONTHS, AND YEARS" TO COME.

DISCUSSING THE PUNTA DEL ESTE SUMMIT CONFERENCE, CASTRO QUOTED A NUMBER OF WESTERN PRESS REPORTS WHICH HE SAID PROVED THAT IT WAS A "RESOUNDING FAILURE." THIS "FAILURE" WAS INEVITABLE, CASTRO SAID, BECAUSE U.S. INTENTIONS IN FOSTERING A LATIN AMERICAN COMMON MARKET WERE MERELY TO CONTINUE U.S. ECONOMIC EXPLOITATION OF ITS LATIN NEIGHBORS. ASSERTING THAT LATIN AMERICAN POPULATION FIGURES CONTINUE TO OUTSTRIP PRODUCTION CAPACITY TO MEET THEIR NEEDS, CASTRO SAID THE "ONLY WAY OUT" IS REVOLUTION.

100. 1967: Fidel Castro's radio speech of April 20, 1967, transcribed by FBIS, which takes particular note of Che Guevara's "Message to the Tricontinental" and Castro's assertion that "approximately one thousand Green Berets have already been sent to Bolivia."

GUEVARA IN BOLIVIA, OVANDO CANDIA CLAIMS

Lima EFE in Spanish to EFE Buenos Aires 1420 GMT 13 Sep 67 C (~~FOR OFFICIAL USE ONLY~~)

3K

[Text] Lima--The Castro-communist Ernesto "Che" Guevara is in Bolivia, Gen Alfredo Ovando Candia, commanding general of the Bolivian army, told a special correspondent of the Lima morning paper LA PRENSA, Mario Castro Arenas, in an exclusive interview which the Lima paper is publishing on its front page.

"We have credible proofs that Guevara is directing the international guerrillas in the Nancahuazu canyon," Ovando says in the interview.

Ovando adds that "Che" Guevara entered Bolivia legally with a passport, but with his features altered by special makeup, and that other guerrillas have entered in the same way. Ovando says that among the guerrillas in his country are Argentines, Peruvians, and communists from other Latin American countries, all of them trained in Vietnam.

Finally, the commanding general of the Bolivian army declares that the guerrillas operating in his country are part of the advance guard of the Latin American Liberation Army (ELLA), planned to erupt throughout the continent. He says that ELLA components have been especially selected in Vietnam.

101. 1967: FBIS reports a dispatch from Lima's morning paper *La Prensa*, in which a correspondent "breaks the story," fed by Bolivian commanding general Alfredo Ovando Candia, that Che Guevara is commanding guerrillas in Bolivia. Preying on anti-communist prejudices and fears, Ovando states falsely that Che's group had been trained in Vietnam and that they were "part of an advanced guard of the Latin American Liberation Army (ELLA)," an imaginary organization which Ovando states had plans "to erupt throughout the continent."

10 October 1967   BOLIVIA

CLASH IN HIGUERAS LEADS TO GUEVARA'S DEATH

Account of Battle

Buenos Aires ANSA in Spanish 1515 GMT 9 Oct 67 P (~~FOR OFFICIAL USE ONLY~~)

[Excerpt] La Paz--In another bloody clash between army troops and guerrillas yesterday in Higueras, south of Vallegrande, a 14-man Ranger patrol suffered two soldiers killed and four wounded. The rebel losses were three killed and two wounded, according to the first reports. The clash began at 1300 hours on Sund: and lasted until 1900 hours.

It is believed that Che Guevara may be among the guerrilla casualties. To try confirm this, Generals Ovando Candia and Lafuente, commanders of the air force army respectively, are going to Vallegrande with a group of investigators. A reliable source reported that the guerrilla group operating out of Higueras is surrounded and completely unable to escape. "We are going to eliminate them co pletely," added the source.

---

102 (a). 1967: FBIS reports on Che Guevara's death in La Higuera, Bolivia.
Che Guevara was captured and his troops nearly wiped out on October 8, 1967. Bolivian Rangers surrounded Che after a shepherd, tending his flock in the middle of the night, noticed the guerrillas and informed the Rangers of their whereabouts. He did so to collect the publicized reward, according to Michèle Ray's account published in *Ramparts*, March 1968. Che was wounded in the leg in the battle that ensued, but not mortally, and was captured by Captain Gary Prado. He told his captor simply, "I am Guevara." He was taken to a two room schoolhouse in the village of La Higuera where he was bound and spent the night. The next day, two CIA agents arrived on the scene to oversee his execution. They were Felix Ramos, age 26, and Eduardo Gonzales, age 32. Ray explains what happened: "The orders have come down to the junior officers. Three of them are competing for the privilege and honor of murdering Che. The door to the school opens and Mario Terán enters with a M-2 Carbine on his hip. He paces to the other end of the room and turns around. 'Sit down,' he says.

"'Why bother? You are going to kill me,' Che answers calmly.

"'No — sit down.'

"Terán makes as if to leave. Suddenly a burst of fire and Che crumples. Behind him, in the wall next to the door, the bullets have made two bloody holes, each as big as a fist.

"Terán puts up his gun and calls outside: 'That's it, that's it. I got him.' Then he goes out to drink a beer.

"Che lies on the floor in agony. Second Lieutenant Pérez comes into the room, a revolver in his hand. He walks over and puts a bullet in Che's neck."

Thereafter other soldiers were allowed to shoot him but told to aim only at his legs. His body was never discovered. Whether he was buried or cremated became a source of controversy, but his hands were chopped off and a finger was sent to the CIA headquarters in Langley, Virginia.

Announcement of Death

Buenos Aires ANSA in Spanish 2244 GMT 9 Oct 67 P (~~FOR OFFICIAL USE ONLY~~)

[Text] The news of Che Guevara's death was announced in Vallegrande by Col Jo: Zenteno Anaya, commander of the army's Eighth Division. Guevara died in a cla: near Vallegrande. According to the Bolivian authorities, five other guerrilla: in the same clash.

It was revealed that Guevara's body will be taken to La Paz shortly by helicop

Correspondent Views Body

La Paz INTERPRESS in Spanish to INTERPRESS Santiago 1238 GMT 10 Oct 67 C (~~FOF OFFICIAL USE ONLY~~)

[Excerpts] Vallegrande--by Jose Luis Alcazar--Last night I saw, lying on the in the Vallegrande hospital morgue, the body of Che Guevara. It could be no c Death could not change his always scrutinizing, cynical expression. His half-mouth seemed to miss the pipe which was with him in the last few years and whi never was without while he was living in Nanchuazu, as the many photographs wh taken by his companions--and which were later found by the army--will attest.

Together with this correspondent was Edwin Chacon, correspondent for the dail: PRESENCIA, with headquarters in Santa Cruz, and we could both see Che's body. were in the company of Gen Alfredo Ovando Candia, commander in chief of the armed forces, and other high-ranking military chiefs.

Gen Alfredo Ovando, looking at Che's body, said: There is nothing to say. H what was not believed. The guerrillas have been annihilated in Bolivia, alth: a small group of six, commanded by (?Inti) Peredo, is still operating. It wi: be destroyed in the next few hours. Once again, the bravery and love of coun of the Bolivian soldier has been shown. He has succeeded in destroying the theoretician of the Castro-Communist guerrillas--something that it was not po: to do in other countries with more modern armies and better equipment.

102 (b). 1967

FBIS

ARGENTINE MINISTER ON GUEVARA

BUENOS AIRES ANSA IN SPANISH 10 OCT 67

BUENOS AIRES — ARGENTINE FOREIGN MINISTER COSTA MENDEZ HAS
CONFIRMED THAT ERNESTO GUEVARA'S FINGERPRINT CARD WAS DELIVERED TO
THE BOLIVIAN EMBASSY IN WASHINGTON BECAUSE THE BOLIVIAN FOREIGN
MINISTER WAS IN THE UNITED STATES AT THE TIME. 'IT WAS ALSO GIVEN
TO OTHER COUNTRIES,' ADDED COSTA MENDEZ.

NEWSMEN BESIEGED COSTA MENDEZ WHILE COMING OUT FROM A MEETING WITH
PRESIDENT ONGANIA WHICH HE TERMED A ROUTINE MEETING. WHEN ASKED
ABOUT GUEVARA'S DEATH, HE SAID HE HAD NO 'OFFICIAL REPORT TO THAT
EFFECT.' 'ON THE CONTRARY,' HE SAID, 'THERE ARE DOUBTS ABOUT
WHETHER HE IS DEAD OR A PRISONER.' TO ANOTHER QUESTION HE SAID: 'AT
THIS MOMENT THE DOUBT INCREASES BECAUSE I DO NOT HAVE PRECISE
INFORMATION THAT HE HAS BEEN OR NOW IS IN BOLIVIA, OR THAT HE HAS
BEEN KILLED OR TAKEN PRISONER.'

103. 1967: FBIS report: On October 10, 1967, the day after Che Guevara's death, the Bolivian foreign minister who is reported, coincidentally, to have been in the United States "at that time," delivers a copy of Che's fingerprint card to the Bolivian Embassy and to "other countries." This was done to confirm Che's death. The FBI has been in possession of Che's fingerprints since 1952 when he was in Miami. Evidently the fresh fingerprints from Che's corpse were to be compared for confirmation.

```
FBIS

GUEVARA REMAINS

BUENOS AIRES REUTERS IN ENGLISH TO REUTERS LONDON 13 OCT 67


LA PAZ —  THE REMAINS OF FORMER CUBAN REVOLUTIONARY ERNESTO 'CHE'
GUEVARA WERE CREMATED BUT AUTHORITIES PRESERVED HIS HANDS OR AT
LEAST HIS FINGERS AS PROOF OF IDENTITY, INFORMED SOURCES HERE
CLAIMED TONIGHT.

THE CLAIMS FOLLOWED CONFLICTING REPORTS ON THE FINAL DISPOSAL OF
THE BODY OF THE ARGENTINE [ILLEGIBLE] GUERRILLA LEADER, FATALLY
WOUNDED IN A CLASH WITH ARMY TROUPS SUNDAY. BOTH PRESIDENT RENE
BARRIENTOS AND ARMED FORCES COMMANDER GEN ALFREDO OVANDO CANDIA
WERE QUOTED AS SAYING THE BODY OF 39-YEAR OLD GUEVARA HAD BEEN
CREMATED. THE REPORTS CONFLICTED WITH A STATEMENT MADE WEDNESDAY BY
OVANDO THAT THE BODY OF CUBAN PRIME MINISTER FIDEL CASTRO'S FORMER
RIGHTHAND HAD BEEN BURIED.

TODAY SOURCES SAID THE HANDS OR FINGERS HAD BEEN SENT [ILLEGIBLE]
FOR PRESERVATION.

A TEAM OF ARGENTINE POLICE EXPERTS ARRIVED YESTERDAY AT
VALLEGRANDE, NEAR WHERE GUEVARA WAS REPORTEDLY BURIED IN AN
UNMARKED GRAVE, TO CHECK THE IDENTIFICATION AND ALMOST CERTAINLY
ATTENDED THE CREMATION, THE SOURCES ADDED. BUT NO OFFICIAL
CONFIRMATION OF THE CREMATION REPORTS WAS IMMEDIATELY AVAILABLE.
```

104. 1967: FBIS report that four days after his murder, "informed sources" tell Reuters that Che Guevara was cremated and that his hands or at least his fingers were kept for identification.

B O L I V I A

20 Octiber 1967

PRESS VERSIONS OF GUEVARA'S DEATH DENIED

Army Communique

Buenos Aires ANSA in Spanish 1444 GMT 18 Oct 67 P ~~(FOR OFFICIAL USE ONLY)~~

[Text] La Paz--The command of the Army's Eighth Division has expressed indignation at Buenos Aires reports that Capt Gary Prado shot Che Guevara in the heart. In a communique the command stresses that Captain Prado did all he could to help Che when he was seriously wounded at Higueras. The statement says that lack of a doctor and the severity of Guevara's wounds precipitated his death. The communique concludes by offering support to Captain Prado in view of this foreign calumny.

Doctors' Denial

Buenos Aires ANSA in Spanish 1415 GMT 18 Oct 67 P ~~(FOR OFFICIAL USE ONLY)~~

[Text] Vallegrande, Bolivia--Drs Moises Abraham and Jose Martinez of the Senor de Malta Hospital in Vallegrande have emphatically denied reports circulated by foreign press agencies that Ernesto Guevara died of a bullet wound in his heart. They also denied that they gave the exact time of the guerrilla's death. Both physicians confirmed their statements on the death certificate and the autopsy report. They also stated they had not made statements to the foreign press.

PRESIDENT BITTERLY ATTACKS CASTRO IN SPEECH

Buenos Aires REUTERS in Spanish 0312 GMT 20 Oct 67 C ~~(FOR OFFICIAL USE ONLY)~~

[Text] La Paz, 19 October--President Rene Barrientos Ortuno tonight said that if guerrilla activities should increase in Bolivia, Bolivians should be disposed to go to the Caribbean to attack Cuba, which is the instigator of the extremist movement. In a speech to the nation over a national network, Barrientos said: "If the defiance, the provocation, and the guerrilla activity of the intruder increase, we should be ready to conquer distance and attack the aggressor on his own soil, which should not be a sanctuary from which anguish, mourning, and bloodshed originate."

The Bolivian President bitterly attacked the Cuban premier, pointing out that "Castro ignores the fact that Bolivians are making their own revolution." Regarding the recent death of guerrilla leader Ernesto Che Guevara, Barrientos said that the Argentine-Cuban revolutionary was betrayed and that he had nothing to teach Bolivia. "The men of the Sierra Maestra were heroes because they fought against tyranny, but they deviated and fell into the Castro-communist adventure." The greater part of the speech was intended to exalt the Bolivian Army and its chiefs who "defeated the intern..."

105. 1967: These press versions monitored by FBIS of Che Guevara's death circulating a week and a half later, are not fully accurate. Although he was initially captured by Captain Gary Prado, he was not seriously wounded. Che was mortally wounded by a bullet wound, not to the heart, but to the neck.

MEXICAN PAPER INTERVIEWS BARRIENTOS, OVANDO

Havana PRENSA LATINA in Spanish 1300 GMT 31 Jul 68 C (FOR OFFICIAL USE ONLY)

[Interview with Barrientos and Ovando by a special correspondent of EXCELSIOR, Mexico City]

[Text] Mexico City, 30 July--"I believe that there are members of the CIA everywhere," confessed Gen Rene Barrientos in La Paz to a special correspondent of the daily EXCELSIOR of Mexico City when the newspaperman questioned him regarding Gabriel Garcia, principal adviser to Antonio Arguedas and a well-known agent of the CIA in Bolivia.

The exclusive interview by Angel T. Ferreira took place in the La Paz Quemado Palace's Red Room, decorated with statuettes from China and Japan. The military Chief of State and Commander in Chief of the Armed Forces Gen Alfredo Ovando Candia, took part.

"Is it true that the Bolivian Armed Forces received arms from the U.S. Army and instruction from U.S. guerrilla experts?" The Mexican newsman asked.

"Che's guerrillas were equipped with automatic weapons.
From that moment, our forces also were equipped with modern weapons. It is true that 12 or more U.S. guerrilla warfare instructors came. We have a U.S. military mission here, as do all other countries in Latin America."

"There is no permanent U.S. military mission in Mexico," the reporter pointed out.

"I did not know that," answered Barrientos, while Ovando remained silent.

"How did Che die?"

"From the serious wounds he received in battle," answered the military Chief of State, repeating the information on which he has insisted since the day Guevara was assassinated.

106 (a). 1968: FBIS account of an interview for the Mexican paper *Excelsior* of the Bolivian President Barrientos and the country's chief general, Ovando. They admit to having been in receipt of U.S. weapons and anti-guerrilla warfare instructors, but would not comment on Fidel Castro's charge in his introduction to Che Guevara's *Bolivian Diary* that "non-commissioned officer Mario Terán fired a machine gun burst at Che." When asked the location of Che's grave they said he was cremated.

"Fidel Castro says in his introduction to Che's diary that Noncommissioned Officer Mario Teran fired a machinegun burst at Che, who was being held prisoner in a school in the town of Higueras." Barrientos and Ovando both remained silent.

"Who received the 4,200-dollar reward that had been offered for Che?" This question was not answered, but the reporter insisted on an answer. Barrientos finally said, "First, we dropped leaflets asking all of them to surrender. On a certain occasion, the guerrillas approached our forces. They thought the guerrillas were about to surrender, but instead, they opened fire and killed some of our men. Then the matter of the reward came out. But we wanted Mr Guevara alive."

At this point, Gen Alfredo Ovando intervened for the first time during the interview. More cautious than President Barrients, he said: "Eight days before the Higueras battle, I said in La Paz that the end of the guerrilla was near. We had discovered Che's tactics. He always made an eight. He would attack at a certain point then he would withdraw into the sierras only to return to the same place, having traced a kind of eight (this he drew on the sofa on which he was seated) to confuse us."

Ovando admitted that Che had been a brave man and that as such he died. He later said that the armed forces had in their possession other valuable documents written by Che. This is in addition to the diary, of which a photostatic copy was turned over to the Cuban Government by former Government Minister Antonio Arguedas, who disappeared mysteriously in London after leaving Chile, where he had obtained political asylum.

"Where is Che's grave?" asked the EXCELSIOR correspondent.

Ovando and Barrientos remained silent for a long time; then they answered, "He was cremated." Barrientos then added something completely unrelated to the interview.

In his usually precipitate and extroverted tone he said, "Our efforts will continue to modernize industries, nationalize others, proceed with agrarian reform, and build roads and schools. We shall not pay heed to those who are always discontented or to anarchists. We hope to end the state of siege very soon."

DAILY SAYS GUEVARA'S BODY WAS TAKEN BY CIA

Lima AFP in Spanish 1921 GMT 26 Jul 68 P (FOR OFFICIAL USE ONLY)

[Text] Lima--Che Guevara's body was taken to the United States by members of the CIA. According to a local daily, members of the Bolivian security police revealed this information to a high-ranking Peruvian security officer. The body, buried somewhere in Bolivia, is that of another person.

The news item, unconfirmed by official sources, says that the body buried in Bolivia had its face shot up and its hands cut off in order to prevent identification. The report concludes by saying that this was done to prevent Guevara's followers from using his body for propaganda purposes.

                              Report Denied

Lima AFP in Spanish 2331 GMT 27 Jul 68 P (FOR OFFICIAL USE ONLY)

[Text] La Paz--A report published in Lima stating that the body of Argentine-Cuban revolutionary Ernesto Guevara was taken to the United States by CIA agents was categorically denied today in Bolivia. The three security officers who escorted President Barrientos on his visit to Peru vehemently denied that they had made any statements in this respect or had had an opportunity to speak to Peruvian investigation police.

It was learned from other sources that the Bolivian Foreign Ministry will request the government of the neighboring nation to reveal the name of the police official to whom the members of General Barrientos' personal escort had allegedly given the information attributed to them. It was also disclosed that the commander in chief of the Bolivian Armed Forces will issue a communique denying that Che Guevara's body had been transferred to the United States and reaffirming that it was cremated and the ashes buried someplace in Bolivia.

107. 1968: FBIS reports a paper in Lima, Peru, via AFP dated July 26, 1968, has alleged that Che Guevara's body was taken to the United States. The next day AFP reported from La Paz that three Bolivian security officers denied making this statement.

ANTONIO ARGUEDAS EXPLAINS HIS RECENT ACTIONS

Havana PRENSA LATINA in Spanish 1355 GMT 12 Aug 68 C (FOR OFFICIAL USE ONLY)

[Text] Lima, 11 August--Former Bolivian Government Minister Antonio Arguedas, talking today to reporters in Lima, said: "There is an important statement which must be published in accordance with an agreement if something happens to me, or if what I eventually have to say to the court in my country should disappear without trace or cannot be made known." Arguedas said that he gave that statement to the U.S. magazine RAMPARTS and the Chilean PUNTO FINAL, but that it cannot be published before one of these possibilities occurs. The former Bolivian minister declared that the spectacular nature of his actions, especially his sudden, precipitate flight to Chile, is due to the need he feels to call continental attention to his person so that later, once he is before the court of his country, he can reveal many things of special importance which affect the interests of the Latin American peoples and which need to be told to an attentive audience and to a prepared continental public. In his statements, Arguedas admitted the possibility that his aims may be destroyed by "a decision similar to that which the court-martial trying Regis Debray adopted--evicting reporters from the courtroom and hearing the French intellectual's allegation behind closed doors."

Moreover, he indicated that in his case, an effort was made first to present him as a simple traitor and later, when certain facts were known, to pass him off as insane. In regard to various charges made against him, he said that he is not a CIA agent. "That is slander," he added. "What is happening is that people are no longer accustomed to seeing men act independently and being guided strictly by their personal convictions." He pointed out that the contradictions which were formerly seen in his statements are beginning to be cleared up now. He later explained that he left Bolivia when he judged that his life was in imminent danger; he made his first statements in Chile to clear up important questions; and he did not accept the asylum offered him by Cuban Prime Minister Maj Fidel Castro for two reasons: "My absolute belief that I am more useful to the revolution by returning to Bolivia than by living in Cuba, and my need to clear up doubts about the motives that led me to make available to Fidel Castro the diary of Maj Ernesto Che Guevara in Bolivia. If I had gone to Cuba," he said, "suspicions that I had gone to collect my pay would not have been lacking." Arguedas added: "I am hoping that my country's court will call me to reply to the charges of which I am guilty."

The former high-ranking Bolivian Government official charged that a counter-revolutionary conspiracy orchestrated by the CIA and the State Department tends to disparage and divide the revolutionaries of America and the world. He pointed out that in line with the defamatory campaign, an effort has been made in the past to make people believe that it was the French revolutionary writer Regis Debray who caused the Bolivian military authorities to learn of Maj Ernesto Che Guevara's presence in Bolivia--"an absolutely false report." Arguedas also said that "at present, an effort is being made to stain the reputation of another great revolutionary figure, Tamara Bunke, who entered Bolivia with the fictitious name of Laura Gutierrez and died in an ambush which the Bolivian army laid on 31 August for Major 'Joaquin's' guerrilla group. "Now," he pointed out, "the people are trying to say that Tania, the combat name for Tamara Bunke, was really infiltrating Maj Che Guevara's guerrilla force, which is another imperialist slander and shows to what extent these figures, Debray and Tania, continue being dangerous even after their imprisonment or their death."

108. 1968: FBIS monitors a *Prensa Latina* report from Havana that Che Guevara's diary from Bolivia was given to Cuba by Bolivian government minister Antonio Arguedas, who then fled to Chile. In this report Arguedas, in Lima, tells reporters he might be killed or tried secretly. He gave an important statement to the U.S. magazine *Ramparts* and to the Chilean magazine *Punta Final* in the event something happened to him.

9

1968

Richard Goodwin briefs the New York Times

★ ★ ★

Richard Goodwin and two of his aides met in 1968 with Ben Wells, an editor of the *New York Times*. Goodwin was now in the employ of President Lyndon Johnson's administration. The memo of the meeting, written by one of Goodwin's aides, is interesting in that it lifts a corner of the curtain on just how public opinion is shaped in America. Noam Chomsky has frequently commented on this process. Background briefings are held with the "newspaper of record," the line is set, and then, once enunciated, it is echoed across the country by the lesser papers. Even the front page of the *New York Times* is transmitted across country prior to their deadline so as to give guidance to other newspapers.

This particular briefing was held for the purpose of educating Wells on the possibility of a "split" between Moscow and Havana. By "split" Goodwin means that the revolutionary internationalism of the Cuban Communist Party is causing mounting "hostility between Castro and the Orthodox Communist world," which includes divisions within the Cuban Communist Party itself, the Communist Parties of Eastern Europe and the Communist Parties of Latin America, who regarded the Cuban "determination to continue export of the revolution" as "adventurism."

Goodwin's aide, who is knowledgeable and cynical, points out the opposition of old-line members of the Communist Party of Cuba to armed revolution. He notes the "lukewarm support for the Che Guevara mission in Bolivia and expressions of satisfaction in the USSR and by Moscow-line leaders in Latin America when it failed." Goodwin claims that the Communist Party's opposition extended back to 1953 when they opposed the Castro-led attack on the Moncada barracks.

The memo writer likens the internationalism of Castro to "the early days of the USSR," saying "the regime had trouble with the same kind of people, and those were the Trotskyists." He emphasized to the *Times* editor: "How seriously things must be regarded in Moscow when they applied the name Trotsky in this situation."

In 1927 the Left Opposition, led by Leon Trotsky, maintained, contrary to Stalin, that it was utopian to believe that socialism could be built in one country, particularly in an underdeveloped one like the Soviet Union. This was so, they argued, because of the superior economic development of the West. The forces of the world market would eventually restore capitalism to the Soviet Union unless the Russian revolution broke out of its isolation and was extended abroad.

★ ★ ★

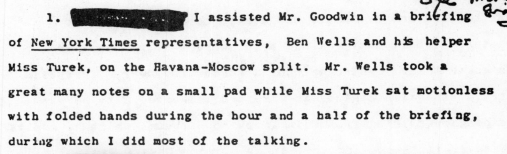

MEMORANDUM FOR: ▮▮▮▮▮▮▮▮▮▮▮

SUBJECT   : Briefing of <u>The New York Times</u>
                  on 22 July 1968.

1. ▮▮▮▮▮▮▮▮ I assisted Mr. Goodwin in a briefing
of <u>New York Times</u> representatives, Ben Wells and his helper
Miss Turek, on the Havana-Moscow split. Mr. Wells took a
great many notes on a small pad while Miss Turek sat motionless
with folded hands during the hour and a half of the briefing,
during which I did most of the talking.

2. ▮▮▮▮▮▮ opened the briefing stating that very recent
events ~~may get~~ appear that the Havana-Moscow split, which would
have seemed impossible even a few months ago, is now entering
the realm of the possible. He explained how the Cubans are
running a summer youth camp in direct competition with the
Moscow-line youth congress being held in Bulgaria, and pointed
out that Castro is thus challenging Moscow for the leadership
of young minds throughout the world.

3. At this point I took up the briefing mentioning
that the origins of the split go back to at least 1953, but
that the tempo of events has rapidly increased in the last
few months. To further interest Mr. Wells in the topic I stated
that no coverage in any depth has ever been given to the Havana-
Moscow split, but clearly it is the next episode in one
already covered amply in the <u>Times</u> and other publications
beginning with Tito and coming down to the present Czech crisis.

109 (a). 1968: Briefing of Ben Wells and his assistant from the *New York Times.*

- 2 -

At this point, Mr. Wells took out his notebook and seemed
to take a more serious interest in the matter. He asked
whether we thought Castro had always been a communist or
whether Herbert Matthews had been correct in his earlier
assessment that Castro was not a Moscow follower. I replied
that at the time Castro was arrested in Mexico City he was
reading everything from Mein Kampf to Marx, which he admits
he never finished, and that in my opinion Castro was not a
Moscow-line communist then and certainly is not now.

4. I pointed out that Moscow is under a three-fold
pressure in its relations with Castro: Castro himself puts
Moscow on the spot by his violent words and deeds and may
even try to frame the Soviets from time to time by arming
guerrillas with Russian-design weapons, thus complicating
their diplomatic relations; Moscow is under pressure from
its bloc allies who wish to waste money and effort
on the wild Cubans; and Moscow is under pressure from the
Communist Parties of Latin America to discipline Castro or
to get rid of him entirely because the attacks he is making
against them and the inroads he is making their power
especially among young people. I quoted an unnamed leader of
a Moscow-line party as saying there must be some deal between
Castro and the CIA because there is no other explanation
for what he is doing to us.

5. Among the historical events illustrating hostility ~~between~~ Castro and the orthodox communist world I ~~said~~: brought up the following.

a. On the eve of the assault on the Moncada Barracks
according to the declarations of one of Castro's
~~communist~~ military chiefs, the "26th of July Group"
did not want to inform Raul Castro of the plan because
of his associations with the Communist Party. Later,
in 1958, the World Federation of Democratic Youth, referring
to Fidel's struggle in the mountains, pointed out that
Fidel was well-known because he was Raul's brother.

b. The Communist Party espionage against the students
conducted by Marcos Rodriguez in 1957 culminating
in the Humboldt Street massacre. I gave a rather
lengthy description of this episode and its aftermath.

c. In a communist conference in Mexico in 1958, Carlos
Rafael Rodriguez attacked Castro and said the Party
would ~~did~~ send someone in to the mountains to take over
the movement and organize the infiltration agents
already in it.

d. The short-circuiting of Castro's attempt to mount
a general strike in April 1958 by the Old Guard Communist
Party. ~~As a means~~ They used to demonstrate to him that (This in a mess)
he could not succeed independently of them.

e. The visit of Carlos Rafael Rodriguez himself to Castro
in the mountains during which Rodriguez succeeded in
placing a fairly strong grip on the leader's mind and

shaping his ideology.

f. The statement of Severo Aguirre in 1960 that
the Old Communists hoped the U. S. would attack
Cuba so as to give the USSR an excuse to intervene.

g. The dispatch of "Tania" to Cuba in 1961 by the East
German Intelligence Service. We noted that she was
probably but one of many Soviet and Bloc agents running
to Cuba to conduct independent operations.

h. The Anibal Escalante affair of March 1962, which
we signaled as a Soviet effort to take over Castro's
government from the inside. We pointed out that ~~the~~
~~Castro~~'s exile of Escalante was a desperate defensive
move and was the maximum ~~he~~ Castro could do as long as the
Soviets were making ~~Castro~~ him a nuclear potentate. Wells
asked if Escalante was an "old-time" communist and we
replied in the affirmative with a brief biographic sketch.

i. The Missile Crisis. We pointed this up as the great
sellout by Moscow and a fact ~~dealing~~ leading to permanent ~~distress~~ distrust
~~for~~ of Moscow on the part of Castro. The attempted inside
job by Escalante and the Crisis together combine! to bring
Castro to the point of initiating an offensive against the
Old Guard Communists.

j. A report from inside Cuba in the summer of 1963 that the
Old Guard Communists expected Castro to mount a provocation

109 (d). 1968

agains them. We gave a little aside on how we
came by this report from a well-placed agent in
a nearby country. The Paraguana arms cache, late 10-3-
We pointed out how furious the Soviets had been
upon learning that arms traceable to Cuba had
been used in this celebrated episode and how the
Chief Soviet advisor had given a tongue-lashing
to the Cuban External Service for its bungling. (2)

1. Juan Marinello's removal as rector of Havana
University and his declarations early in 1964 that
he would like to see Fidel Castro dragged by his
beard thru the streets of Havana.

2. The trial of Marcos Rodriguez, March-April 1964. We
went into great lengths to explain why this frame-up
was mounted, namely as a prelude to the removal of the Vice-
Minister of Defense who was the most important
Moscow-line communist in Latin America. Wells asked
for the name of this man; and we replied Ordoqui. He
spelled the name out loud for us correctly and we
observed that Juan de Onis had reported quite fully
from Havana on all this. We compared this trial to
"Darkness at Noon," and pointed out the parallels with
Tukachevsky case even to the point that both targets
were 2nd Vice-Ministers of their respective armed forces.
We noted that just prior to this, Fidel Castro had
said he would kill Old communist leaders.

A. The removal of Ordoqui from the Armed Forces Ministry in November 1964. We know that this was a completion of phase one of Castro's offensive against the Old Communists and corresponded to the provocation feared by them per the report of more than a year before. We noted that Ordoqui was not and never has been accused of anything in particular and his removal as announced in the Havana press was merely for investigative reasons. We pointed out he is subject to whatever Action Castro may feel politic.

B. We noted that during 1964,65, and 66, Castro removed Old Guard Communists from positions of real power, sending Some them abroad and putting others in positions where they were separated from real power and money. We know that as an example Blas Roca has not an effective function, that he is allegedly rewriting the constitution which will probably result in zero meaning, and that according to one of our highly-placed contacts in Cuba "he is always alone."

p. Towards the end of 1965 new plotting by the Old Guard
began again. We cited various remarks from the
Microfaction Purge of January 1968 to bear out this
statement and we gave a rather lengthy discourse
on the three-fold plan to isolate and liquidate Castro

which he had picked up from an Old Guard leader
towards the end of 1956. ███████████████

████████████

q./ The Tri-Continental Congress of January 1966.
We showed this was Castro's assertion of independence
in the foreign field.

r. The establishment of the Douglas Bravo faction of
the FALN) We showed how Castro deliberately broke
in the spring of 1966.
the unity of the Venezuelan Communist Party by backing
Bravo's faction against the will of the Party. We
described how Castro had resupplied the group in
May 1967 losing three Cubans and some Soviet-designed
weapons in the process. Mr. Wells asked if these were
Soviet made. We replied they were of Soviet design
but actually made in North Korea. We hazarded
guessed that the Cubans deliberately risked these
weapons to muddy Soviet attempts to establish diplomatic
relations with Venezuela in the event of their compromise

5. Intensification of Castro's public attacks on
the USSR for maintaining diplomatic and trade
relations with other Latin American governments.
These increased in 1966 and 1967.

4. Lukewarm Soviet support for the Che Guevara
mission in Bolivia and expressions of satisfaction
in the USSR and and by Moscow-line leaders in
Latin America when it failed. We brought up references
to the Czech Communist Party's position of mid-1967
condemning Castro for adventurism.

12. The LASO congress of Havana, August 1967. We pointed
out this was another declaration of independence by
Castro and mentioned his statement that some Moscow-
line leaders in Latin America had asked the Soviets
to discipline him.

13. The deliberate Castro slighting of the 50th Anniversary
of the Russian Revolution. We dwelt on the low level & ⌐
members of the Cuban delegation, their departure prior⌐
to the final ceremony and the simultaneous pro-Trotsky
press campaign in Havana.

14. The prolonged and stormy trade negotiations with the USSR
in 1967 and 1968. Mr. Wells asked if it was true the
Soviets still give a million dollars a day. We said
this is a sort of a figure which is convenient to use.
We said that Castro had asked for an 8% increase in
petroleum deliveries but was given only 2%. Wells asked

how many Soviet technicians both military and civilians remain in Cuba. We replied about 2,800 and slowly diminishing.

X. The Microfaction Purge of January 1968. We gave a lot of information about this and its background emphasizing that it was really a warning by Fidel to the Russians to get off his back. We stressed how well the Cuban internal services had learned their lesson from their Soviet advisors. We highlighted Castro's statement in February 1968 stating the (worms)
"gusanos" and the Microfaction had the same umbilical cord. We think we made our point with Mr. Wells that Castro regards the US and the USSR as about equally hostile since he has used this theme several times. Mr. Wells asked about the origin of the term microfaction and we explained that this is what Raul Castro himself called it in his speech at the trial.

Y. Pravda criticsim of Castro in March 1968. We referred to the Volsky article which criticized Castro as bourgeois, etc.

Z. The article in Kommunist of May 1968 which assailed unnamed national liberation revolutionary "adventurers" in Asia, Africa and Latin America. We went on to say that the article relates how in the early days in the USSR the regime had trouble with the same kind

of people, and these were the Trotskyists. We made
every effort to emphasize "CASTRO - TROTSKY" and
emphasized how seriously things must be regarded in

Moscow when they applied the name Trotsky in ~~this~~
situation. We noted that in May a couple of articles
sponsored by the Castro government in Mexican
magazines emphasized Cuban determination to continue
export of the revolution.

d'd. The violent anti-Soviet preface Castro wrote for the
Che Guevara diary. We put this into the same
general perspective ▬▬▬▬▬▬▬▬▬▬▬▬▬
▬▬▬▬▬▬▬▬▬▬ mentioning that Castro
blamed the Communists even more strongly than the
"imperialists" for Guevara's failure.

6. By this time we had returned to the present day
and our initial remarks about Castro's youth camp. In ~~the~~
closing ~~remarks~~ we gave a bit more information on Guevara,
including the statement by one of Castro's present military
leaders during the civil war to the effect aht Guevara was
a dirty Communist bohemian.

7. It is my impression that the audience listened closely to the message , but through lack of knowledge about Cuba probably missed a lot of the good points.

On 25 July Mr. Goodwin informed me that Mr. Wells had told him that morning that he had not been able to use the material yet. Mr. Goodwin reads this to m that Mr. Wells seriously plans something but no one knows when.

Also published by Ocean Press

CIA TARGETS FIDEL
The secret assassination report
Only recently declassified and published for the first time, this secret report was prepared for the CIA on its own plots to assassinate Cuba's Fidel Castro. Under pressure in 1967 when the press were probing the alliance with the Mafia in these murderous schemes, the CIA produced this remarkably frank, single-copy report stamped "secret — eyes only." Included is an exclusive commentary by Division General Fabián Escalante, the former head of Cuba's counterintelligence body.
ISBN 1-875284-90-7

ZR RIFLE
The plot to kill Kennedy and Castro
by Claudia Furiati
Thirty years after the death of President Kennedy, Cuba has opened its secret files on the assassination, showing how and why the CIA, along with anti-Castro exiles and the Mafia, planned the conspiracy.
"Adds new pieces to the puzzle and gives us a clearer picture of what really happened." —
Oliver Stone
ISBN 1-875284-85-0

THE SECRET WAR
CIA covert operations against Cuba, 1959-62
by Fabián Escalante
The secret war that the CIA lost. For the first time, the former head of Cuban State Security speaks out about the confrontation with U.S. spy agencies and presents stunning new evidence of the conspiracy between the Mafia, the Cuban counterrevolution and the CIA. General Fabián Escalante details the CIA's operations in 1959-62, the largest-scale covert operation ever launched against another nation.
ISBN 1-875284-86-9

IN THE EYE OF THE STORM
Castro, Khrushchev, Kennedy and the Missile Crisis
by Carlos Lechuga
For the first time, Cuba's view of the most serious crisis of the Cold War is told by one of the leading participants. Rushed to New York during the crisis to take up the post of Cuba's ambassador at the United Nations, Carlos Lechuga provides a coherent history of what really occurred when the world was on the edge of a nuclear catastrophe. Lechuga also reveals exclusive details of his participation in a secret dialogue between Washington and Havana immediately prior to the assassination of President Kennedy, discussions that could have led to a thaw in U.S.-Cuba relations.
ISBN 1-875284-87-7

AFROCUBA
An anthology of Cuban writing on race, politics and culture
Edited by Pedro Pérez Sarduy and Jean Stubbs

What is it like to be Black in Cuba? Does racism exist in a revolutionary society that claims to have abolished it? How does the legacy of slavery and segregation live on in today's Cuba? *AfroCuba* looks at the Black experience in Cuba through the eyes of the island's writers, scholars and artists. The collection mixes poetry, fiction, political analysis and anthropology, producing a multi-faceted insight into Cuba's rich ethnic and cultural reality.
ISBN 1-875284-41-9

HAVANA–MIAMI
The U.S.–Cuba migration conflict
by Jesús Arboleya

What were the origins of the 1994 "rafters crisis"? Why did the U.S. government decide that those Cubans would not be automatically admitted as they had been previously, and instead intern them at the Guantánamo Naval Base? How has this migration — and the Cuban émigré community — been used by Washington against Cuba since the 1959 revolution? And why has this policy become such an important U.S. domestic issue? This book examines the origins of the migration conflict and why it remains one of the most difficult issues in U.S.-Cuba relations.
ISBN 1-875284-91-5

GUANTANAMO
Bay of Discord: The story of the U.S. military base in Cuba
by Roger Ricardo

This book provides a detailed history of the U.S. base on Cuban soil that has remained from the beginning of the century to the present day. It documents how the base has been used for continued violations of Cuban territory and why it remains a sticking point in U.S.–Cuba relations.
ISBN 1-875284-56-7

ISLAND UNDER SIEGE
The U.S. blockade of Cuba
by Pedro Prada

Cuban journalist Pedro Prada presents a compelling case against this "last wall" of the Cold War, showing how the 35-year blockade has affected life in the tiny island nation.
ISBN 1-875284-88-5

FIDEL AND RELIGION
Conversations with Frei Betto
A best-seller throughout Latin America on the relationship between church and politics.
ISBN 1-875284-05-2

CUBA AND THE UNITED STATES
A Chronological History
by Jane Franklin
Based on exceptionally wide research, this updated and expanded chronology by U.S. historian Jane Franklin relates day by day, year by year, the developments involving the two neighboring countries from the 1959 Cuban revolution through 1995. An introductory section chronicles the history of Cuba from the time of the arrival of Christopher Columbus.
ISBN 1-875284-92-3

"Whether one reads this as a history, or keeps it handy as a ready reference... this is a book that no serious student of U.S.–Cuba relations can afford to be without." — Philip Brenner

CUBA AT THE CROSSROADS
by Fidel Castro
What future lies ahead for Cuba as it faces the new millennium? Must it now turn its back on the past four decades since the 1959 revolution? In a series of speeches over recent years, including his address to the United Nations in October 1995, President Fidel Castro of Cuba discusses the main issues confronting the small Caribbean nation as it tries to adjust to a changing world.

In a rare personal mood, Castro reflects on his university days, the influences on him and what drew him into student politics and then national political life.
ISBN 1-875284-94-X

CUBA: TALKING ABOUT REVOLUTION
New, expanded edition
Conversations with Juan Antonio Blanco by Medea Benjamin
A frank discussion on the current situation in Cuba, this book presents an all-too-rare opportunity to hear the voice of one of the island's leading intellectuals. Blanco discusses the fall of the Soviet Union and its impact on Cuba, the possibility of a multi-party system being introduced in Cuba, the historical experiences of socialism, and provides a penetrating assessment of Fidel Castro's role and the steps being taken to prepare for a generational transition of power. This expanded edition features a new chapter by Juan Antonio Blanco, "Cuba: 'socialist museum' or social laboratory?"
ISBN 1-875284-97-7

"A reformist, a hard-liner, a radical, an idealist, a pragmatist, a futuristic historian, Juan Antonio Blanco is a fascinating product of fascinating nation." — Medea Benjamin

FACE TO FACE WITH FIDEL CASTRO
A conversation with Tomás Borge
The issues confronting a changing world are frankly discussed in this lively dialogue between two of Latin America's most controversial political figures.
ISBN 1-875284-72-9

Che Guevara titles from Ocean Press

CHE GUEVARA READER
Writings on Guerrilla Strategy, Politics and Revolution
Edited by David Deutschmann

Three decades after the death of the legendary Latin American figure, this book presents a new selection of Ernesto Che Guevara's most important writings and speeches. It is the most comprehensive selection of Guevara's writings ever to be published in English.

This wide-ranging selection of Guevara's speeches and writings includes four sections: the Cuban guerrilla war (1956-58); the years in government in Cuba (1959-65); Guevara's views on the major international issues of the time, including documents written from Africa and Latin America after his departure from Cuba in 1965; and a selection of letters written by Guevara, including his farewell letters to Fidel Castro and his children and family.

This anthology provides an opportunity to assess Guevara's contribution to the Cuban revolution in its early years. As the most authoritative collection to date of the work of Guevara, the book is an unprecedented source of primary material on Cuba and Latin America in the 1950s and 1960s. As well as an extensive chronology and glossary, included is a complete bibliography of Guevara's writings.
ISBN 1-875284-93-1

CHE — A MEMOIR BY FIDEL CASTRO
Preface by Jesús Montané
Edited by David Deutschmann

For the first time Fidel Castro writes with candor and affection of his relationship with Ernesto Che Guevara, documenting his extraordinary bond with Cuba from the revolution's early days to the final guerrilla expeditions to Africa and Bolivia. Castro vividly portrays Che — the man, the revolutionary and the thinker — and describes in detail his last days with Che in Cuba, giving a remarkably frank assessment of the Bolivian mission.
ISBN 1-875284-15-X

A NEW SOCIETY
Che Guevara on the Cuban Years 1959-65
Edited by David Deutschmann

This book is the product of Che Guevara's experience as the President of the National Bank, the Minister of Industry and as a central figure in the Cuban revolutionary government in the years 1959-65.

FOR A LIST OF OCEAN PRESS DISTRIBUTORS: see copyright page
Ocean Press, GPO Box 3279, Melbourne 3001, Australia ● Fax: 61-3-9372 1765
Ocean Press, PO Box 020692, Brooklyn, NY 11202, USA ● Fax: 1-201-864 6434
E-mail: ocean_press@msn.com